Experiencing Regeneration

Equipping Our Personality For
Living In The Afterlife

Leon James, Ph.D.

Experiencing Regeneration

REGENERATION MEDIA
Kailua

God, Immortality and Theistic Psychology Series

© Leon James 2015

http://www.theisticpsychology.org

This is the Second Edition published in November 2015

Print and Kindle Digital versions at Amazon.com

ASIN: B013J85SFQ
ISBN-13: 978-1515380450

Dedication

This book is dedicated to my spiritual brother

Rev. Dr. Ray Silverman

*Associate Professor of Religion and English
Bryn Athyn College, PA*

*Chaplain, Professor, and Creator of spiritual growth
courses on the Ten Commandments*

Life is a Journey. Travel with purpose.

— Ray and Star Silverman

Contents

Experiencing Regeneration

About This Book

Experiencing Regeneration: Equipping Our Personality for Living in the Afterlife (2015) Leon James

For many centuries people have searched for the secret of immortality. This book shows that there is no such secret because every human being is born into immortality and eternity.

This book presents a radical new psychology of self in a dualist and theistic context. For the first time in the history of modern psychology the afterlife of eternity is defined as the shared collective mental world in which every person's mind already exists since birth. We are not aware of each other's presence in this collective mental world until after the three-day dying-resuscitation process that separates our mind from the physical body and world. We then awaken in our spiritual body and continue experiencing an immortal life in the collective mental world where everyone can see and interact with each other through the spiritual body. People in the afterlife of mental eternity congregate on the basis of interests and loves, and live in spiritual communities that are either in heavenly mental states or hellish. Heavenly communities are in mutual love and in love to God, while hellish communities are in selfish love and hatred of God. People choose to live in one or the other type of community on the basis of their personality preferences.

This book explains how to acquire personality traits that will allow anyone who desires to live eternally in a heavenly state of mind and community life. This spiritual preparation is called experiencing regeneration and consists of cooperating with God in the gradual lifelong process of personality change from our inherited and acquired selfish loves to mutual love and love of good and truth. Without undergoing regeneration, eternal life in a heavenly mental state is not possible because our selfish personality cannot be happy where mutual love is present. Living in a hellish mental state is marked by suffering and insanity and is to be avoided through equipping our personality with heavenly loves. This book

Experiencing Regeneration

unlocks the secrets of rational enlightenment that is used to defeat our weaknesses and negative dependencies.

It is generally believed that heaven in the afterlife is for those who have earned that reward by living according to the commandments of God, while hell is the final punishment for living a sinful life. This book shows that a rational analysis reveals an entirely different explanation, one that is consistent with God's infinite love for every human being. After describing the three-day dying-resuscitation process that everyone goes through upon death, the author shows that we awaken in our immortal spiritual body that contains our mind, and continue eternal life from there on. After trying out the two available mental states of heaven and hell, everyone then chooses which mental state they are going to enter forever. This book examines that critical choice in the afterlife, and shows that we can prepare for that choice by equipping our personality with traits that can live and fit in a community of heavenly people. This process of personality change is called experiencing regeneration.

For the first time in the history of modern psychology the afterlife of eternity is defined as the collective mental world in which every person's mind exists since birth. We are not aware of each other's presence in this collective mental world until after the three-day dying-resuscitation process that separates us from the physical body and world. We then awaken in our spiritual body and continue experiencing an immortal life in the collective mental world of eternity where everyone can see and interact with each other through the spiritual body that contains our mind and personality. This book explains how to acquire personality traits that will allow anyone who desires to live eternally in a heavenly state of mind and in a community life of mutual love and love to God.

This book presents a radical new psychology of self in a dualist and theistic context. For the first time in the history of modern psychology the afterlife of eternity is defined as the shared collective mental world in which every person's mind exists since birth. We are not aware of each other's presence in this collective mental world until after the three-day dying-resuscitation process that separates us from the physical body and world. We then awaken in our spiritual body and continue experiencing an immortal life in the collective mental world where everyone can see and

7

interact with each other through the spiritual body that contains our mind and personality.

This book resolves and explains in simple rational terms the major issues and concerns that people have about God, salvation, being a good person, love, truth, and eternal happiness. After reading this book you will understand and be able to discuss the following topics:

> salvation; atonement; enlightenment; liberation; resurrection; sin; heaven and hell by choice; three-day dying-resuscitation process; afterlife; immortality; eternity; self; mind; spirit; spiritual body; consciousness raising; dualism; materialism; rationality; spiritual; supernatural; theistic; creation; God; Sacred Scripture; angel; devil; marriage; mental anatomy; love; truth; selfishness; regeneration; daily emotional spin-cycle; self-witnessing; spiritual-natural correspondences; feeling bad by being negative; feeling good by being good;

About the Author Leon James

Since 1971 Dr. Leon James has been Professor of Psychology at the University of Hawaii. He has also held academic positions at McGill University, Laval University, University of Wisconsin, and University of Illinois. Since 1962 he has conducted research, published articles and books, and taught courses in several scientific specialty subjects that include the following:

social-personality theory and measurement; statistics and research design; psycholinguistics and ethnosemantics; ethnomethodology and intersubjectivity; discourse analysis; language learning and teaching; library and information science; driving psychology; road rage; sidewalk rage; air rage; the spiritual psychology of Emanuel Swedenborg; cyberpsychology; marriage and couplehood.

Experiencing Regeneration

He is on the Editorial Board of various academic journals and regularly consults with safety organizations and institutions worldwide on driving psychology. He is considered an expert on "road rage", "air rage" and "sidewalk rage", and has given over one thousand newspaper interviews and media appearances. In 1997 he gave expert testimony to the Transportation Sub-Committee in the U.S. Congress on the topic of road rage and aggressive driving.

In fifty years of scientific research and writing he introduced more than two thousand *neologisms* or novel expressions that refer to new scientific ideas that he discovered. Some of these expressions have been picked up by others and are in use today. The oldest and most successful of his neologisms is the expression *"semantic satiation"* which was the topic of his Masters Thesis and Ph.D. Dissertation at McGill University in 1962. Semantic satiation refers to the change or loss of meaning of a word when it is repeated beyond a certain frequency (see Wikipedia article). He demonstrated how this neuro-semantic phenomenon applies to various situations, including vocabulary learning, doing arithmetic, enjoyment of popular songs, stuttering on the phone, bilingualism, remembering TV commercials, and focusing on visual displays. In the past few years semantic satiation has been researched in dozens of articles in psychology, instruction, business, art, music, and aesthetics. It has now become a popular topic of chat discussions and name for bands and albums. It is also entering the vocabulary of ordinary speakers in everyday use.

Another of his neologisms that entered into popular use is the expression *"road rage nursery"* to refer to the back seat of a car. This was meant to alert parents that how they verbalize and behave behind the wheel in traffic will function as a model for the children in the back seat when they grow up and start driving. An expression he coined that became very popular in the language-teaching field is *"communicative competence"*. This idea was meant to make a distinction between mere linguistic competence and the actual ability to use the language for communication.

However most of his neologisms remained unaddressed by others. Some of these are: *"cross-modality transfer effect"*, *"ethnosemantic hexagram series"* (trigram, hexagram, ennead, double hexagram, electric couple), *"existential neologisms"*, *"mental anatomy"*, *"the mental world of eternity"*, *"vertical community"*, and *"self-witnessing"*. The full list of his neologisms

with explanations is available on the Web at:
http://theisticpsychology.org/books/neologisms/neochartp1.htm

For the past thirty years he has focused his research especially on the *Writings of Swedenborg*, looking for ways to transform Swedenborg's ideas into the language and theory of modern scientific psychology. Leon James coined the expression "theistic psychology" in 1990. He acknowledges E. Swedenborg (1688-1772) as the actual Founder of theistic psychology, though Swedenborg himself did not use this expression. This book on experiencing regeneration is the latest instance of that continuing task. Several useful spiritual ideas emerge from this effort. Just four of these ideas will be mentioned here, as they are discussed throughout this book.

(a) Born Immortal

A central idea elaborated by Leon James is the novel principle, which is unheard of in modern psychology, that *the spiritual world of the afterlife is the mental world of eternity*. This may be the greatest discovery of his career. The consequence of this equation is that *every human being is born into eternity and thereby is immortal*. Every mind and its personality or self is immortal because it already exists in eternity. Therefore instead of "death" Leon James discusses in this book the "three-day dying-resuscitation process" by which our spiritual body is disjoined from the dead physical body. We then immediately gain consciousness of the surrounds and begin to interact with the people who are already in the afterlife. Our spiritual body upon resuscitation has the same appearance as our former physical body, but this changes after a little while.

(b) Vertical Community (spirits)

A second insight from Swedenborg needed a new name to express the idea in the language of modern psychology, namely, the existence of the *vertical community*. This idea describes how every individual's mental life is anatomically connected to the mental life of those who are already in the afterlife. There is therefore a hitherto unknown anatomical interconnection from each human being to every other. This amazing new view expands the meaning of community from "horizontal community" that depends on geographical place and time, to "vertical community" that is independent of fixed time and place. The psychological implications of this discovery are numerous and remain to be followed up. The concept of a vertical community opens up whole new areas of study, research, and application in human mental health and in community organization.

(c) As-of Self (Instead of Self)

The third new concept proposed by Leon James for modern psychology is the idea of the *as-of self*. This concept replaces the idea of the self, or more precisely, proposes the next phase of human evolution. When we think of ourselves as an "as-of self" we are able to overcome the illusion that our mental life is from ourselves. This illusion ignores the actuality of the vertical community, and this results in many debilitating symptoms in psychological functioning and interpersonal relations. Equally important, the "as-of self" concept clarifies the relationship between individual freedom and God's omnipotence. Experiencing regeneration is possible with the "as-of self" concept because it allows us to separate ourselves from selfish loves and inherited evil inclinations. Psychologically we can now stop identifying with negative feelings and intentions, and this gives us the freedom and opportunity to adopt new altruistic traits. This process equips our personality with positive traits that will allow us to enjoy the life of heaven in the afterlife.

(d) Mental Anatomy

The fourth concept is the idea that *mind has an anatomy and organic structure*. Without organs the mind is not real. Hence arose materialism and reductionism in materialistic science whereby the mind is tied completely to the physical brain and not actually existing in its own realm, world, or substantive permanence. In that materialistic view, when the brain dies, so does the mind. This idea is disturbing to people because it gives them the idea of being impermanent, and this is the experiencing of death. Everything

12

changes when we consider the new proposal of *mental anatomy*, which restores scientific dualism to historical psychology. Now for the first time psychology of mind is discussed as anatomy of the spiritual body and its threefold system of affective, cognitive, and sensorimotor.

Dr. James started studying *Swedenborg's Writings* in 1981. Full text access to most of his Swedenborgian books and articles is available at the Theistic Psychology Web Site: http://theisticpsychology.org/index.htm

Chapter 1
God, Mind and Human Immortality

Are We to Think of God as a Man or a Woman

Increasingly people are wondering why God is defined and represented as male. As more women are elevated to important cultural and religious positions, there has been a movement to have God be declared as a woman. This idea and motive are natural extensions of natural consciousness. It comes up in the mind when God is an abstract idea in people's thinking.

This section will analyze the issue from the perspective of spiritual-rational consciousness.

A concern has been expressed by some that it's detrimental to the mental development of girls to think that men are more "in the image of God" then women are. According to this idea, if God is a man then men are more important than women because they are more like God. Another argument has been that since God created human beings in God's image, it must mean that God is both a male and a female. Hence it would be beneficial to represent God as either a man or a woman. It is believed that women would be able to relate more intimately and lovingly to God-as-woman than to the current God-as-male.

The idea that God is both male and female, or man and woman, does not take into account the fact that God created human beings as male and female. *The Creator cannot be the created.* God created human beings, animals, plants, and planets. It does not follow that God is one of these things or all of them together. Rationally we would say that God is none of

14

these since the Creator cannot be the created. Hence it is not rational to say that God is male or female or both.

Some religions insist that it is wrong to try to describe God as possessing this or that trait because God is above and beyond all things that we can see or think of. Other religions portray God as man, sometimes old with a beard, sometimes young with long hair. Still others describe God as a man with three heads, or else, one head and three bodies. Sometimes they are portrayed as three separate Gods but acting together in unison as one God. These portrayals and descriptions are fantasies. Sometimes God is described as shapeless and no different than the universe itself.

This type of thinking is strictly immersed in the lowest level of natural consciousness called corporeal consciousness. It fails to take into account the different levels of existence that God created and is maintaining in both worlds.

People who avoid this type of corporeal thinking about God feel inspired from within to think of God as a Divine Human person or God-Man. In order to have a reciprocal relationship with God it is necessary to inhibit all natural and corporeal ideas of God that are discussed by people. If you think of God in natural terms then God is no longer omnipresent. It is impossible to be in all places when one is in one of the places. The only way God could create spaces, time, and two worlds is from outside spaces, time, and either world. This goes back to the rational precept that the Creator cannot be the created. To be omnipresent God has to be apart from time and space. If God were in space or in time, God would no longer be infinite and omnipresent. To be in time or in space would be limiting God's infinity, which is erroneous.

People often accept the idea that God is infinite and perfect in love, goodness, truth, wisdom, and rationality. This idea gives us the departure point for understanding rationally what God is and is not. Note that love, goodness, truth, wisdom, and rationality are human qualities that must be located in some human person. Can you think of these traits as abstracted or separated from a human person? Can these traits exist if they are not in God and not in some human being? They cannot. And so God must be thought of as a human person possessing a character, mind, and

15

consciousness that are identified as love, goodness, truth, wisdom, and rationality.

Once we think of God as a human person in whose mind there is love, goodness, truth, wisdom, and rationality, we must add the idea of substance to God. Since God exists from eternity to eternity and therefore already existed before all creation, we can ask what was God made of since nothing was yet created. You can see that a human person with mental traits cannot exist in nothing.

It must be therefore that there existed in God things that were not created but have always existed in God from eternity to eternity with never a beginning or an end.

We conclude therefore that there exist both uncreate and created things. Each and all uncreate things must be Divine and infinite having existed in God from eternity to eternity as part of God's mind. We have mentioned love, goodness, truth, wisdom, and rationality as some of the uncreate things in God. But since God is infinite we must conclude that each uncreate thing is also infinite and eternal.

Taken all together, we can think of God as a human person in whom infinite uncreate human things are held together as one. This is God's conscious human mind.

When we are initiating a reciprocal relationship with God this is the God whom we love and depend on. To love God therefore means to love God's love, God's goodness, truth, wisdom, and rationality. When we love all these things we love God.

You must exercise care here to avoid the awful conclusion that some people draw from this infinity of God, that therefore in God there must be both good and evil, otherwise where did evil come from? This idea is irrational and therefore wrong because, if there were evil in God, then we could not think of God as perfect in love and goodness. We must therefore find another explanation for where evil came from, if not from God. Once we go a little further in our analysis, and introduce the idea of God's substance and anatomy, we will see clearly that evil originated in the minds of human beings and not in God.

God's Substance and Divine Human Anatomy

Now we need to consider what is the substance and anatomy of the infinite uncreate things that are eternally in God's mind.

You'll need to allow in your mind the idea that minds have an anatomy. Since we are raised in a materialistic culture immersed in natural and corporeal consciousness, we have gotten into the cognitive habit of thinking of our mind as less real than our body. This is an error due to our cultural and educational materialism that irrationally assumes that mental activity can operate within physical materials such as the physical body and brain. This is the error of "reductionism", a term that is known in the history of psychology and has been used throughout modern contemporary neuroscience. According to this flattened view, mind has no anatomy of its own other than that of the physical brain. Hence when the physical body dies, so must the mind, the self, the person, and the human being. There is no room here for the idea of the immortality of the mind and person.

But if you can let go of this materialistic prejudice and error you can then begin to understand that the mind has an anatomy of its own since without an organic structure there can be no mind and no mental activity. Feeling, thinking, and sensing are mental activities. Since the mental cannot exist in the physical, the rational conclusion must be that the mind exists apart from physical time and space and their gross material substances. The only way such a mind can exist is if there is world of its own in which mental activities can exist. This world is not physical, therefore not in space or in time.

The rational conclusion must be that God created two worlds, one physical and the other mental.

This idea is known in the history of science as "dualism". The details of dualism and how they relate to the anatomy of our mind is treated of throughout this book. If for now you are willing to accept the idea of scientific dualism then you can begin to see how the human mind and God's mind must have a mental anatomy that is organic and structural. All the infinite uncreate things in God's mind mentioned above are therefore living organic substances. They have a form that is organized into an

17

anatomy, which as we have seen above is a human anatomy, thus like our mind and its mental anatomy.

Human mental anatomy is easy to picture and study once you realize and accept the idea that the mind is actually a mental body. This is a critical but necessary component of the total picture, if it is to be understood scientifically and rationally. What is a "mental body"? You can also call it a "spiritual body" since mental and spiritual are closely connected and overlap in meaning, though this is still not known to many people. If you say the "spiritual world", you can also say the "mental world" to refer to the same thing. Consider for instance love and truth. These are mental concepts of things that are in the mind. Since they are of substance, we conclude that mental substance is the same as spiritual substance, and mental world is the same as spiritual world. Hence when we say the "spiritual world of eternity in the afterlife" we can equally say the "mental world of eternity in the afterlife".

This is an awesome conclusion! It means that our mind or spiritual body is born into eternity and hence is immortal.

We are immortal human beings, each one of us. There is no way of dying or escaping immortality. For human beings, once alive always alive. This is clear when we consider again that our mind is made up of the uncreate and eternal substances called love, goodness, truth, and rationality, which are in God and out of which God created the mental world and the physical universe.

All human traits originate in God's mind and flow out into the mental world where everyone's mind is born and exists forever. God does not create objects out of nothing, as this is rationally impossible. Yet everything God does is rational as indicated by the order of things in reality. In God's mind infinite things make one. Everything in God's mind is uncreate and eternal. Hence the source of all things that have been created are the uncreate things that existed always from eternity to eternity.

God used the uncreate things in his mind to form and build all the created things in the universe.

The first of all creation was the mental sun of eternity. This is also called the spiritual sun of the afterlife of eternity. This Divine living mental sun

18

contains the substances of God's mind. From this spiritual sun all things were created. It is called a "spiritual sun" because it emits spiritual heat-substance and spiritual light-substance. This Divine mental heat and light expand around the spiritual sun and create atmospheres in which spaces and objects can exist and have their being. First, spiritual heat-substance and light-substance create the expanse that we call the mental world of eternity. This expanse is made of living spiritual heat and light. Our mind therefore exists and survives in this collective mental world created and intended for the human race.

It takes a while to get used to thinking about spiritual heat as love-substance and spiritual light as truth-substance. We can do this if we abandon the prejudices of our materialistic natural consciousness. Love is often used as a word referring to what we are feeling, and truth is often used to refer to what we are thinking. It's normal to talk this way about love and truth. But now we are asking a scientific question when we desire to know where does the feeling of love come from, and where does the thinking of truth come from. The answer will take us to the issue of the difference between a man and a woman, and whether God is to be thought of as male or female.

Love-substance and truth-substance are uncreate eternal and living substances in God's mind, as discussed above. God is the Divine Human that existed from eternity to eternity and prior to all creation. God is called Human prior to all creation because God acts from love according to truth. *This is the spiritual definition of what it means to be human.* God the Divine Human person experiences the desire to create human beings in the image of God. Human beings are called "human" because we act with conscious purpose from the will by means of our understanding. This is the definition of being human. This is why we say that human beings are created in the "image and likeness" of God who is the first and only original human in itself. All other humans are derivative from the original Human.

Animals do not act with conscious purpose from the will by means of the understanding. They are therefore not human. We can love God consciously and thus reciprocate God's love for us, and thereby we are conjoined with God and live forever. Animals do not have the mental anatomy capable of understanding of who God is and how to have a conscious reciprocating relationship with God.

19

Experiencing Regeneration

In natural consciousness it is common to think that human beings are human because of their physical body. Materialistic psychology has fully accepted the theory of evolution, which says that the human body is anatomically and genetically derived from an animal non-human ancestry. This confusion comes from denying the existence of the mental world as a separate world from the physical. In spiritual-rational consciousness we can see that the physical body is a derivative and a representative of the spiritual body, which is our mind in the mental world. *It is the spiritual body or mind that makes us human.* Our physical body is indeed human but it is an image in physical matter of our spiritual body, which is of mental matter or substance.

When we awaken from the two-day dying-resuscitation procedure we appear in our spiritual body exactly like our former physical body since they are images of each other. People who knew us on earth will know us in the afterlife because they can recognize us in our spiritual body. What makes us human when we no longer have the physical body? It is our mind. That is what defines being human. Animals do not have a human mind and this is why they are not human. If we remove the reality and anatomy of our mind or mental-spiritual body, then we have no choice but to falsely conclude that human bodies are derived and evolved from a lower species, that is, from animals. Our physical body may be seen as continuous with the body of certain animal species like chimpanzees and gorillas, as long as we fail to define the human mind as having real and permanent spiritual existence separate from the physical body.

Now we can come back to the question we posed at the outset: if there is one Divine Human who created men and women in God's image, then what is God's gender: male, female, both, or neither?

We now need first to define male and female anatomically and mentally. God created the human mind from the spiritual sun of eternity from which stream forth love-substance and truth-substance. In God's mind love-substance and truth-substance are united as one. When exiting the immediate sphere of the spiritual sun, love-substance and truth-substance are separated and act as two instead of one, each having their own distinct function in creation. Love-substance in created atmospheres and objects of the mental and physical worlds seeks out truth-substance that is also in them, and strives to reunite with it. There are two distinct mental-spiritual forms in which this reuniting process takes place genetically and

20

anatomically. One is for the love-substance to surround and completely cover up truth-substance and incorporate it within itself. Love-substance is then on the outside of the organic structure, while truth-substance is contained on the inside. This love-truth mental gene is the form of the female mind. Everything whatsoever that exists in the female mind is composed only of such female genes. The reverse anatomy forms the gene of the male mind, namely, love-substance covers itself up with truth-substance, like a cocoon, and all further things in the anatomy of the male mind is composed only of such truth-love genes.

In other words, a woman's mind is love-substance on the outside and truth-substance on the inside. A man's mind is truth-substance on the outside and love-substance on the inside.

You can see from this that both men and women were created in God's image, from the love and truth in God's mind, but arranged in reverse anatomical order.

When we relate to God in a sensorimotor or corporeal consciousness, which is the lowest form of human experiencing, we can wonder whether God as a male Divine Man can really understand a woman's perspective and experiencing. Hence some women in certain churches want God to be a woman. But this natural desire ceases when men and women learn to be conscious of God in a universal sense as Divine Human love-substance and truth-substance. We can then realize that God is not on the outside looking in, but is just as much on the inside looking out. In that perspective it can't be that women can relate better to a God who is pictured as a woman. God is inside a woman's mind, just as much as outside as long as you see God as love-substance and truth-substance. God is a partner and actuator of the individual's thoughts, feelings, and sensations. God is inside the woman's sensations or feelings and is actuating them, and managing them, just as God is inside the man's sensations and thoughts. It then makes no sense to think that our experiencing of God might be less intimate than it is.

How God Created the Universe

Every human being consists of two things: a physical body and a spiritual-mental body. These two bodies are discrete to each other, which means they each belong to their own realm, world, or substance. *The physical body is born and dies in the physical world of time-space, while the spiritual-mental body is born and exists in the mental world of the afterlife that is in eternity.* The two discrete worlds, each with the materials or substances they contain, cannot be mixed or intermingled. One cannot go from one to the other for there is no connecting bridge. The interaction between the physical world and the mental-spiritual world is by built-in correspondence. This means that they act synchronously or at the same time, starting from the spiritual body, which then affects the physical body.

The mind is located in the spiritual body only, and none of it in the physical body. If I think in the spiritual body of raising my hand, the physical body reacts and my hand is automatically and unconsciously raised. When we will or intend some goal in the mind or spiritual body, along with a plan, the physical body executes that plan. In this way we gain knowledge and experience, which develop our natural mind.

The maturation of the natural mind with its natural consciousness takes place in early adulthood and at that time we are immersed in natural consciousness from the experiencing of our natural mind for two decades. Everything we think and understand connects to the physical and natural world of fixed time, space, and quantity of materials. In the natural mind we have no ability to understand what is a "mental world of the afterlife". It seems like it is nothing. *If we accept the idea of an afterlife, then we place it here on earth.* In natural consciousness we cannot realistically imagine an afterlife that is not on earth and is not in fixed space or time. Similarly, when we relate to God in natural consciousness we do so through performing collective ritual worship and scripted verbal declarations of prayer. The idea of a different and separate "personal" relationship with God does not seem likely or feasible in this state of mind.

When we are in natural consciousness and are considering the idea of God and the afterlife, we often ask for some proof that there is a God or the afterlife. Later when we are experiencing regeneration and are entering the awareness of spiritual consciousness, we can see the lack of logic of wanting a physical proof for the existence of a mental reality such as God or the afterlife. Physical realities or facts need physical proof, not mental, while spiritual realities or facts need spiritual or mental proof, which is also called *rational proof*.

Experiencing Regeneration

Rational proof of the existence of God and the afterlife of eternity is easy to obtain in spiritual consciousness, which allows us to assume the existence of God as a rational premise that does not need to be proved. Natural consciousness rejects this assumption and illogically insists on physical proof of the afterlife, which is irrational.

The rational proof of an afterlife and of our immortality is as follows. It involves four steps up from natural consciousness and into spiritual consciousness, which is based on spiritual-rational perceptions and understandings that cohere into a unity of diverse parts.

(Step 1) Confirming the premise of scientific dualism

In spiritual-rational consciousness we can consider the distinction between physical and non-physical, which is called mental or spiritual. When we say "spiritual" or "mental" it is the same thing. So the first step is to acknowledge two distinct worlds or dualism, which is the separation between the physical, which is in fixed time-space, and the mental, which is apart from fixed time in eternity. Dualism is a rational necessity once we accept the existence of God as a premise since in order to create the world of fixed time-space God had to be apart from fixed-time space. This "apart from" is eternity in the mental world.

(Step 2) Confirming the idea that the "spiritual" is the same as the "mental" and that both are in eternity apart from fixed time-space.

It is a logical error to say that God created the universe "out of nothing" since from nothing, there can be derived or composed nothing. Whatever exists must have something it is made of, and this is called its *substance*. "Nothing" is not a substance, and therefore God had to use some substance to create the world and the objects that are in it. What was this substance?

Since the world was not yet created there was no substance except the Divine substance that was in God and was part of God. Hence it logically follows that God created the universe out of the Divine substance that always was and existed within God Himself. We need to consider what was this Divine substance in God that He used to build up everything created.

Experiencing Regeneration

The primary substance within God's mind is *Divine Love*. The secondary substance united with the first is Divine Truth. Love is the action of the will in the mind and expresses itself as an intention to do something specific. Love specifies the goal that is desired, therefore the motive that is involved in the execution or performance, in which the love is embodied and consummated. God's motive and intention in creating the universe was the desire to create human beings with a mind that is an image of His Divine Human mind, and is capable of receiving His love and of loving Him in return.

God wanted a reciprocal relationship with conscious human beings who could receive God's goodness and thereby be made happy in conjugial heaven to eternity. And this He still wants today, and will want forever. Hence the creation of the universe never ended and will always be going on.

In natural consciousness we reject the idea of "love as mental substance" out of which things can be built like those there are in our world. We prefer to think of oxygen as a physical substance that is a component in many things on earth. But love-substance and truth-substance appear as nothing since they have no physical embodiment, like oxygen does. These limitations in natural-rational thinking are not present in spiritual-rational thinking in which we can perceive the universal idea of discrete degrees in creation, from higher to lower. At each discrete level there are different forms and functions of love-substance and truth-substance. Through this mechanism of causation in creation, Divine love as mental substance can undergo transformations of itself into lower and lower discrete steps, until at the bottom, the living substance of love has been covered over by several levels of substances and materials. Love is still the inmost level of any object but it is no longer visible in the lower levels as with air or stone. Physical objects have lost all living mental properties and have taken on the appearance of lifeless and rigidified properties of materials on earth. *A dead stone is therefore created out of the living mental substance of Divine love when it is embodied in a lower degree of existence.*

The substance of Divine truth is united to Divine love-substance that exists in God's mind. But as it exteriorizes from God into the created universe love-substance and truth-substance are separated and take part in different functions. This is like the heat and light from our natural sun that reaches our earth. In the sun the heat and the light act as a unified matter,

Experiencing Regeneration

but when its rays hit earth's atmosphere and surface of the earth, the two are no longer unified. Light has its distinct properties and functions and so does heat. Divine love-substance has a specific activating power on our affective system, while truth-substance is received by our cognitive system and activates it. Our mind must therefore have an anatomy with receptor organs such as the affective and cognitive systems that provide us with the experiencing of feelings and thoughts. This mind's anatomy is called the spiritual body, which is born along with the physical body but in different realms or worlds. The spiritual body is in the realm called the mental world of eternity, while the physical body is in the realm called the natural or physical world. You can see why the spiritual body or mind cannot exist in the natural world since nothing mental can exist in the physical as they belong to discretely different realms from creation.

The reason the mental world is called eternity is very well known to everyone though few people may think about it until a discussion on it comes up as here. Everyone can confirm the fact that there is no fixed time or space in our thoughts and dreams. Psychological time varies with mental states but physical time is fixed and determined by the motion of stars and the vibration of atoms. Our thought can travel from one part of our globe to another in an instant, the same as when we think about the refrigerator in our kitchen. Our daydream or imagination can construct a room of any size, as needed by the arriving visitors. So there is no physical time and physical space in our mental world, which includes our feelings, thoughts, and sensations.

The world that has no fixed time, no fixed space, and no physical materials, is called the mental world of eternity.

(Step 3) The third step in the rational justification of God is to rationally connect the mental world of eternity to the afterlife world of eternity.

From a rational perspective there is only one eternity possible, just as there can be only one infinite. *Hence it logically follows that the mental world is the same as the spiritual world of the afterlife.*

Human beings are born into the mental world of eternity. Our spiritual body or mind is immortal since it is born outside time. Only that which is born in time can die or be temporary. For many centuries people have been searching and hoping for finding the secret to immortality not knowing that they were already immortal to begin with.

(Step 4) The fourth step is to acknowledge the meaning of mental "anatomy" and love as substance.

It is impossible in natural consciousness to make sense of the idea of love-substance and truth-substance as the basic building blocks and underlying framework of human minds and the physical world. But for now you can allow yourself to put this limitation aside and to imagine that love is not just a feeling in our mind but a substance that originates from outside of ourselves that flows in and creates that feeling in our mind. It is analogous with the various objects that we see around us. What is it that allows us to see them? It is the light that shines of the objects and their reflection then flows into the eyes. Light and heat from the sun are actually physical substances. Similarly there is a sun in the mental world of eternity and its heat and light are spiritual substances originating from the love and truth in God's mind.

You can see now that if the mental world of eternity is constructed out of Divine love-substance (or spiritual heat) and Divine truth-substance (or spiritual light), then the collective mental world and our personal mental world overlap and form part of the mental anatomy of the universe.

These four rational confirming steps will be further elaborated and integrated in what follows.

The Mental World of Eternity

In order to benefit from the awareness of spiritual consciousness we need to know some of the mental anatomy that is involved in the process of elevating our consciousness.

We will then be in a position of reasoning with universal principles that take into account the anatomy of the human mind. We speak of the "anatomy" of our mind because the mind is an organ and all organs have a structure or an anatomy.

Experiencing Regeneration

The organ of the human mind is the spiritual body.

All human beings are born with two bodies, one physical, and the other spiritual. *The mind is not physical hence it is impossible for its objects like sensations, thoughts or feelings to be in a physical realm such as the physical brain or body.* Our entire mind is the spiritual body. The appearance of the spiritual body if you could see it would be that of yourself in a mirror, with at different times progressive changes that reflect the content and flow of your thoughts, emotions, and feelings. When you are mentally a mature adult your spiritual body appears as yourself in a full adult state.

Our two bodies are functionally and synchronously linked, muscle-by-muscle, organ-by-organ, cell-by-cell, gene-by-gene, and atom-by-atom. The difference is that the physical body is made of matters from earth and the planet, like carbon, hydrogen, and oxygen, while the spiritual body is made of matters from the mental world like truths, loves, and meanings. This is a difficult idea to grasp at first, namely how mental objects like thoughts and feelings can be made of some material or substance that is formed into a structure like an organ. And yet rationality requires that if something is something then it must be made of something.

What then are mental sensations and thoughts made of?

At birth our spiritual body is born with the organs of the human body. These organs are made of the materials or substances that are available in the mental atmosphere of the spiritual environment. These spiritual materials stream out from the spiritual sun as spiritual heat and spiritual light. So our mind and its mental organs are made of these two mental materials or substances which can be varied infinitely, so that no two mental organs or minds are ever the same to eternity.

Now here comes the mind-stopper and heart-quickener: Spiritual heat is nothing else than pure Divine love and goodness, and spiritual light is nothing else than pure Divine wisdom and intelligence.

So our mind and its organs are made of pure Divine love-substance and pure Divine intelligence-substance.

Experiencing Regeneration

This is the anatomical reason why human beings are automatically born into immortality.

Now here is another amazing spiritual revelation: There is only one mental world or spiritual world, and only one spiritual sun.

We are each born into the same communal mental world of the entire human race! No one has ever been born anywhere else, regardless of where in the universe their physical body is sourced and attached to the spiritual body or mind.

Every human mind is born into the one mental world of eternity.

There is nothing of our mind in the physical body or world.

The fact that there is only one mental world for everyone is an amazing fact that kept on amazing me for a long time, and still does after many years of thinking and saying it to others. We can confirm this fact by direct experiencing the instant we are resuscitated through the two-day dying-resuscitation process. We then have spiritual consciousness and live in a mental world in a spiritual body. Everything around us is now visible and touchable. There are no physical distances or limits since this is a mental world with its rules of navigation. In this world you have instant access to anyone who ever lived in the human race because the mind of all human beings is in the one shared collective mental world.

This means that when you think of someone with the desire to be closer, you and the person now appear together up close and face-to-face. You can hear and touch each other and feel everything you felt while connected to the physical body on earth. But now the sensations are much keener and purer than was possible through the mediation of the gross material body.

The mental world of humanity is therefore the mental world of each of us, and we are all together in that one mental world.

We cannot consciously experience this fact until the dying-resuscitation process that liberates our spiritual body from being tied down to the gross physical. Then upon resuscitation or awakening a few hours later, we are fully in the experiencing of the mental world of eternity where everyone is who had already "passed on". An eyewitness report of the dying-resuscitation process is presented in the Appendix at the end of the book.

The spiritual world was created in a certain organic shape that is familiar to us as the human form or body. It is a mental world because its atmospheres and composing elements are all mental, namely (1) love-substance or goodness-substance and (2) intelligence-substance or truth-substance. These love and truth are mental objects and mental materials or substances. *Everything composed of these will also be mental.* Hence the entire universe has been created out of mental substances that belong to God's mind.

But obviously these mental substances can appear with many properties and in different shapes, and make up the composition of the two basic building blocks of reality, namely mental objects and physical objects. Although both categories are sourced in mental substance, nevertheless physical and mental objects appear outwardly as very different. We experience this when we compare in our mind things that we know and feel, which are mental objects, to things in the physical world that are material, like a chair or a mountain.

Everyone's mind or spiritual body is shaped along the common human anatomy of the body. For instance, the circulatory system of blood and cell nutrition in the physical body corresponds in the spiritual body to the *affective system* whose operation provides us with what we experience as sensations, emotions, or feelings. The respiratory system of oxygenation and voicing in speech in the physical body correspond to the *cognitive system* in the spiritual body, whose operation provides us with the experiencing of thoughts, images, representations, meanings, and understandings.

For instance, when breathing ceases, so does all cognitive activity and thinking. Our two bodies are connected by the spiritual laws of correspondence that are built in from creation, and govern the relationship between mental and physical things. When spiritual heat or love-substance ceases to flow into the affective system of the spiritual body, the heartbeat in the physical body stops and all its life activity ceases. This is immediately followed by the two-day dying-resuscitation procedure by which God extirpates the spiritual body and separates it from the physical body and consequently, the physical world. We then awaken in awareness in spiritual consciousness and continue our immortal life in the mental world of eternity.

The mental world into which our spiritual body is born and lives forever, is divided into anatomical regions and zones of operation. Our consciousness has permanent anatomical access to any part of the mental world. The highest regions of the human mind have traditionally been called "heaven" or "the heavens" while the lowest regions have been called "hell" or "the hells". You can experience at any time either heaven or hell in your mental regions. On a really good day when you feel great you are experiencing some of the heavenly mental states, and on a really bad day in your life when all goes wrong and your heart is in the dumps, you can experience hell.

But most of the time most of us find ourselves here on earth neither in heaven nor in hell, but in some in-between mental region that may be called the *regeneration zone*. This is the anatomical region that gives us the ability to be dual citizens, possessing a permanent spiritual body for our mind and a temporary physical body for our years on earth. In this dual anatomical mental state we have open communication and connection with both our upper regions and lower regions, thus, with both heaven and hell. Our experiencing moment-by-moment results from alternations between heaven and hell in our mind. In any one situation we may have open communication with heaven and closed with hell; or vice versa. Hence comes our experiencing of mood swings such as being in a good mood in one moment and exploding with rage in another moment. Peace with calm and confidence is experience from heaven, while disturbing and unpleasant emotion is experience from hell.

Every person's spiritual body inherits from parents and ancestors specific mental fibers that connect anatomically to heavenly and hellish societies. Everyone after resuscitation undergoes mental changes that bring out one's chief loves to the surface of the personality where they are expressed and consummated in social interactions with those who are also in the mental zone of regeneration. All the hellish loves that we have accumulated in our personality are then gathered together in a bundle, and so are all the heavenly loves. Each love is an anatomical connection to either heavenly or hellish societies that exist in our mind by inheritance and by acquisition in daily living.

Experiencing Regeneration

The two-day dying-resuscitation process separates the spiritual from the physical. In that new anatomical mental state there is experienced a gradual but persistent change in our dual relationship to heaven and hell. Our more interior loves push their way through to the surface of our personality as they are no longer kept hidden for fear of the law or social persecution. Soon there is one chief love that takes over all of our life and becomes the ruling love of our personality. Nothing else matters unless it promotes this ruling love.

Our chief love is that which we love more than anything.

After resuscitation everyone's chief love comes out to visibility and decisive action. *This begins our anatomical rise-or-slide in the mental world of eternity.* The anatomical end point for every human being is either heaven or hell in the mental world of eternity. In the regeneration zone of the afterlife we gradually lose the ability to be dual citizens and to alternate experiencing either the upper or lower regions of our mind. Love is acting forever. Our chief love never gives up.

In eternity the quality of our life, consciousness, and experiencing are totally determined by the quality of our chief love.

As you proceed through this book much more will be said about the mental world of eternity and how our mind fits into it. *If you keep this knowledge alive in your thinking you will possess the tools you need for undergoing your regeneration successfully.* The whole purpose of this book is to give you the knowledge and skills needed to experience your regeneration. Anatomically examined our inherited mind is like a large and mature plant that has grown across the field and valley and now spreads out and connects to all its many branches near and far. But this large plant is doomed and cannot survive because another large plant of an invasive species is growing all around its branches, which have now begun to suffocate.

Regeneration is the anatomical process of pruning these two plants. The suffocating plant species must be disentangled and cut, freeing the good plant and giving it new life to expand and propagate. We are born with a mind that contains heaven and hell. We are born with inherited genetic connections to societies in both these regions of the human mental world.

Experiencing Regeneration

The required spiritual job in this life for every individual is to prune one's personality and to disentangle it clear free from involvements with the suffocating and invasive species of negative emotions from hell. When we undergo the dying-resuscitation process we awaken to a regenerated personality that has solid ties with the heavenly regions in our mind and is now willing to let go and give up whatever ties still remain to hellish emotions and lusts.

We have the choice now, to slide or to rise, but not later.

Experiencing Our Dual Nature: Natural and Spiritual

We are all familiar with the spiritual -- once we realize that the spiritual part of us is *mental* while the natural part of us is *physical*.

We experience the spiritual every time we are aware of what we are thinking or feeling. What can be more familiar to every human being than the mental world? This becomes obvious as soon as we realize that the expression "the mental world" is to be interpreted as being a real world that is distinct and different from the physical world. Those who base their thinking on only what is natural observation define the mental world as a subjective or illusory perspective that emerges from the physical brain and its operations. Therefore, they say, when the physical body dies the thoughts, feelings, knowledge, and memory that we call the mental world then vanishes into nothing. So it's not really a world of its own like the physical world is, according to this view.

However this materialistic idea of our mind is clearly inadequate and unconvincing to anyone who thinks in terms of the experiencing of reality.

If we are willing to make the observation we can actually experience our dual nature and reality. Some people talk about "that little voice in my head", explaining that when they listen to it as a warning about some act they can avoid trouble or an accident. Some people can mentally hear an entire song by the original artist, and most people can hear fragments. We can think back on an encounter with someone, and see the face and mentally hear the voice of that person. The voices in our mind are real mental events taking place in the mental world.

The world of the "internet" is analogous to this. Everything we do online happens in the *cyberworld* which exists in "digital cloud" that can be seen or reached from an appropriate device located anywhere on the planet. The virtual cloud is the repository of information that may be your own, having placed it there yourself, or other people's. There is only one cyberworld, which may also be called virtual world or digital world. Whatever you and others do online it happens in the same online world. Hence anyone can reach or communicate with anyone else regardless of their physical location. People thinking with a materialistic consciousness deny that there is such a thing as a cyber world. They point instead to computers and say that the cyber world is nothing but these computers who get interconnected by wires or Wi-Fi.

But in spiritual consciousness one can see that the cyberworld or "infosphere" does not refer to the connected computers that form the Internet grid. This is merely the skeleton or hardware. Roads and streets do not make traffic, but only the cars and their drivers trying to get somewhere. Interconnected computers do not make the cyberworld, but only the information and the minds of people consuming it.

Time and place in the physical world are defined as fixed according to the planet's rotation or according to the vibrations of a tiny piece of quartz. On the other hand, time and place in the mental world are not fixed. Psychological time can stop, or go either slowly or fast depending on the mental state that we are in. Mental place is not fixed on a map, and any mental distance can be traveled in an instant. Travelling with our physical body must be mile by mile, while travelling with our spiritual body depends on changes in our mental states, which can be either immediate or by gradual intermediate steps.

Objects in the physical world such as a lake, a house, or money in the pocket, are fixed according to quantity or numbers, while objects in the mental world are created instantaneously in any quantity or shape by our wishes or loves. We know this from dreams, daydreams, and fantasies. These are real mental objects and operations in a real world. Our loves and desires are mental powers in that world by which we can produce any object or act upon the mental objects that exist in the mental world created

Experiencing Regeneration

by the minds of other people. People's fantasies and emotions are actually visible in the mental world after resuscitation. This phenomenon takes place because thoughts and emotions are real mental substances in their particular form, and emit themselves in the mental atmosphere that is all around the person's spiritual body for others to witness.

In order to think of mental objects and operations as real and as occurring in a real world *we must think of them as occurring in an organic atmosphere.*

The human mind is a spiritual organ constructed out of elements or substances in the mental world of eternity. Every human being is born to function in the two worlds. Therefore we possess from birth a spiritual body to function in the mental world and a physical body to function in the natural world. These two bodies are identical in form and function but different in composing elements. The spiritual body is composed of the matters and substances that exist freely in the mental world and originating from the spiritual sun that exists in that world. This Divine sun is an outpouring into creation from God's own mind or spirit. It is made of spiritual heat, which is pure love-substance or "good", and of spiritual light, which is pure intelligence-substance or "truth". These two mental materials are substantial and when they change state and degree they become physical and solidified in the form of stars and planets.

The infrastructure of the physical universe is therefore constructed out of the mental substances of love and intelligence.

The spiritual heat and light from the sun of the mental world supply all the mental atmospheres and objects that surround the spiritual body, and including the spiritual body itself. Similarly, the physical body is composed of the matters and elements that exist in the atmospheres and earths of the natural world that originate in the natural sun and other stars.

Our two bodies from birth develop synchronously and change in a corresponding manner. As the physical body grows through the organic chemical nutrients of the planet and sun, the spiritual body grows through the mental nutrients that stream into the mental world from the spiritual sun.

Experiencing Regeneration

The mental nutrients that grow our spiritual body are the infinite variations of spiritual heat and light that fill the atmospheres of the mental world. Spiritual heat is received by the affective organ of the spiritual body, and spiritual light is received by the cognitive organ. These two organs are mental receptor organs. They are organically structured to receive either spiritual heat or light from the spiritual sun. Spiritual heat is God's love in the form of atmospheric substances. When spiritual heat or love-substance inflows into the affective system, our will springs into life and is activated by loves and emotions.

The experiencing of this activation provides the consciousness of love, which involves feelings, intentions, attractions, sensations, emotions, desires, longings, pleasures, delights, and all things affective, including the opposites of these such as pain, fear, sadness, hatred, cruelty, etc.

Spiritual light is God's wisdom or intelligence in the form of atmospheric substances. When this truth-substance inflows into the cognitive system, our consciousness springs to life and is activated. The experiencing of this activation provides the awareness of thinking, which involves thoughts, knowledge, reasoning, language, memory, imagery, symbolic representation, counting, and all things cognitive, including the opposites of these such as unintelligent, foolish, illogical, false, deceitful, etc.

People who are functioning in natural consciousness will find this description of the mental world unclear and improbable. The reason is that we are taught to think materialistically from childhood onward in our enculturation and instruction. And so the mind and its mental world seem less real to us than the solid objects of the physical world. But we can overcome that limitation in our thinking, if we want to. This would be of great benefit to everyone since materialistic thinking about the mind has resulted in so much misery and mental un-health and powerlessness.

One way you can approach the issue of a substantial mental world is to think of your dream body and self that allows you to have experiences while asleep. As a dream character you are real to yourself and the objects around you are real. You can touch them, you can sense their touch and experience pleasure or pain. *These dream experiences are real and are occurring in a real world.* People say "they are just dreams" when they think of the material world as the only real world. The fact that dreams are real events in the mental world is proven to us by experiencing. We

35

actually experience the feelings and thoughts in dreams. We know this when we remember the dream after awakening from sleep. Experiencing cannot be based on nothing or on physical things. It is illogical to think this.

Hence from now on you can begin a new life that is based on knowledge and awareness of experiencing. If we rely on the rationality and logic of experiencing we cannot continue to be fooled and exploited by the ideas of materialism that have cost humanity such a tragic price in suffering, negativity, and confusion.

Why the Mental Is Real
While the Physical Is Not

Everyone's mind is trained to think upside down when immersed in natural consciousness. One instance of this fact is that "mental" things are considered "just" mental while physical things are considered real and solid. People sometimes say, "It's just a wish" or "just a hope". We hear others say "It's nothing. It's just something in my mind." And everyone is taught that "dreams are not reality" and that "reality is rock bottom". Most people think that the expression "mental world" is a metaphor or simile and not a real world in which there are people, cities, and activities. Education and science in natural consciousness are both so ignorant about reality that they have withdrawn and exiled all information and thinking about God and the afterlife of eternity where all human beings congregate through the dying-resuscitation process.

Although all of us have been raised in this upside down thinking our rational mind retains the ability to think spiritually. This capacity is never lost in a human being because our mental anatomy is built with that capacity and for that function. Anyone of us may luck upon a book such as this one that presents in spiritual consciousness genuine information and knowledge about spiritual consciousness. Genuine spiritual consciousness is that which is based on the spiritual sense of all genuine *Sacred Scripture. No one can experience this sense without maintaining a daily reciprocal relationship with God.*

In spiritual consciousness we think immersed in spiritual-rational thinking. Everyone is born with the capacity to live in spiritual consciousness. Our

36

Experiencing Regeneration

natural consciousness is only the first phase and is the exact inverse of the second phase, which is the stage of completion of becoming a full human being. In natural consciousness we are not quite complete human beings. We are a lot like animals, especially the so-called intelligent species like chimpanzees and dolphins. No wonder that materialistic science classifies human beings along with animal species. We are indeed animal before we become fully human when we raise ourselves to spiritual experiencing.

Once we stop rejecting spiritual ideas we give ourselves the opportunity of examining what is spiritual consciousness and how we are actually related to the world.

Spiritual-rational consciousness is based on this one ruling principle that defines all human rationality and meaning: Everything starts with God and everything ends with God.

If we are willing to approach this idea with a positive bias we can raise our experiencing from animal to true human, that is, from natural to spiritual. The idea starts in its most general form and if we favor it then we can begin to fill it with particulars and more meaning.

The general idea about God is that He is a Divine Person with a human mind and feelings, but who is infinite, omnipotent, omnipresent, omniscient, and perfect in love and compassion for us whom He created out of Himself.

If on reading this you feel awe, reassurance, and tearful happiness at this idea, you are on your way to more spiritual excitement and fulfillment.

Indeed, is it not remarkable and awesome that God is like us having feelings and thoughts, but without limit? And it is reassuring that God is moved by love and compassion for us, not by His own glory and by experimentation in creation. God is the original and only human in itself. He created the human race by replicating Himself in each person but on a finited plane of experiencing. As human beings each of us can experience what God experiences, but on a finite basis. *God is moved by love in creating us because His Divine Human love is such that it desires reciprocation in relationship with created human beings.*

37

Experiencing Regeneration

By entering spiritual consciousness we are entering into that reciprocal relationship that God longs for by which He can fulfill His Divine Human love and wisdom.

To fulfill this love God has created two worlds and manages their every detail. The first world was the mental world created out of the mental substances that God has in Himself. Since God is infinite He cannot be directly perceived by human beings who are created finite. But since God wants a reciprocal relationship with each human being that He creates, it is necessary for God to provide an appearance of Himself in the created world so that the individual with whom He has a relationship may be able to see God and have a reciprocal relationship with Him. Therefore He created the human mind with three anatomical levels of operation called the spiritual mind, the rational mind, and the natural mind.

God appears to our consciousness at each of the three levels, but in different modality or manner.

Each of us experiences these three levels of operation all the time but we are mostly aware of our natural mind's operations and its level of consciousness. We are however able to elevate our awareness from our natural consciousness to our spiritual consciousness. To our spiritual mind God appears as the Divine Human in whom infinite love and wisdom make one. In this spiritual (or celestial) appearance, God is nothing but the omnipresent love and wisdom as Divine substance that fills the created worlds. Since nothing existed except God, everything that was created was constructed out of God's Divine mental substance. This is how the mental world was first created out of the substance of love and wisdom.

Our mind is actually a spiritual body that we have since birth. Our mental organs cannot exist in a physical world. Everyone is aware that thoughts and feelings are mental, not physical. Our brain is physical and scientists who live in natural consciousness locate the mind in the physical brain. This is of course an impossibility and to believe it is to be spiritually insane. Our spiritual body (or the mind) and our physical body are born together but in different worlds. They are connected to each other by the built-in creation laws of correspondence. This connection is so all encompassing that our natural mind has no sensation or perception of this union or conjunction. To our natural consciousness our mind is in the physical body somewhere or everywhere in it. To believe this is to deny the afterlife of

Experiencing Regeneration

eternity, which is where the mind continues life after the two-day dying-resuscitation process that separates our physical body from our spiritual body. An eyewitness report of the dying-resuscitation process is presented in the Appendix at the end of the book.

The mind, or spiritual body, once separated from the physical world, at last can see the others in the mental world of eternity. Here we discover that the so-called "spiritual world after death" is nothing else then the mental world of eternity into which we were born and have always lived. It feels very familiar to us to live consciously in the collective mental world where all human beings live. Now we feel irresistibly attracted to certain mental states and spontaneously seek and find others who share this same love. We now realize that all along while on earth and in our natural mind we were connected with the same spiritual society and their loves. It is their loves that we identified as our loves. Now in their company we come fully into our loves and are in them to eternity. Our life is then a heaven if those loves are compatible with mutual love and love of God. But if the loves are incompatible with heavenly loves, our life is then a hell.

Hence is the critical importance of equipping our personality with loves that are compatible with mutual love and love of God.

We accomplish this by resisting and hating our selfish loves. Doing this would make room for mutual love to replace the self-love in our personality. Mutual love and love of God is the spiritual order into which God has created us. Therefore if we arrange our mind in that order we can receive and experience the eternal life of conjugial happiness. If we have not equipped our personality for mutual love and love of God we are unable to survive in the atmospheres of heaven because these are contrary to the selfish loves that we have within ourselves. The two battle each other in our mind and destroy our happiness and desire to stay in that state.

Even in natural consciousness the information provided above about God and the mental world can be understood with the natural-rational mind. However it cannot be believed and is therefore dismissed as nothing. But if we compel ourselves to use our rational ability to examine spiritual ideas, then we can understand these details, and therefore believe them to be true reality.

Experiencing Regeneration

The three anatomical levels of operation in our mind are arranged in a "vertical" order of complexity and perfection. First comes the spiritual-celestial mind at the top; then the rational mind in the middle; and at last the natural mind lower down. Below that is the corporeal mind which is the level of mental operation in hell. God provides the experiencing of a reciprocal relationship with Him at each level. When God appears to us at the spiritual-celestial level, which is the highest, we see and perceive God's mental substance of love and wisdom in every object and event. Below that level God appears to us at the rational level in which we can see and perceive that the meaning of *Sacred Scripture* is God's mind appearing to us through spiritual truths. Examples of these include the commandments and the miracles. Below the rational level God appears to us at the sensuous level in which we can see and perceive God in His Divine Natural Body, thus with our physical eyes and ears. This evidence overcomes our doubts and allows us to worship Him as God-Man and be persuaded to obey His commandments written in *Sacred Scripture*.

All the commandments can be fulfilled if we merely fulfill the "*Two Great Commandments*". The first is that we are to love God above all things. The second is that we are to love others as much as we love ourselves. The beginning of loving others is to stop doing them harm or to show disrespect.

Some people might wonder about the idea of seeing God in His Divine Natural Body, thus with our physical eyes. Where do we get to see God this way? The incarnation and birth of God as a human on earth, which is described in *Sacred Scripture*, is perceived as a spiritual truth when we are in spiritual-rational consciousness. Hence we can understand that God's Divine Natural Body exists as a historical and scientific reality. We accept the idea that Julius Caesar or William Shakespeare had a physical body that would be visible to our physical eyes had we been there or had they been here. The difference is that Julius and William lost their physical body at death while God took His Physical Body with Him into the afterlife of eternity. Following the two-day dying-resuscitation process you too will be able to visually confirm that God's Natural Body exists. Of course at that time we will be looking with the eyes of our spiritual body.

People might wonder why God created two bodies for human beings and a suitable world for each of them. Could we not have been born only with our spiritual body? Why do we need a temporary physical body and its subsequent death and separation?

The reason involves the need to equip our personality with heaven-appropriate loves and ideas.

Consider these details. In the mental world incompatible loves repel each other, and if they are forced to be together, they destroy one another. This means that the love and truth die and only hatred and falsity is left in the mind, and this is hell. This is why heaven and hell are absolutely separated from each other in the mental world, one functioning above, and the other functioning below with no bridges or atmospheres to cross from one to the other. *But in order to acquire loves to be as our own, we need to be able to practice them from free choice.* This is not possible in the mental world where heaven and hell must stay separated. But while we are connected to the physical body on earth we can experience freedom of choice for either good loves or bad loves. We can then equip our personality with good loves, which we must have in our personality in order to live in heaven in the afterlife of eternity.

People might also wonder why can't we "repent" or change our loves after death. Is this even fair or just or loving? The answer is that God would love nothing better than to bring everyone into heaven after death. But you need to realize the order of reality that God has created. In this order the human mind has an anatomy to allow it to be permanent and immortal. This anatomy is made of mental organs that function to allow us to experience feelings, thoughts, and sensations. These mental organs are like our physical organs built up slowly from progressive growth of fibers and cells. Good loves in our spiritual body develop mental fibers that grow from left to right clockwise and upwards, while bad loves develop fibers that coil from right to left or counterclockwise and downwards. It is similar with the growth of plants where early growth patterns establish organ structure that cannot be altered later without tissue destruction.

Hence it is that God does not judge people to hell for any reason. It is the anatomy of the individual that determines where life is possible. People who have not undergone regeneration prior to death cannot change their loves since in the afterlife the spiritual body can no longer be persuaded to change its loves. This is only possible while the spiritual body is still conjoined to the physical body, thus while living in this world. Now we are

41

in freedom to choose to experience good or evil loves, but after death we must give one up to keep the other. Which loves we are then willing to give up and which ones to keep is determined by regeneration.

Our loves do not become our very own until we are separated from the physical world.

In this world our loves flow in from this or another spiritual society to which God connects us moment by moment. *This switching around allows God to infuse us with different types of loves and ideas at various moments in our regeneration process.* For example, smokers who quit smoking for spiritual reasons undergo spiritual temptations about it. *Natural* reasons for quitting involve health considerations when the person becomes convinced that to continue smoking will be very injurious. But spiritual reasons for quitting involve not just health considerations but also interpersonal. A father and husband might feel a spiritual obligation to his wife and children to be around to help them lead happy lives. And so quitting smoking is for their sake and not just self. A temptation to light up involves therefore both natural and spiritual consequences.

In order for us to experience the spiritual temptation, God connects us to hellish societies whose thinking flows in and inspires doubt in our mind about the smoking. For instance the thought might enter that it's really up to each person to balance other people's needs for him and his needs for himself. Wanting to accept this idea is a spiritual temptation. It is overcome with the spiritual idea from *Sacred Scripture* that no one is born for self and that everyone is born for others.

Regeneration proceeds by facing all sorts of spiritual temptations in the course of our lifetime.

Experiencing Natural
vs. Spiritual Consciousness

In physical growth we distinguish between physical childhood and physical adulthood according to age. Similarly in mental growth we distinguish between mental childhood or immaturity of mind, and mental adulthood or the age of reason, responsibility, and accountability. Thus the main

Experiencing Regeneration

divisions of physical and mental growth correspond to each other. Experiencing mental adulthood involves undergoing two major changes. The first phase is the state of experiencing self as the center of one's love and devotion in life. The self is adored and loved more than others or God. This type of experiencing produces the natural consciousness of adults with which we are all familiar in everyday living, each in our own communities and lifestyles.

Experiencing in natural consciousness involves seeing everything in relation to self as the center, especially whether it promotes or hinders the consummation of one's selfish loves and longings. Everything is loved that benefits the self and promotes the individual's power, reputation, gain, and honor. Nothing is loved unless it benefits the self. One's children are loved to the extent that one sees oneself in them and they in us. Thus it is a selfish love opposed to mutual love, which involves loving others and God as much as self or more than self. Parents in natural consciousness stop loving their children in this way when they no longer see themselves in their children's appearance and traits, and then they even hate their children for being different than them.

When we are experiencing our life in natural consciousness we only care about ideas and practices that allow increase in our reputation, power, and admiration. The experiencing of daily life minute by minute is encapsulated in the attitude that is expressed through the following experiencing windows into the logic and motives of natural consciousness:

What is this to me? Why should I care?
If they don't like me I don't need them. Let them rot.
Why should I follow this rule? It's not fair to me. Besides, I will
    cover it up so no one will know.
I can't stand it how they turn on me now. Let them rot.
Who are these people? Why should I care about them? What are
    they to me?
Oh, I see, you are close to so and so. Of course I will hire you.
I know I should wash my hands before I examine the next patient
    (or handle that piece of food), but I think I can be forgiven for
    just not being perfect all the time.
How can they win and me lose? Let them rot.
I want all of it, all of it. I don't want anyone to have as much as I
    have.

Experiencing Regeneration

Chastity? What is it? Loyalty? What's that? Let's just do it you and
    me, forget about others right now. You're with me and that's
    all that matters now.
Let them volunteer and get killed. Not me.
I don't deserve this. I deserve to make as much as any other guy.
I can't help you. Anyway what's in it for me?
How come an ugly guy like that gets to date a gorgeous girl like
    that?
Etc.

Natural consciousness and spiritual consciousness are two radically
different modes of experiencing. Spiritual consciousness gives us the
ability of experiencing and perceiving things that we cannot even
understand or believe in natural consciousness. Our lower mode of
experiencing involves only physical or sensory perceptions. Our concepts
and ideas in that state are tied to the material world and its materialistic
reasoning that involves time, space, quantity, distance, and limits. When
we are experiencing our life in that mode we do not believe that there is
anything beyond sensory input, and what appears otherwise is taken to be
an illusion or wishful thinking without basis in reality. The mental world
does not seem to be real in that mode, so it is referred to by negative bias
scientists as an "epiphenomenon" or an "emergent phenomenon" that is
based in the operations of the physical brain.

Spiritual consciousness sees that mental experience such as sensing,
thinking, emoting, loving, intending, etc. are mental objects rather than
electro-chemical operations.
Natural consciousness rejects this idea and equates mental with electro-
chemical. This reduction or flattening of the experience eliminates the
mind or mental world as a distinct world of its own. It is not possible for
natural consciousness to understand what it means that thoughts cannot
be physical or natural, nor that they cannot be derived from what is
physical. Spiritual consciousness sees that what is "emergent" or derived
from the physical remains physical.

Consequently the experiencing of natural consciousness denies life after
death. And those who do not deny the resurrection of the dead see this
event as natural only, happening in this physical world. When heaven in
eternity is not a meaningful idea it cannot be believed.

Experiencing Regeneration

Materialistic science as it has been taught in schools for the past century or two is opposed to the introduction of scientific dualism because this supposes what to it is impossible, namely a reality or world that is not in physical time, space, or composed of material substances. But spiritual consciousness affords the experiencing of ideas and intentions that are "beyond this world" and includes the idea of God, the afterlife, spirituality, and morality based on conscience for what is universally and objectively good and true. Spiritual consciousness sees the validity of our two natures, one natural external, and the other spiritual internal. Furthermore, spiritual consciousness sees the connection between our two natures and ascribes a higher position to the spiritual. It sees clearly that the mind is the actual source of the physical body's animation and operation. By itself the physical body is not living but it receives its living property from the mind, which is spiritual.

Awareness of the operation of conscience provides the experiencing of spiritual consciousness and thus the realization that we are of a dual nature and citizens of the dual universe. Spiritual reality is objectively experienced as spiritual conscience. We can perceive the operation of spiritual conscience as originating from a higher place in the mind than our own thinking in natural consciousness.

For instance, the man who plans to cheat on his wife thinks and argues what harm can it do as long as the wife is kept from discovering or suspecting it. But then he may experience regret or pain from his conscience for considering breaking his promise and for not being true and honest in the relationship. This experience is the elevation of his consciousness to the spiritual level. Even when there is no visible physical harm done to the wife spiritual conscience perceives that it is wrong to deceive. This perception of mental pain constitutes the experiencing of spiritual consciousness.

In the afterlife, people who have disregarded the voice and perception of their conscience in this life are unable to stop their devolution into more and more insane and shameful activities with others whom they encounter in the spiritual societies. At the same time they are compelled by their mad desire to possess all power by which to dominate and torture anyone in their environment who does not favor them as an ally and servant. This sliding down into the hell regions of the mind is inevitable and unconscious. It is caused by the individual holding on to the evil love. But those who allowed their conscience to remain intact while living in the societies of the physical world, now in the afterlife can experience the operations of the mind known as the heavens and their heavenly bliss.

Natural consciousness also has a conscience but it is external to the person and consists in giving warnings about something natural that might hurt one's selfish goals. Natural conscience functions to protect the person's selfish life while spiritual conscience functions to protect altruism and mutual love, by prompting the individual to look out for the welfare of others in addition to one's own. For example, a person engaged in business transactions may see an opportunity to cover up and withhold information from the buyer that would hurt the sale. Natural conscience gives the businessman a warning 'heads up' about the risks of the subterfuge being discovered later, hurting the reputation of the business. The decision to act honestly in that case is motivated by self-preservation. In contrast, the businessman who has an active spiritual conscience decides to remain honest to protect the buyer from becoming a victim of the dishonesty. Even when the dishonesty can be completely covered up and done in secret it is nevertheless rejected because it is contrary to what is good and true.

When we act from a spiritual conscience to protect others as well as ourselves we are experiencing inner satisfaction that originates from the higher regions of the mental world. This heavenly happiness and contentment cannot be part of a mere natural conscience that can provide us only with a shallow or degraded happiness that is never fully satisfied, always wanting more than what one already has. This kind of happiness despises the inner happiness as nothing, since they cannot experience it.

The Five Modalities
of Experiencing Regeneration

Have you ever thought about what is your experience made of? We can realize that experiencing is the very life itself that we have. If we stopped experiencing our life would no longer be living or human. We start as infants to become aware of our experiencing. Following that nothing can be more familiar to us than experiencing. It is our very own mental life and consciousness.

Experiencing Regeneration

Experiencing is done by our mind, which anatomically is our immortal spiritual body. No experiencing whatsoever is done by the physical body. Our mind makes use of our physical body to detect how the body is affected by its environment. Our mind detects changes in the physical environment through sensory receptors that form part of the anatomy of the physical body. We are familiar with five categories of sensing through the physical body. Starting from the top and going down we have the eyes by which we can detect changes in light and their reflection. We can see things around us if there is enough light in the surrounding space or atmosphere. This provides us with visual information.

Next in line we have the ears or organs of hearing by which we can detect sound vibrations coming into our ear. Our mind then interprets these physical vibrations and represents them by correspondence as mental sound. This is our sensation of hearing. It resides in spiritual body, and none of it in the physical body. People often do not make this distinction. They are focusing on the appearance that we can hear the sound. But when you analyze the process rationally, ignoring the appearance, you can realize that sounds are mental phenomena and cannot exist in a physical environment. The physical body can only support the mechanical vibrations of the air outside and the movement of the electrical components inside the ear and brain. This is not sound.

The spiritual body, or our mind, is so connected to the physical body that the two react to each other according to the laws of correspondence between mental and physical operations. The sounds we are aware of are mental correspondences to the physical vibrations. Our awareness and our experiencing is therefore through the mental organs of hearing that belong to our spiritual body. In the afterlife we are no longer connected to the physical body and yet we can hear sounds as before, and probably much more clearly and purely than what we knew before through the physical body.

Going next lower we have the organs of smell and the olfactory apparatus in the nose that makes it possible. The spiritual body does the actual smelling or experiencing the odor. In everyday language we speak by appearance and we say: "I detect a bad odor here. Let us leave." But in actuality we detect the changes in the chemical receptors caused by air and particles entering the nose. We then experience these changes in the

47

spiritual body by correspondence, and that's where we sense and feel the odor or smell. The physical chemical properties that affect our physical olfactory sense are not the smell or the odor. To experience smell or odor our mind needs to analyze the corresponding representations. "What is this? It is sharp. I don't like it. Yuk! Let me turn away or fan it away." Smell and odor are psychological or mental phenomena, not physical.

Going down next we have the taste receptors in the mouth, tongue, and throat. Through these by correspondence, our spiritual body senses the changes in taste, texture, and temperature. These last two – texture, temperature, actually belong to the next and last category of sensation called the touch. This is a broad category that includes sub-categories well known to everyone: texture, temperature, softness, proprioceptive movement, vibration, rhythm, area, chemical quality, tenseness, and others.

These are then the five broad categories of sensing by correspondence many of the changes in the physical body. Each modality of sensing corresponds to a specific category of mental activity and experiencing in the spiritual body. Here is a table that can help you remember this information for later use.

Experiencing Regeneration

Table Showing the Five Modalities of Experiencing Regeneration

Physical Operation in Physical Body	Mental Operation in Spiritual Body	Mental Correspondence in Natural-Rational Consciousness	Mental Correspondence in Spiritual-Rational Consciousness
Eyes	Seeing	Desire to understand	Love of spiritual truths in Sacred Scripture
Ears	Hearing	Desire to obey	Love of being guided by spiritual truths
Nose	Smelling	Desire to analyze	Use of self-witnessing for reformation
Mouth	Tasting	Desire to appropriate	Love of practicing heavenly traits
Body	Touching	Desire to conjoin	Love of God and considerate of others

Inherited and Acquired Role Enactments

Ideas in spiritual consciousness can greatly help us to live more effective lives even in our natural consciousness, as long as we retain an open mind to spiritual rationality.

Regeneration is an organic anatomical growth process that progresses throughout our entire lifetime here on earth, and then it continues to eternity in the afterlife.

49

Experiencing Regeneration

This is because God created our mental anatomy to be capable of endless improvement, and yet without ever approaching perfection, which is infinite and therefore can be applied to God only. *When our natural consciousness adopts an open attitude to spiritual ideas we can see more of reality.* Our natural consciousness then receives spiritual light from our spiritual consciousness. This process continues gradually to the extent that we resist our selfish ways of thinking and feeling every day. As we progress in experiencing regeneration, more and more of our natural consciousness in daily life becomes enlightened through the growth of our spiritual consciousness.

For example, a spiritual idea that enlightens our natural consciousness is the idea of viewing our daily interactions as *role enactment*. People are familiar with the saying that "the world is a stage". Stagecraft has been with the human race on this planet since its earliest generations. In natural consciousness we interpret the saying "the world is a stage" as a metaphor. No one thinks that the streets and the houses are actually a stage, which designates a platform inside a theater or outside where a performance or ceremony takes place with an audience watching. Hence we tend to conclude that "the world is a stage" must be a metaphor.

That the world is a "stage" implies that people in daily living are actors each playing their roles. Here is the famous poem by Shakespeare that many know:

All the world's a stage,
And all the men and women merely players;
They have their exits and their entrances

The analysis of daily life activities viewed as stage was scientifically explored in great detail by sociologist E. Goffman in the 1950s and afterwards. His first and most popular book had the title "*The Presentation of Self in Everyday Life*" in which he illustrated how face-to-face interactions can be understood in terms of dramaturgical performances of the conversationalists, whom he called the "actors". He argued that people try to control the impression they make on each other and as a result they put on a role performance to influence that process. Conversation consists of taking turns putting on a performance and being an audience to each other.

Experiencing Regeneration

If you take the expression "*All the world's a stage*" literally rather than as a metaphor, you can perceive the spiritual insight in it. You and I and everyone around are actors performing appropriate and normal roles while we are an audience to each other. We recognize this in the expression "the *father* was not home at the time" or "the *driver* of the car was stopped by a police *officer*" or "the *voters* go to the polls tomorrow", etc. Those of you who have taken Social Science in school or college are familiar with the idea that every individual in society has *roles* to perform, and that each role has a set of prescriptions or a "protocol" that must be followed in order to fulfill that role acceptably. This is true of both private roles like being a parent, and of professional roles like being a mechanic or teacher.

Most people understand this idea of *task related role performance*. However, most people are unaware that the idea of role performance also applies to how we think and react privately in our own mind. This is where the spiritual-rational insight begins. The initial thought is explosive: "*What! You mean when I'm upset I'm just playing a role? No way!*" or some other "formulaic expression". Start observing how predictable everyday exchanges are at work, in public, at parties and receptions, at museums or sports, or when contemplating, planning, and returning from travel, when watching someone's slide collection after the trip, etc. You can also observe public gatherings, ceremonies, and speeches how they follow acceptable standards of role performance.

The more you consider this idea in some spiritual-rational light the more you can confirm the *scripted or formulaic role enactments* in everything that we do socially in interactions with others under all circumstances.

It is not so surprising that this role enactment procedure is also going on in our thinking when we are experiencing our daily activities in natural consciousness. Sometimes you can actually mentally hear the voices of your parents, mentor, spouse, or leader, saying the lines of your role in your mind . Out loud we might say, "Grandfather used to say..." Sometimes you can hear children and adolescents being interviewed in the media and it is very plain that they are repeating lines they have learned from adults as if they are not aware of this input, or as if they themselves feel this way and so express it from themselves.

Experiencing Regeneration

It is normal to forget the input of our innumerable thoughts, ideas, and speech acts. But when some of these thoughts or scripts begin to be bothersome to you there is a way of getting rid of them. Many kinds of mental neuroses that people "suffer from" are initiated and maintained by particular *dysfunctional mental role enactments*. One such bothersome syndrome that many people put up with is "being in a bad mood" and experiencing the double blows of dissatisfaction and resentment. "*Being in a bad mood*" is a mental role that many people are enacting, to the distress of the people they interact with. Their distress then impacts negatively on your mood and peace of mind.

Often some person of importance in our past, perhaps even in childhood, has modeled for us the role of "being dissatisfied" as a reaction to anything and everything. It's as if that person has learned to apply the *dissatisfied role script* to everything, and now is enacting it for other children and adults. Thus it is that particular role enactments are passed on from generation to generation and cumulate over time. We can use the expression *standardized imaginings* to refer to the ideas, solutions, daydreams, and fantasies that we construct as-if they came spontaneously from us and were not merely learned as a formulaic expression or script. It seems to us that we are just imagining or making something up, but in actuality we are merely modeling and enacting roles and scripts that come to us from others.

Becoming aware of the ubiquity of role enactments in our mind is like brushing aside and clearing the space from cobwebs that obscure what's there.

It opens up a new way of interacting and living in daily life. *Without this awareness we become victims of our own mental role enactments. We take them seriously.* We react to them emotionally and defensively as-if they were real, not play-acting. It's as if the actors on stage forgot that they are on a stage and reading scripted lines written by someone else. As long as they remember being on stage they do not react defensively to what others say or do.

As Shakespeare has reminded the world "All the world's a stage, And all the men and women merely players". Why "merely" do you think? Perhaps he meant that no one is sincere. But in our discussion here we can say that if we really are "merely players" and doing role enactments, then there

Experiencing Regeneration

is no reason to be defensive, discontent, resentful, in a bad mood, angry, spiteful, etc., as a result of what something said or did. These will remain dysfunctional defensive role enactments until we remember that everyone is role-enacting and that life is a stage.

Next time you experience a rude person being in your face, simply remind yourself that the rudeness is a scripted act. *It is not personal against you or about you.* You are merely the target that conveniently presents itself for the occasion. Thinking this gives you an option as to how to react and feel about the situation. You can enact the defensive script, which spins you into emotional discontent, resentment, and the compulsion to retaliate and mentally ventilate. Or you can enact the script of empathy by displaying understanding of what the rude person must be going through, and if you don't have the details at least you can imagine that it's been a challenge for that person.

Enacting rudeness is merely a stage play so there is no real point in reacting to it defensively.

We sometimes become despondent or depressed when we don't receive compliments or expressions of appreciation for what we accomplished or for what we did for someone. This reaction of despondency and dissatisfaction quickly spins into resentment and even anger against the people involved. These bothersome and tedious mental role enactments can be stopped and replaced with more agreeable and effective role-play alternatives that are available. In spiritual consciousness we persuade ourselves to give up these pointless role-binding acts that involve the useless defense and aggrandizement of self.

In spiritual consciousness we set ourselves in daily life to do things because they are for the sake of others, not just for self. When we do something useful because it is useful to somebody, we do not do it for the sake of acknowledgement or thankfulness. If these are not given, it is of no import to our ego. The use that we performed remains, with or without acknowledgment, and that's our ultimate motive and the built-in reward. This way of thinking is called spiritual-rational. given that it is immersed in spiritual consciousness. It contrasts with natural-rational thinking that is immersed in natural consciousness, which constantly immerses us in the experiencing of discontent and resentment.

Mental disturbances that people experience on a daily basis are variously discussed by mental health professionals as neuroses, psychoses, behavioral disorders, mental illness, defense mechanisms, learned helplessness, emotional impairment, irrational thinking, dysfunctional habit, etc. *Role enactment enters into most of these types of mental routines and emotional spin cycles by which people torment themselves with standardized imaginings.* People can create these negative symptoms in their mind only when they stay immersed in natural consciousness. By raising their consciousness to the level of spiritual-rational thinking, these negative role enactments cease to be active in the natural mind. This book attempts to show you how you can raise your consciousness to the spiritual level.

Many mental disturbances in daily living are not classified by mental health professionals as "abnormal" or "maladjusted". These include feeling envious and despondent over other people's good fortune, feeling angry and resentful of people who don't reciprocate our advances, frequently buying clothes and returning them, repeatedly calling the police over your noisy neighbors, owning six cats, always carrying an umbrella just in case, shopping only when there is a special sale, etc. A lot of negative emotions and needlessly cumbersome and impaired thoughts go on every day, but these are not considered in the category of mental illness. However, when we consider the issue from the perspective of experiencing, it is clear that one's living quality would greatly improve if all types of mental disturbances were eliminated or filtered out of our experiencing.

It is liberating to realize that our inner mental life, just like our external social life, is constructed out of inherited and learned role enactments. They are borrowed feelings and thoughts and nothing of them is really our own.

Basic Definitions:
Consciousness, Conscience, Spiritual

Consciousness is the awareness of experiencing. In other words, human beings are born with the capacity to experience and to be aware of that experiencing.

Experiencing Regeneration

Conscience is a portion of consciousness. Human experiencing includes the reception of inflowing stimuli from both the natural and spiritual worlds. Awareness of the spiritual inflow into the mind is spiritual conscience.

Spiritual is anything from the spiritual world, which contrasts with the natural world. We use the natural mind and its natural consciousness for our everyday functioning prior to experiencing regeneration. All our ideas and feelings in *natural consciousness* are materialistic, time-bound, numerical, self-centered or "humanistic", and opposed to spiritual truths such as inherited evils, spiritual regeneration, God, and the afterlife of eternity. In contrast, all our ideas and feelings in *spiritual consciousness* are theistic, other-centered or altruistic, and opposed to principles that are based on natural appearances.

Consciousness, conscience, the natural mind, and the spiritual mind are organic anatomical structures that make up our spiritual body, which is born at the same time as our physical body. But the two are in different worlds. They function together and act synchronously through the cause-effect laws of correspondences that bind together the natural and spiritual worlds. The physical body does not have the capacity to receive stimuli from the spiritual world and vice versa, the natural world stimuli do not register on our spiritual body.

When the physical body is no longer in correspondence with the spiritual body it ceases to function and disintegrates. This happens in the two-day dying-resuscitation process, after which we awaken in our spiritual body and continue life in eternity. *The spiritual world of the afterlife is a mental world in the shape of the human body.* This is because the body and the mind are constructed in the same image or form, which is that of God the Divine Human. The spiritual body is an image of the spiritual mind while the physical body is an image of the natural mind.

The rational mind is anatomically midway between the natural mind at the bottom and the spiritual mind at the top. The rational mind itself functions at two sub-levels. The lowest is called "natural-rational" and the highest is called "spiritual-rational". When we think at the lower level of our rational functioning we use only concepts and ideas that pertain to the natural world, namely to time, space, quantity, and material. This is the thinking level when we are experiencing natural consciousness.

Experiencing Regeneration

But when we think at the upper level of our rational functioning, all the ideas and concepts are devoid of what is natural. This provides us with the experiencing of spiritual consciousness. For instance, some people think of heaven and hell as places of punishment and reward in the afterlife for how one has lived in this world. This is a natural-rational idea because it attributes to God the desire to punish and reward. This is merely a natural idea of God, as if God were similar to a judge or king on earth. Now remove from this idea the notion of God being like a king or judge on earth, and think of the spiritual idea that selfish and evil deeds have their built in punishment, while mutual love and love of God has its built in reward. The punishment of selfishness is that the selfish person will not regenerate in this life and in the afterlife will choose one of the hellish societies to live in to eternity. On the other hand the built in reward for living a good life and undergoing regeneration is that the good person in the afterlife will choose to live in heaven and enjoy its eternal blessedness. This is a spiritual-rational idea of heaven and hell.

We learn to develop our rational mind by means of three kinds of daily practices that may be called civil rationality, moral rationality, and spiritual rationality. Each type of rationality has its own type of conscience. *Civil conscience* pertains to the regulations and laws that apply to private, public, professional, and community life. This includes laws, standards, and norms that regulate the business transactions and trade agreements between citizens, insuring their protection through justice and equity. *Moral conscience* pertains to the motives for which we do things, and the intentions we pursue, whether we consider only our own gain or whether we also look out for the interest of others who are affected. This also involves the performing of moral virtues such as honesty, sincerity, compassion, loyalty, generosity, marital chastity, etc. *Spiritual conscience* pertains to the nature of our loves, whether they are sourced in hell or in heaven, and the content of the thoughts that they produce, whether rational or false.

There are three levels of consciousness in our rational mind. Each level is opened or activated by its own level of conscience. When we practice obedience to civic conscience the first level of rationality becomes active and develops through that practice. Practicing moral conscience develops and strengthens the second level of rationality, which is a discrete degree higher and more perfect than the first level. Similarly, our third and highest rational consciousness develops through the practice of spiritual conscience, which involves experiencing regeneration. Once spiritual rationality is activated it can descend and enlighten the second level, and after that, it can descend to the lowest level and enlighten that.

Self-Witnessing
and the Awareness of Experiencing

The goal of this book is to communicate to interested readers the details of experiencing regeneration. This involves self-witnessing.

Self-witnessing is the process of becoming as-if a witness to our own mental life in daily living.

To see our own mental life from the perspective of another person may be called *objective self-witnessing*. It is a method we can use to obtain objective information about our mental activities. All mental activities are real and go on in a world shared with others in their mental activities. This is the mental world of eternity into which every human being is born with an immortal spiritual body, which may also be called our *mental body*. All our mental activities go on with this spiritual body, which is our mind. At death the spiritual body is separated from conjunction with the physical body and we "awaken" in spiritual consciousness, no longer in contact with the physical world. Such as our mental life was until then, such it remains to eternity. Hence comes the critical need for practicing a life of self-witnessing now. In this way we gain the opportunity to equip our personality for living in the afterlife. This process of mental change is called experiencing regeneration.

The usual way that we gather information about our life is to make *subjective* assessments of our situation and accomplishments. An example is to make lists of things we think and do, or to check off lists prepared by others about some activity. Our answers, choices, and check marks are called here "subjective" because people are merely reporting something about their behavior, speech, or plans. No one has actually made any objective or independent observation. This kind of information is selective and biased in favor of people's loves that are current or ongoing.

Experiencing Regeneration

It is not an accurate or true description of what mental states people are actually experiencing.

Human beings have the innate capacity to observe their own mental operations, what is sometimes called *metanoid perception*. Anatomically viewed, metanoid perception involves our higher rational mind looking down on our lower sensory-motor mind. Every individual performs metanoid perception almost all the time but without necessarily being consciously aware of it.

The benefits of increasing and elevating your awareness of mental operations are many, as you will come to happily discover. *The goal of self-witnessing is to gain manageable control over our mental operations.* Along with this critical benefit of living better, comes the accumulation of new information and knowledge that is not obtainable by any other source or method. Gradually you become aware that your unique individual mental operations day-to-day, and minute-by-minute, take place objectively in a world shared with all human beings, past, present, and future still to come. The entire human race was created to live mentally in the same mental world, in the same way that the entire physical world, from immense galaxies to tiny sub-atomic particles, were created to move in the same physical space.

This means for instance that a sub-atomic particle can travel to meet any other sub-atomic particle in the universe as they are all in the same physical space. Similarly, any individual human being has access mentally to any other because all human beings are born and operate in the same mental space. Of course there are laws, natural and mental, that determine under what conditions or states one object or person can come into connection with any other.

The practice of self-witnessing builds up people's ability to liberate themselves from life's most common spoilers of their happiness, contentment, and creativity. Each of us inherits from our parents and genetic ancestors a very large number of physical and mental traits. *This means that every human mind is packed with both good or healthy traits, as well as bad or unhealthy traits.* We also inherit the ability of metanoid perception. Mental traits are anatomical properties of mental operations in our mind. It is necessary understand that our mental operations fall into two distinct categories. One involves what we *feel*, and the other involves what we *think*.

Nothing is more important in regeneration than to understand how feeling and thinking operate together.

Feeling and thinking are two distinct mental activities. Most people confuse these two or mix them up, but this gradually changes as one begins the practice of objective self-witnessing. Feeling operations in the mind are called *affective,* while thinking operations in the mind are called *cognitive.* Affective mental operations provide us with the experiencing of sensations, emotions, intentions, dreams, fantasies, loves, desires, pleasures, delights, wishes, motives, preferences, and so on. These affective mental operations can be positive and healthy for individual development and community or negative and unhealthy. For instance, the desire and contentment of being accepted socially is a positive affective activity, but the enjoyment of being cruel when hurting others is a negative affective activity.

Cognitive mental operations provide us with the experiencing of thoughts, mental images, meanings, information, logic and reasoning ability, memory, knowledge, and so on. These cognitive operations can be rational, sane, and realistic, or they can be irrational, delusional, and contrary to fact and reality. For instance, it is false and misleading to think that being selfish leads to greater success and contentment in life than being altruistic. As people begin practicing objective self-witnessing they are spontaneously led to discover many false beliefs they hold, along with the negative and prejudiced attitudes that are attached to the false beliefs.

There is no limit to the information and knowledge that are available to human beings through the discipline and practice of self-witnessing.

There is only one body of knowledge in the human race that is accumulated from past, present, and future self-witnessing. *Everything is accessible to anyone.* This is the universal law of humankind. *The entire human race evolves and accumulates as one person.* Every mental operation of every individual in every generation that ever lived or will live accrues together into one connected and integrated unit that may be called the Grand Human. In the Grand Human every person exists and contributes to the whole. Your own unique individual mental operations that you experience minute-by-minute, add themselves to the integrated Grand Human. You are part of the whole but without losing your unique individuality and consciousness of self.

Furthermore, your individual progression and growth in abilities and powers are communicated to everyone else in the Grand Human. In the same way, your individual mental growth benefits from the mental growth of others in the Grand Human. *Thus, everything in the mental world is shared with everyone.* In this manner there is an endless enrichment of heaven as more people become part of it every day. In this manner the evolution of the Grand Human continues forever to ever higher and more advanced levels of humanity and community.

The organic anatomical growth or evolution of the human race is two-valued, positive and negative. Evolution is proper to the Grand Human while devolution is proper to what might be called the Grand Monster. The universal laws of human mental anatomy is exhibited in the individual's body, which may be healthy throughout or it may be mixed healthy and unhealthy. A person may continue to be healthy overall even though bacteria and viruses have invaded the body. As long as the body continues to oppose and neutralize these harmful organisms, the body remains healthy.

It is similar with the mental body or spiritual body with which everyone is born. Affective and cognitive mental operations are of two types, healthy and harmful. All the healthy positive feelings and rational thoughts are culled together by spiritual laws and integrated into the evolution of the Grand Human where it is shared and communicated to every individual. Likewise, all the unhealthy negative feelings and false thoughts are culled together by spiritual laws and integrated into the devolution of the Grand Monster where it is shared and communicated to every individual.

It is critical for everyone to understand that the dying-resuscitation process changes forever how an individual is mentally connected to the Grand Human and the Grand Monster. When our spirit body or mind is still connected to the physical body here on earth, the anatomical condition allows the active operation of both positive and negative feelings, and both rational and irrational thinking. But this changes anatomically when the physical body is separated from the spiritual body through the two-day dying-resuscitation process. The spiritual body or human mind then

Experiencing Regeneration

undergoes a filtering process that centralizes all positive and healthy traits in one place and all unhealthy traits in another place of the mind's anatomy.

Before this filtering process takes place while we are still connected to the physical body, we experience both positive and negative mental states in alternation according to the events in our lives. One day we may be unhappy and filled with resentment, discontent, and anxiety, but the next day we may feel happy, contented, and safe. This kind of alternation may occur from one hour to the next, or even from one minute to the next. We are in a good mood and some little accident occurs and we are suddenly in a bad mood. And so on. This alternation is familiar to everyone who practices self-witnessing.

But this process ceases when the filtering functions are activated by the dying and separation of the physical body. When regaining consciousness after the two-day dying-resuscitation process, we are in our spirit body and are leading an active life in the spiritual world in company with others who are also in a similar state. This is a transitional state in which the ongoing anatomical filtering process is experienced as experimental interactions with many others with whom we seem to be connected in a spiritual community, society, or city. Our affective and cognitive operations in these social interactions give us experiences that are more and more one-sided with respect to healthy and unhealthy. There are two directions available to the as-of self preferences. One direction is closer and closer to the Grand Human, while the other is closer and closer to the Grand Monster.

Getting closer to the Grand Human means the gradual operational silencing or "inhibition" of negative feelings and irrational thoughts. And similarly, getting closer to the Grand Monster means the gradual operational silencing or "inhibition" of positive feelings and rational thoughts. This directional change in our mental anatomy is exhibited by correspondence in the appearance of the spiritual body. The closer people get to the Grand Human the more they appear young, healthy, and beautiful. The reverse is the case with those who move closer to the Grand Monster, appearing in their spiritual body with various horrible deformations and ugliness. Selfish loves and their connected negative sub-loves or affections move people closer to the Grand Monster, while altruistic loves and their connected positive sub-loves or affections move people closer to the Grand Human. Everyone after death becomes a pure version of himself or herself, angelic if positive, monstrous if negative.

The practice of self-witnessing in this life gives you the opportunity to determine by choice which direction you will take after death.

What would happen right now if God were to remove all at once your unhealthy and negative loves and thoughts? What would remain is an incomplete person who cannot survive and grow. This becomes evident when you start your self-witnessing practice and discover that your experiencing must be mixed in order to feel like a complete person. In some areas you may be knowledgeable and practical but the reverse in other areas.

For example, suppose you are a successful plumber making an excellent income. When you are doing a plumbing job you are meticulous, practical, and neat, being polite and pleasant to the people who pay you for your services. But when you drive home you get angry at other motorists, and when you get home and begin to relax you are indulgent and lazy, eating inappropriate foods, acting in a bad mood and being quarrelsome in your interactions with those around you. If you removed all your indulgent and self-centered traits you would still be an effective and successful plumber but you'd feel like there is no fun in your life and you would find it impossible to overcome your growing depression.

The only way that life can work is for you to gradually by choice and preference eliminate one by one the many traits that involve self-indulgence, self-centeredness, and ignorance. Such gradual change by choice over your lifetime will insure that your future in eternity will be a happy one in the Grand Human, avoiding an unhappy one in the Grand Monster.

External and Internal Conscience

For a number of years I've asked various categories of people of all ages to describe to me what they mean by "evil" and to give me examples of evil people. The majority answers identified evil with mass murderers, cruel dictators, terrorists, and demons, and giving instances of historical figures that are traditionally described as evil. Of course these descriptions and people are indeed evil. But this type of dramatic and obvious evil is comparatively rare compared to the evil that most people do on most days of their lives.

Evil is the constant experiencing of the selfish person.

And since we are all born selfish we are all evil. We don't need to go far and search for evil elsewhere than where we are and what we are. The consciousness experienced in our selfish mental states is a natural consciousness in which we are completely unaware of the existence of anything that is spiritual within us. For example, think about when and where you have been annoyed and disturbed by people playing their music or TV beyond the volume of decency. Or think of people talking on their cell phone in a waiting room or elevator. What is it that prevents inconsiderate noisemakers from perceiving that they are being inconsiderate? When you start thinking about your experiences over the long haul you will recognize and become aware of yourself as a victim of people's inconsiderate behavior in many areas of daily life.

We can wonder why or how it is that people are inconsiderate to those around them. Are they aware that their behavior is causing others discomfort and annoyance? To answer this question we need to experience how and when we are being inconsiderate to others. For instance an acquaintance sees you while shopping in the aisle of a supermarket and approaches you with greetings and a smile. You may be aware that your cart and your friend's cart are blocking the aisle so other customers have to back out and use the next aisle. This may continue for four or five minutes while several customers back out or simply wait for you to move out of the way. You are experiencing their annoyance but you are engaged with your friend and do not wish to put her off by asking her to move. Thus, you are being inconsiderate and you are aware of it.

This answers the previous question about the noisemakers' inconsiderate behavior, whether or not they are aware of it. They are aware of it but they do not act upon that awareness. That is the key to understanding our selfishness and everyone else's. At that level of natural consciousness there is no power available to us to oppose the selfishness. Our mental state must exit from mere natural consciousness into a higher consciousness, perhaps what could be called in this case moral consciousness. Our experiencing in the mental state of moral consciousness provides us with the desire or motive to put an end to our disregard of others.

Moral consciousness is a mental state of power over our conduct. It is a higher perception and awareness than we have in mere social consciousness.

Moral consciousness has two distinct mental states, a lower and a higher. In the lower state of moral consciousness we experience a concern for our reputation or a fear of retaliation. We inhibit our inconsiderate behavior as long as we feel ourselves exposed. But when anonymity gives us protection we are unable and unwilling to cease our behavior that inconveniences or harms others. But in the higher state of moral consciousness we experience the desire to avoid being inconsiderate because we are bothered by our conscience. We experience the annoyance or distress that others are experiencing and this affects us with mental pain. We feel uncomfortable seeing ourselves as the cause of their distress. It is empathy and sympathy operating together.

In the lower state of moral consciousness we experience empathy, knowing full well what it feels like to be annoyed by someone's inconsiderateness. Tut this fails to affect us, other than a shrug, or some convenient justification like "I have the right to do this. Let them adjust to it." *This is empathy without sympathy.* The ability to be affected negatively by the distress we cause to strangers is the experiencing of sympathy. To be considerate for the sake of one's reputation or safety does not require sympathy or love.

The highest form of sympathy is the experiencing of mutual love. This requires that we be in a mental state called spiritual consciousness. It involves the desire or motive to be a good person, a decent person, an individual of integrity and sincerity. Spiritual consciousness provides us with the power to be a good and truthful person. The experience of being inconsiderate immediately arouses the impulse to cease because it is contrary to being good and decent.

It's important to keep in mind that everyone is born selfish as part of our inherited *mental* traits that contain not only the selfish traits of the immediate parents, but cumulatively what they inherited from all the prior generations.

Experiencing Regeneration

Definition of selfishness:
Selfishness is the unwillingness to be affected by *sympathy-for-others* unless it benefits oneself or benefits what is associated with oneself such as family, friends, and those who may potentially benefit us in some way in the future. In a selfish mental state we are able and willing to act and think in this way. *This is the experiencing of our external natural mind.*

The external mind does not feel and think about selfishness that it is necessarily bad. This is the experiencing of life in natural consciousness in which there is nothing of spiritual perception or perspective. To our external way of thinking and feeling being selfish brings us influence, power, wealth, pleasures, and safety. This result appears to us as good. Hence selfishness can bring us goods of life. *But all individuals regardless of what mental traits they inherited retain their human ability to enter the experiencing of their choice regardless of any inherited preferences.* This is possible due to the activity of our inner or spiritual mind with which everyone is born.

Our inner mind is always and continuously in spiritual consciousness.

Our way of thinking in this mode is called "spiritual-rational" in contrast with the "natural-rational" way of thinking that we are experiencing in our external natural mind. *To be in spiritual consciousness means that the inner mind and the outer mind are made to correspond to each other.* The natural-rational thinking of our daily lives reverses itself from looking to self only, to looking to others as well as self. This new love of doing is activated by the inner mind that has now established a functioning anatomical connection with our external lower mind. This means that our perception, thinking, attitude, loving, speaking, and doing all change radically towards the direction of mutual love and altruism *in every task we accomplish in the course of the day.*

In this mental mode our spiritual consciousness is activated and receives inflow from the mental world and its heavenly societies as they become anatomically connected to us more and more fully. There is a new unwillingness to satisfy selfish loves that hurt others and ourselves. Spiritual conscience highlights and exposes selfish loves that hide in the background of our personality. These are self-promoting affections to which we are oblivious, and perhaps were never conscious due to undesire for understanding rationally.

Until the inner spiritual mind is activated, the outer self remains in the illusions that are created by the appearances of the senses. One such illusion was pointed out just above, namely the conviction that being selfish can be good because it brings us what we want and need. Without our spiritual conscience being activated we cannot overcome this illusion and we die in it, bringing it with us to the afterlife in our personality, and there it becomes a huge problem to the individual, as is explained throughout this book.

Spiritual-rational thinking in the inner spiritual mind is based on principles of theistic psychology that every individual acquires by studying *Sacred Scripture* while maintaining a daily reciprocal relationship with God. Only through this practice can anyone have life in eternity. Our immortality and awakening from the dying-resuscitation process gives us a choice that we are unable to avoid regarding our living style in eternity. But it should be known that we are not doing the choosing, but it is our love that is choosing for us. Such as is the love in our personality, such is our choosing in eternity.

Being born with the need and delight to love self only is therefore not the only inheritance. We also inherit the good traits of our parents and ancestors in a long cumulative genetic chain. Without these good traits society would be impossible. Mutual love and respect for all is the bond that holds society together as one functional unit that protects the innocent and exercises justice. Each of us human beings experience the consciousness of the giant battle that constantly is waged between our external mind filled with selfish traits and our internal mind filled with nothing but spiritual truths from *Sacred Scripture*, and hence from heaven and God.

This inner battle between feeling sympathy for others on the one side, and on the other, feeling nothing for them, is the life or death struggle that is waged within our mind between heaven and hell.

Indeed, our mind is literally and anatomically between heaven and hell, being pulled outward and downward vs. inward and upward. The spiritual societies in hell are connected to us anatomically through the selfish affections that we are unwilling to give up. And the spiritual societies in heaven are connected to us anatomically through the mutual love affections to which we are dearly holding on. The experiencing of these battles is called being in spiritual temptations. We ourselves are not doing any of the battling though it feels like we are. But in fact what we are experiencing is the battle that the spiritual societies are waging against each other in our mind as a battlefield.

The evil societies call up from our memory the selfish desires and interests, and they also drum up anxiety in our mind about our safety and benefit, doing this through recalling to our awareness things we thought in the past or doubts we've had about God. For instance, a common idea people retain in their memory is that God's omnipotence is limited by people's freedom of choice, which God is committed to uphold and maintain as part of our being truly human. This idea brings with it a generalized and disturbing fear that something might happen to us or to someone that God could not prevent. The evil spirits drum up this idea and hold it in front of the consciousness of the person who is undergoing a spiritual temptation.

But the balance in decision-making is once again restored when the heavenly spirits activate in our awareness spiritual truths that we acquired in our memory from study of *Sacred Scripture* and insights received from a reciprocal relationship with God. For instance, we know from spiritual-rational thinking that omnipotence cannot involve exceptions or else it would not be omnipotence. *This thought reassures us that nothing can happen due to God's inability to prevent it.* This experiencing in the spiritual mind chases away the fear and anxiety in the external mind. Along with this spiritual truth come others that are related to this situation. For example, we know from spiritual truths of theistic psychology that the only evil events that can occur are those that God turns into a blessing for the victims and helps prevent them from experiencing something much worse.

Experiencing relationship to God as person takes place not only by dialog and at the same time by personal worship. God is holy, omniscient, and perfect in love and wisdom. Hence to reject God's Commandments of living and thinking is to deny the reality of this relationship that we actually have with God. We worship God by being willing to submit ourselves to

Experiencing Regeneration

His will, as expressed in the Commandments of *Sacred Scripture*, both in the literal sense and in the spiritual sense.

Not many people have understood that God gives Commandments because they are the method of weakening and silencing our inherited loves that are selfish.

For instance the *Ten Commandments* of the *Decalogue* in the *Old Testament* of the *Bible* prohibits the common things people do to each other out of lack of compassion and selfishness. This includes lying and deceiving, hating and murdering, cheating in marriage, robbing and stealing, denying God.

Now what would happen if we fail to fight against these selfish loves? They will prevent us from entering a happy mental state in eternity. *If we did not fight against our selfish loves before we get to the afterlife, we will remain in them forever.*

God not only creates us but sees us through the difficult spiritual battles that we must fight in our mind in order to become considerate and loving individuals.

It is critical to understand that heavenly happiness is something that we already have built into our mind from birth. Heaven is not a place somewhere for which we have to look. Heaven is an anatomical level of functioning in our spiritual body of our will and understanding. When we neutralize our selfish loves by fighting against them, our consciousness is raised from natural to spiritual. The hells in our mind remain at the bottom. If we hold on to selfish loves we hold down our consciousness to remain at the materialistic level of thinking and experiencing life. At this level when we hear or read the idea that *"to live in heaven we must love others as much as ourselves"*, what is it that we think or say? I have heard people say things that may be summarized as follows:

Well it doesn't sound like I am a heaven person. I'll take my chances with hell. Heaven sounds boring and unattractive, but hell is fun and exciting. A place where you can never lie or cheat does not sound like fun. A place where you always have to be considerate sounds too rigid to me.

Experiencing Regeneration

In spiritual consciousness this type of talk is experienced as spiritual insanity. Life in hell cannot possibly be fun and exciting, and to believe that is insane. Communities of people who are immersed in selfish loves create a social-psychological environment of hell for each other that is horrible and tragic to contemplate. *Selfish loves degenerate into ever worse sub-human conditions of interaction.* Competition turns into warfare, which turns into hatred, which unleashes unbridled rage, which ends in mayhem, torture, and butchery. Since every human being is immortal in eternity there is no escape or end to the experiencing of hell as it devolves into lower and lower levels of human depravity.

What would happen if God removed selfish loves from those who are in their hells?

Since they do not have remnants of altruistic feelings such as sharing and wishing others well, or being honest and faithful, there would be a void or emptiness of all of loves for that person. All loves being hellish, there would be nothing left there if God removed these. Being in nothing is not being human and excludes the possibility of positive change and a return to humanity and happiness. *Hence Divine love and wisdom require that those in hell be left with their selfish loves.* This at least keeps the possibility of return a theoretical possibility. Eliminating all selfish loves and substituting them with heavenly loves would result in the experiencing of a worse hell than they are in. Their mental organs would be crushed and would implode by the inherent opposition that is built into selfish loves and mutual love. In the afterlife of eternity they cannot exist together or alternately, and so they annihilate each other leaving a potential human but not a real one.

And so the only way to eliminate selfish loves and acquire heavenly loves is to compel ourselves over and over again to resist selfish loves, thoughts, and deeds.

This resistance gradually gains ascendance, so that selfish loves are replaced by altruistic loves with more and more regularity as we proceed in life and growth. God must be a conscious factor in this attempt. God is willing and eager to supply us with the power to defeat selfish loves. All we need in order to use this power is to maintain a daily reciprocal relationship with Him. In this way when a situation arises where a selfish love takes over our thinking and willing, we can counteract it by relying on God to give you victory over yourself.

Loving Our Neighbor:
Whom, How and Why

Heavenly loves are altruistic, rational, and spiritual.

All loves are arranged in a hierarchy or rank order of importance and power over other loves. At the top of the list of heavenly loves is the chief heavenly love, which is to love God more than self and to love others as much as self.

"Loving others" or "loving the neighbor" is to do no harm to them for the sake of self.

This is done by considering the welfare of others in whatever you intend, enjoy, think, say, and do.

When we intend something we must consider whether such an intention is fair, honest, or inconsiderate. For example we might plan to close a business and not give the employees involved sufficient advance knowledge of it. To love your neighbor means that you must balance your benefit with the loss to others who depend on you. In this case you want to make sure that the affected workers have time to find other jobs. This is to love the neighbor.

When we enjoy something like having friends over for dinner we need to balance that desire with the caution that our next-door neighbors are not unduly inconvenienced by noise past bedtime hour and smoke from outdoor cooking. To love the neighbor means to consult the neighbor's welfare for the ordinary needs of life, thus to balance as much as possible your need and theirs.

When we think that the government is requiring us to pay a tax or license that we consider unfair or excessive, we cannot give in to our desire to avoid that payment by some subterfuge or false declaration because that would be cheating the common welfare and process of law. To make all legally required payments is to love the neighbor.

Experiencing Regeneration

When strangers in a parking lot yell at you and insult you for taking a parking space they apparently thought was theirs, you cannot allow yourself to retaliate by insulting them back or picking a fight to punish them. To act peacefully for the sake of public peace and safety is to love the neighbor.

Finally, you may wake up one morning and just not feel like going to work. On top of that you're giving your best friend a dinner party later that day and you'd like more time for preparing. You think about calling in sick but you remember that today is a planned sale with a crush of customers expected. You then compel yourself to get up and go in so that your boss may not experience a financial loss due to your convenience. This is to love your neighbor.

Some people think that loving the neighbor means treating everyone the same way. But this is an error. Spiritual-rational thinking indicates that it's not charity to treat dangerous criminals or nasty "occupiers" on your lawn the same way as you treat your neighbors or co-workers at work. Similarly when you see a neighbor's adolescent son packing into a car with friends and drinking what looks like alcohol, you make yourself call the parents even though you're already late for an appointment. This is to love your neighbor.

Some people think that loving your neighbor is to contribute to charities and donations for good causes. But one should note that this is a matter of individual choice and discretion. Despite giving away ten percent of your income or even more, it does not mean that you love your neighbor in the sense of God's Commandment. To give for the sake of self is very common in charity works and in volunteering. In general to love the neighbor means first, to resist doing anything that is harmful to the neighbor, and second, to do good to the neighbor, which means to be useful, to be considerate, to be peaceful and tolerant. *First you must resist doing harm to the neighbor, and only after that you can do good.*

We know from theistic psychology that love desires to give to another what is its own and thereby make the person happy from oneself. God's infinite love for the entire human race and for every individual is such that He ardently longs to make all human beings happy by giving them all the good that they can use for happiness. This He can do in heaven to eternity.

71

Experiencing Regeneration

Hence is God's intense desire and involvement with every individual's regeneration, which is the pathway to heaven. To love the neighbor as well as oneself, or more than oneself, therefore means to always wish the neighbor well and to rejoice with the neighbor when it goes well with him or her.

You know that all people are connected and integrated by God. Humanity as a whole moves collectively forward by interconnecting and uniting. You can experience the happiness and bliss when you feel yourself a part of this whole and be contributing to it. The created universe has a built in order and reality. This order represents God's infinite wisdom. Everything that is in this order is good and provides a use for community and individual. Truth is the representation of this Divine order.

This also applies to our willing and thinking. When we intend good to others, feeling glad at their happiness and feeling sadness at their tragedy, we are in the order that God created for the human mind and communities. There is a built in benefit in being in a state of order. There is therefore also a built in disadvantage in being in a state contrary to order. God is in all order, but not in disorder, which is produced in hell by deliberately inverting order. This is the experiencing of turning away from God.

Before we are in the experiencing of spiritual love we interpret the Commandment of "love your neighbor" to mean that we are to love everyone equally without distinction. But this interpretation is completely impracticable, as was just discussed. It is not possible to love everyone the same way. What parent can love a stranger or a stranger's children in the same way as they love their own children? Or, what husband can love other women in the same way as he loves his own wife? Who can love a child molester as one loves a community hero?

It is not reasonable or rational to think that we ought to love everyone in the same way.

It is not human to love a lazy selfish person as one loves a kind and generous person. We love a soldier who risks his or her life for the defense of the country, but not a deserter. We love a mediator who is impartial and helps carve out a needed solution, but we don't love a biased mediator who does not respect equity and fairness. We love a handyman who is punctual and thorough, but not one who is flaky. We love children

Experiencing Regeneration

who are obedient and are affected by good and truth, but we don't love children who are psychopaths and spiteful. We love a country that protects freedom and justice, but we abandon one that is tyrannical and unjust. We love a next-door neighbor who is considerate and sincere, but we don't love one who is inconsiderate and hypocritical.

It is clear that the idea of "loving the neighbor" applies not so much to loving the person but to the good and truth that are in that person.

We are not commanded to love the good and the bad in a person, which would be the case if the commandment applied to loving the person. But it is a contradiction to think that we are to love the bad in a neighbor or in anyone, including our own children. Parents who raise children in natural consciousness experience a selfish love for them since they feel a love for the person of the child. They feel "unconditional" love and loyalty, even when the child is bad or very bad, and treats the parents and everyone else badly. "Parents who don't control their children on the plane" is the second most often mentioned complaint of air travellers these days. Good parents love their children when they discipline them and manage them so that the children are considerate of other people around them. Parents who exercise insufficient discipline over their misbehaving children do not love them, nor do they love their neighbor.

The experiencing of loving people reveals to us that we love a person in accordance with the person's goodness and usefulness to the community. We love a carpenter or painter who is conscientious and skilled, but we do not love one who cheats or deceives and doesn't have the skills that the individual was hired to perform. We love the soldiers who risk their lives to defend their country from attack, but we do not love those who betray us to the attackers. Bad people are not to be loved except to respect the human rights that all human beings are entitled to by virtue of being human. If we keep a traitor and a murderer in jail we are still obligated to feed them and to treat them medically when they are sick. This is to love them appropriately by respecting their human rights despite their hatred of us. We are not commanded to love these categories of people, and if we did love them we would harm the general community and the social order, and this would be to *not* love them.

You can see from all this that God commands us to love the good in the neighbor, and not the person of the neighbor. By loving the good in the neighbor we love God since the good in the neighbor is God's good, hence Himself. But by loving the person as a whole we are not loving God but the person instead, and this is loving what is bad. Only God is good and hence only good ought to be loved. God commands us to love good in others, hence to love Him, because everything God wants to give us in order to makes us eternally happy is through our love of God.

Such as is our love to God, such is our happiness and intelligence.

The Unending Web
of Our Hellish Loves

The afterlife is the mental world of humanity.

We are already in the afterlife now since our mind and our personality resides anatomically in our spiritual body, which is born into the mental world of the afterlife.

We get to experience and confirm this at the completion of the two-day dying-resuscitation process when we awaken in our spiritual body in the mental world of the afterlife. We can then confirm that we are immortal. Being then in our spiritual consciousness we can visually observe the anatomical fibers that connect us to the heavenly and hellish societies.

Now the next phase of our development is to migrate upwards towards the heavenly connections or downwards towards the hellish connections.

To understand this all-important moment of decision we need to be informed about how the hellish and the heavenly societies were connected to us while living on earth. Keep in mind that the shape of the mental world of the afterlife is that of a human body and that this anatomical system operates at lower and higher levels of functioning. For instance the brain in the physical body operates at a higher level than the foot or any other organ. In the mental world of the afterlife the upper regions are those of the head and chest, while the lower regions are those of the legs, buttocks, and feet. The hellish loves and their associated falsehoods operate in the lower region, while the heavenly loves and their associated truths operate in the higher region.

Experiencing Regeneration

As we develop in mental maturity and intelligence here on earth, our spiritual body changes and grows accordingly. The nourishment for the spiritual body is mental nourishment as obtained from the spiritual food that is found in the mental atmosphere surrounding the spiritual body or mind.

This mental food consists of a new consciousness consisting of new perceptions, new thoughts, new understandings, and new feelings.

Our affective system is the organ called the "will", which contains our loves and emotions that motivate us to act and acquire skills. Our cognitive system is the organ called the "understanding", which operates our cognitions, thoughts, reasonings, representations, and so on. Everything we do comes from our will and understanding when they join together to make our muscles move. The organ of the will initiates, motivates, and gives direction, while the organ of the understanding figures out plans and provides knowledge and options.

God created the spiritual body to be activated by the anatomical fibers that connect that body to the rest of humanity. This includes those who are in some heavenly society in the afterlife as well as those in some hellish society. *While we are still on earth connected to a physical body we are unable to have any life of willing and thinking without inflow from both these spiritual societies.*

All of humanity is thus permanently and forever connected with each other, but as you will see, the connections can be influenced by our choices and our loves. All human beings are organic mental plants connected to a shared collective root system that is forever being enlarged from the new births that occur every day on the numberless inhabited planets around the physical universe. When the individual dies there is an awakening of awareness in the spiritual body that is located in the mental world of the afterlife.

All human beings regardless of where they were born congregate and associate together in the same mental world of the afterlife.

This is awesome!

Experiencing Regeneration

You can see that in an anatomical system such as the human race no individual who is unconnected to the whole can survive and exist. This is like what we know from the physical body, namely that when something of our physical body gets disconnected or separated from the whole it decomposes and is devoid of all vitality. An individual mind that is disconnected or separated from spiritual societies instantly stops breathing, loses all vitality, and dissipates.

Anatomically viewed the entire hellish societies operate and function together as one integrated system of selfish loves and their associated falsities and falsification of truths. Similarly, the entire heavenly societies operate and function together as one integrated system of mutual loves and their truths. As we grow up and develop intelligence, God counterbalances the momentary inflow from the good and bad societies into our spiritual body. At one point we are activated by a good love such as children following up on their innate curiosity, and at the next moment we are activated by an evil love such as children fighting with each other and not wanting to share toys. Every activity we do all day every day is activated in this way by God through connecting us and disconnecting us to particular heavenly and hellish societies. God's intention and purpose is to keep us in perfect equilibrium between the power of the hellish societies and the power of the heavenly societies. When we are in this spiritual balance we can make free choices about spiritual matters, free because we can follow our loves whatever they are. *Choices made from loves remain forever.*

When we become adults mentally we are able to use our learned and innate rationality to perceive which things are good and useful and which things are bad and hurtful. We can also perceive our natural consciousness that informs us what is just and moral. In this series of mental stages of our growth, God constantly attempts to draw our awareness of experiencing Him in our life. *Everyone has the idea of God implanted from birth and it is activated in adult life in various ways.* When the individual is ready and sufficiently prepared, God begins the organic process of regeneration. Certain goods and truths begin to flow in from the heavenly societies and establish a basis or foundation in a new mental organ that we receive called the "new will" and the "reborn self". As this affective organ grows it gradually acquires a spiritual conscience and provides us with the experiencing of a life in spiritual consciousness.

Experiencing Regeneration

When we are awakened at the completion of the two-day dying-resuscitation process, we are faced with the all-important choice mentioned above, namely, which spiritual societies we want to join into eternity from among those to which we have been connected, either heavenly or hellish. The choice is up to us. We can even try it out experientially by disconnecting ourselves from the heavenly societies and entering fully into the hellish societies. After that we can reverse the experiment. Ultimately we decide purely on the basis of which loves are stronger in our personality, the heavenly or the hellish. *Whichever loves we finally refuse to give up, those are the ones that we keep forever.* We at last enter the particular spiritual society that contains our chief love. We are then either in heaven or in hell, permanently.

It is permanent not because God keeps people there against their will as a form of punishment, but because they continue to choose according to their chief love. This is the love in our personality with which we arrive into the afterlife from the habits of thinking and doing during our life on earth.

The web of loves in our personality is unified into two collections, one hellish and the other heavenly. Each type of love is united and integrated with other loves that are compatible with it and support it. *It is important for us to understand and be aware of the loves that activate us on a daily basis here on earth.* Here is where we form our personality habits that will stay with us to eternity. Anatomically in terms of the connecting fibers and inflow, all our loves fall into two categories: love of self only vs. love of others as much as self, which is called mutual love and love of God.

Until our personality is regenerated the "love of self only" enters into every thought or act that we do. It may seem that we do "good deeds" or that we entertain thoughts that are considerate of others. People often think that they may sometimes do things for the sake of self only, but that at other times they do things for the sake of others not just self. But this is a fallacy and a misunderstanding. In spiritual consciousness while regenerating we can clearly see that all loves we have are integrated and arranged in agreement with our chief love. If our chief love is love of self then we act for the sake of this love all the time, regardless of how it appears outwardly.

Consider how loves are anatomically interrelated, interdependent, and mutually supportive. Think about a very common group of daily *defensive*

Experiencing Regeneration

loves that may be referred to as the love of *complaining, being resentful, and blaming*. People may not consider these as very "evil" or destructive, but that's because they are not looking at the entire web to which these loves are connected. When we act defensively it is often at the expense of sympathy for others. For instance, after I served my wife some strawberries she said, "*The strawberries are so sour*" and made a sour face. I answered out loud: "*I'm sorry. It's not my fault.*" And inwardly I thought that she is not being very grateful. I was experiencing being at fault and as a result retorted agonistically or showing that I am peeved. This put distance between us in that moment. On the other hand sympathy is to bond closer, which would have happened had I expressed friendship instead: "*Yes! They are! I thought so too.*"

Think about when we are dissatisfied, resentful, and rebellious against order. Conditions under which resentment, complaining, and blaming occur include self-justification, cynicism, and arrogance. We may resent that some people seem luckier than us and live better for no apparent justification. We may wonder why we got stuck with a bad deal. Where is God's justice and mercy in all this? Criticizing God is arrogance, and doubting God's goodness is cynicism. You may be able to see from this that at the back of cynicism and resentment is selfishness and self-justification by merit. It is selfishness or the love of self-only that forces our mind into arrogance and cynicism that provide occasions for complaining and resentment. And finally you may be able to see that selfishness, arrogance, and resentment act together to lead us to break all the commandments against being cruel, hating and murdering, hypocrisy and deception, adultery and criminality.

In other words: *blaming breaks all the commandments*!

Someone might protest: "I'm not punctual. Does my habit of not being punctual condemn me to hell forever? Isn't this a bit unreasonable?"

But now you can have the idea that all selfish traits are interconnected from the "lightest" or least offensive to the "heavier" or most offensive. Ask yourself: *Will I be able to give up my love for the habit of non-punctuality when I'm resuscitated in the afterlife?* This alone and nothing else will be the deciding factor in your eternal happiness or suffering. It is not safe to proceed by making exceptions on account of their appearing as only "light" sins or slight evils. Knowing that everything is connected will help to adopt the mental state of regeneration in which we are committed to fight against all our evils from the lightest to the most severe.

Experiencing a Reciprocal Relationship With God

To understand our relationship to God in a spiritual way we need to define that relationship anatomically.

Sacred Scripture declares that we are to think of God as being the Vine and of ourselves as being its branches. This description shows that our relationship to God is an organic anatomical connection. Or we might say that God is the head and we are the rest of the body. A more technical way of saying this is that God is "in us" and we are "in God", as *Sacred Scripture* also declares. Now when we think about these things in natural consciousness it appears to us that these are metaphorical ways of expressing a relationship. We think of the president or king of a country as "the head" of the nation, which is using a metaphorical comparison.

But in spiritual consciousness we can see that what we call a metaphor is actually a correspondence of anatomical parts and functions. *We are branches or fibers of God in a literal sense, that is, anatomically.* A human being has a unique existence, but not a separate one. Each person is an anatomical part of other persons. All human minds are organs in a mental world. *The entire mental world is an anatomical construction and everything therein is connected anatomically to the whole.* The description of God being "in us" and each of us being "in God" is literally descriptive. Think for instance of your heart and lungs. They are each in the body and connected to each other and to all parts of the body through fibers or vessels. In exactly the same way our organ of the will allows us to love, to hate, to enjoy, to be afraid, to seek out, to intend. These affective functions, powers, and capacities are fueled and activated by the inflow of God's love-substance and its powers. Because love-substance flows into our will, like light flows into the eyes, it is actually "in us", that is, in our organs. Love-substance is God's own substance, and therefore it must remain God's own substance even when it has flowed into our will and is organically active there.

79

Experiencing Regeneration

God's love-substance is in us but is not part of us. This is because the infinite cannot be part of the finite, but it can be adjoined to it so that we may say that the infinite is "in" the finite.

Because God is infinite, every part of God is infinite since there cannot exist any limit in God. *This means that God's love-substance that is in me is also God's love-substance that is in you.* The same Divine love is in every human being. This Divine *love-substance* is the basis or infrastructure of every individual and object, and is infinite in each because the infinite cannot be divided and parceled out by bits, or else it would not be infinite. Since we are organically finite the infinite cannot be an organic part of us. But the infinite can be in us, just as a pebble we swallow is in our stomach but is not part of it. This is because the finite can contain the infinite within itself, or more precisely, the finite and the infinite can be adjoined by God.

The infinite can be "within" or "in" the finite by correspondence, but cannot be part of it by substance.

God is not part of any human being but is within every human being as the infinite is within the finite.

The same infinite God is within every finite human being.

The relationship is anatomical so that we cannot have feelings, thoughts, and sensations other than that come to us from God who is within us as the substance of love and truth. This substance of infinite Divine love and truth flows into the organic receptors of our spiritual body or mind, and activates all our mental capacities and abilities. Our sensations are this substance in our sensorimotor organs. Our consciousness is this substance in our experiencing. Our intelligence and rationality is this substance in our cognitive organ. Our loves, joys, and longings are this substance in our affective organ.

This anatomical relationship between God and each human being is our condition and situation from birth to eternity. It is what makes human beings to be born immortal. God is not a stranger to us. God is our intimate companion who is always present and is a co-participant in every detail of our lives.

Experiencing Regeneration

When we are experiencing spiritual consciousness we are gladdened by the idea that any human being at any place or time has direct mental access to God as the Divine Human person, creator and manager of the universe. It is felt to be such an awesome reality! Our experiencing of God's Human mind brings order and peace into our daily life. Without this experiencing we are like a small leaf on its way to the ocean through wide rivers and mighty waterfalls. This relationship we have to the Divine Human Creator is anatomically and genetically implanted permanently in our spiritual body and forms the basis and axis of our mind, consciousness, and personality. And yet few people are actually experiencing this relationship in awareness. Yet the connection is there from birth and cannot be removed because it is anatomical and organic, like that of a branch connected to the roots through the trunk.

If this direct anatomical connection should be cut off or cease, the individual would then cease to survive, like the branch that is broken by a gust of wind falls to the ground and dries out, ending all sign of organic vitality. Or it is like the light bulb giving light at night and suddenly failing and going dark because the electric power or battery was cut off. Living creatures and human beings are active from the fact that they receive influx of love-substance from God. This influx flows into the receptor organs of the plant, animal, or human being, allowing these organic forms to 'spring to life' according to their form or constitution. The plant springs to life from influx in a different way than an animal since the physical structures of these two are differently created. The human mind as a spiritual body is the highest of all created forms in the universe. In fact you'll discover that everything created in the two worlds was created by God for the sake of human beings.

Given these considerations you can see that every unique individual has a unique relationship to the Creator since "unique" means to be anatomically different from anyone else to eternity. Through this unique relationship to God we receive the Divine influx into our two receptor-systems: the affective and the cognitive. The affective organs of the spiritual body operate from that Divine influx as a result of which we experience sensing of our external environment, feeling of our internal environment of loves and emotions, and picturing of our thoughts and symbolic representations. If the Divine influx stopped for a moment, we would instantly lose all operations in our spiritual receptor systems. This would put an end to experiencing, hence a shutting down of our consciousness and life as a human person. This is the anatomical and genetic reason why every person is permanently connected to God and cannot be disconnected.

For the continuation of this connection with God it is not required that the individual be aware of it or even acknowledge the existence of God. Denying God intellectually and in lifestyle is part of the ability and capacity of the human mind operating in as-of self freedom. God gives you the power to deny Him and the power to believe in anything else whatsoever. However, those who will not acknowledge their connection to God by influx are unable to experience a reciprocal relationship to God.

It is very important to understand that our ability to manage successfully our inherited negative mental traits depends directly on the experiencing of a reciprocal relationship to God.

By denying God as a Human person from whose influx we can have feelings and thoughts, we are denying reality and making ourselves to be spiritually insane.

Our life of willing and thinking is therefore dependent on the continuous and unceasing influx of God's love-substance with its truth-substance. This mental influx gives us the life of our willing and understanding moment by moment from birth onward to eternity. To deny the reality of this Divine influx would be like the tree denying that its life nutrients come from earth and water that is received through the roots. The experiencing of a reciprocal relationship to our Creator begins with the acknowledgement that God exists and is omnipotent, omnipresent, and perfect in love and wisdom.

This acknowledgement brings us into sanity and rationality because it aligns our thinking with what is real and true.

All relationship of love must be reciprocal. Once you acknowledge your mental reality and anatomy, you open up the capacity for God's influx to take you further and further into reciprocal relationship with Him. Experiencing this reciprocal relationship of love between God and a human being opens up many new channels of ability in feeling and thinking. Since God is Human and person it makes sense to talk with God, one on one, face to face, mind to mind. God is perfect unconditional love. *God loves every person from birth to eternity.* God foresees what every unique person needs and how to make that person happy, productive, considerate, and loving.

A direct reciprocal relationship to our Creator is independent of any cultural or religious background.

Absolutely nothing can interfere with this relationship because it is at the center of the person's existence. Everything else whatsoever is around it. What is around is external and cannot interfere with what is internal and central. Religion, ritual, and community prayer are outside this reciprocal relationship to God.

Experiencing a reciprocal relationship to God may vary in intensity in various mental states. You can maintain your focus on God's co-Presence in everything you feel, think, or do. It's like having God look over your shoulder all the time, outside your mind and inside your mind. You cannot hide anywhere, nor would you want to.

God is known also as Lord. He is both. When we talk about God from a distance we use the name God, but when we interact with God more closely and intimately we are inspired to use the name Lord. In the *Old Testament* of the Bible whenever God is used the subject being discussed is Divine Truth, but when the subject is Divine Love the name *Lord* is used. In the *New Testament* only *Lord* is used.

God is known by different names in different cultures and religions.

Why Human Life is Immortal

The early generations of human beings on this earth had both natural and spiritual consciousness. This remains the case on other planets.

People of the most ancient civilization on this earth lived in mutual love and everyone loved others as much as self or more than self, and God above all things. With their natural consciousness through the physical body they had awareness of things in the physical world, and with their spiritual body in spiritual consciousness they had awareness of things in the mental world of the afterlife. They could thus be instructed directly by their ancestors who had passed on and were living in heaven. Eventually however this *dual consciousness* was lost when people started being selfish and loving themselves more than others. This has been called the "Fall of Humankind" or simply the "Fall."

Having lost their spiritual consciousness they became separated from conscious communication with their ancestors. They gradually over the generations lost knowledge of the existence of the afterlife. Eventually they even denied that there is an afterlife and soon after, people started denying that there is a God. This coincided with the rise of science and materialistic thinking.

Today it is still generally not known that all human beings are born immortal and that there is an afterlife of eternity where people live after passing on.

Every human being is immortal and lives forever on account of being conjoined with God. There is nothing living, still less immortal, in human beings.

God's life flows into our spiritual body and wills that we experience this life as our very own.

We have immortal life because God continually wills to give us life and to never stops.

Human immortality is therefore an anatomical property of the spiritual body, which is our mind containing our mental organs and structures of personality.

The idea of God is implanted into every human being from birth.

Even if we deny this awareness later in life nevertheless that idea remains implanted without our awareness. Life and intelligence flows in from God into our spiritual body, which is "inside" our physical body, not in space but in correspondence. This life and intelligence in our spiritual body activate the natural mind and our natural-rational consciousness. This correspondence and relationship is involuntary and does not depend on conscious agreement or participation. Hence it is that atheists enjoy the same mental abilities as those who believe in God.

Experiencing Regeneration

There are two discrete anatomical conditions of life in the afterlife of our immortality. Experiencing the upper regions of the mental world is called living in heaven, while experiencing the lower regions of the mental world is called living in hell. The expression "eternal life" usually refers to life in heaven, which is happy, blissful, and rational. When we sink in experiencing to the lowest regions of the mental world we are still immortal, but instead of the happiness and rationality of eternal life in heaven, there is the misery and insanity of life in hell. In *Sacred Scripture* this is called being "dead," that is spiritually dead. People who reach that mental state in them are called dead because they are forever unwilling to return to human sanity. Thus they make it impossible for God to save them. To be saved by God requires having a reciprocal relationship with God, and this they are forever unwilling to do because they hate God and hate all heavenly goodness, truth, and happiness. The reason of this hate is that heavenly loves are contrary to their infernal loves. People hate what is contrary to their chief love since this threatens the extinction of that love. Only by a gradual process of regeneration can a person's love be changed from selfish and infernal to altruistic and heavenly.

Throughout life on earth God continually strives to guide and direct every individual towards eternal life in heaven. Since the Fall all people strive to follow the selfish loves which they inherit, and this prevents their regeneration and adequate preparation for eternal life in heaven. Everyone who cooperates with God in regeneration of personality succeeds in the suppression and elimination of inborn selfish traits and their replacement with heavenly traits of mutual love towards others and God.

This book describes the methods by which we are being regenerated by God, who is thereby equipping us for living happy lives in the afterlife of eternity. Knowing these methods and cooperating with them is the secret key by which we enter heaven and avoid hell.

Why It's Necessary to Reciprocate God

Experiencing Regeneration

Every human being is born immortal due to the fact that our spiritual body or mind is anatomically connected to God's inflowing spiritual love-substance and its spiritual truth-substance.

These mental substances are in God's mind and are in themselves living and immortal. God cannot divide love-substance into little pieces that can be handed out to human beings. God is fully in every individual and object, and is the same everywhere. God is in all places without being in those places. This is what makes it possible for God to be everywhere simultaneously. If God were present anywhere in space God would be restricted and finited, even trapped in that space, and this is impossible with God. Hence it is rational to think that God is not in physical space, but is *apart from space*, and it is from this that God can be in all space or omnipresent. Another way of representing this might be to think that all space and the entire universe is in God and nothing is apart from God. To think this requires the spiritual-rational idea that "in God infinite things make one".

God is therefore present in our mind and body through the spiritual heat and spiritual light that forms or constructs the human mind into *anatomical organs of reception* for inflowing spiritual heat and spiritual light.

This alone is living within us and from which we have immortal life, spiritual love, and rational intelligence.

Keep in mind that it is impossible for God to give pieces of Himself and thus be divided. Therefore the spiritual heat and light, which are His own substance, flow into our mental organs and are active there as loves, emotions, sensations, joys, and the thoughts that are sourced in these.

Through God's love for the human race He wills that this living substance of His own mind be felt like our own. We definitely feel that the life we have is our own, our very own. This is what God wills for us to feel. He does this out of love and compassion for us, since we would not be inventive and true human beings were we to feel that the life in us is not our own. However it is necessary to know that though we feel that life is our own, it is God's in us.

You can see now that God's own living and immortal substances inflow and form our anatomical organs in the mind, with which we can think, plan,

Experiencing Regeneration

interpret, love, interact, and enjoy everything that God has placed before us as experiencing.

From this you can see how every human being is anatomically connected or conjoined to God and why as a result we are immortal and living eternally.

The human mind has two zones in the upper and lower regions. The upper zone is called heaven and the lower zone is called hell. Everyone can experience heaven and hell on alternate days or even hours and minutes. We can engage in such alternation only in this life, prior to the onset of the two-day dying-resuscitation process. In the afterlife inner loves come forth from the depths of our personality and show themselves outwardly to us in the form of thoughts and feelings of attraction to particular things or situations. These are our chief ruling loves, the highest in the organic hierarchy of loves, and the most powerful in determining what we believe and do. We irresistibly follow these loves while all contrary loves are put aside and disabled. Hence it is that a choice is then made by our ruling loves. If these are loves for the sake of self only, then all altruistic love for others and God are put to the side and rendered inactive. But if they are loves that can live compatibly with heavenly loves then all the remaining selfish loves are put the side and rendered innocuous.

Hence it is that although God is within every human being equally and wholly, still the reception or reciprocation of each individual is unique. Hence is the fact that all human personalities are unique to each person. *Such as is the personality of the individual, such is the reciprocation to God, and consequently such is the regeneration and the salvation.*

You can see from this that all human beings are immortal but that some live a life of mutual love and happiness in heaven, while others live in hell experiencing misery and hatred of each other and for God.

God is anatomically present in the human mind and communicates with every person in two ways: consciously and unconsciously.

The *unconscious* connection is from within or inmost of the soul, mind, and body and insures that we always continue to have freedom of the will and ability to think rationally. God does not allow us to be conscious of this close connection and management of our unconscious mind, through which He also manages the conscious mind. This unconscious connection and management also takes place between God and animals, plants, and indeed all physical objects.

The *conscious* connection with God takes place only with human beings, and only when an individual reciprocates. Reciprocation is achieved by first acknowledging that God is co-Present and managing everything we feel, think, and do. Second, reciprocation is involves acquiring knowledge about God through *Sacred Scripture* and through talking to God and experiencing God as a daily activity.

Initiating a conscious and personal connection to God is the first step to experiencing regeneration.

Since we are born with a selfish character, our willing and reasoning are self-serving and unable to be unbiased. Hence false life principles arise that justify selfish acts and thoughts. At that point the person is no longer able to see what is good or true but sees falsified truth as truth and corrupted good as good. *Whatever the individual likes, he or she calls good, and whatever the person believes, that is designated as truth.* The person is then cut off from conscious connection with God and is unwilling to be regenerated in this life. That person therefore will have ruling loves that avoid heavenly societies and lead the person to the societies in hell. *This is the regrettable lot that awaits the unregenerate person's mind.*

Hence you can see why God is so passionate about getting us out of this spiritual mess. To every culture and nation He gives *Sacred Scripture* in some form that is appropriate and meaningful to that cultural perspective. We need to worship and study *Sacred Scripture* as if it were God Himself because God's mind is in Sacred Scripture as Divine love and Divine truth, just as He is in the human mind.

Experiencing Our Anatomical Relationship to *Sacred Scripture*

All *Sacred Scripture* necessarily exists in two distinct anatomical layers: literal-historical and spiritual-correspondential.

Experiencing Regeneration

God's truths in human words first appear at the highest level of meaning called *celestial-rational correspondences*. Understanding God's words at this level is the experiencing of celestial consciousness, the highest possible to human anatomy. From that inmost level of experiencing, God's words continue to descend by changing form and appear at the next level as *spiritual correspondences*. This mental operation involves the experiencing of *spiritual*-rational consciousness. From there, God's words enter the level of *natural*-rational consciousness and present themselves in the form of *natural correspondences*. At this level the literal-historical meaning of God's words appear in natural languages. At this external or outmost level of consciousness, God's words appear to differ in message and content when compared with the *Sacred Scripture* of different religions and cultures.

Hence it is that religious disagreements arise even though all versions of Sacred Scripture are sourced in the same words of God.

When God speaks, the Divine Human words appear in creation as truth-substance flowing into the mental world and into every individual's mind. This is received as a substantive inflow by the organic structures of our cognitive system. *This anatomical inflow is accomplished through mental fibers that connect God to every person's spiritual body.* The meaning of God's words appears simultaneously at all three levels of human consciousness.

Experiencing regeneration activates in people the spiritual level of consciousness so that they are able to comprehend the meaning of God's words at the spiritual-rational level. Those who are still in their natural consciousness are unaware and unable to comprehend spiritual truths in God's words. Instead, they understand God's words as a historical narrative. This is how all *Sacred Scripture* was written by prophets who were prepared by God to receive God's words as mental dictation in their natural language. This is what they wrote down, not being aware that there was a very different meaning to those words that could be retrieved and understood in spiritual-rational consciousness through the knowledge of correspondences.

There is therefore a three-way anatomical connection between God, God's words in Sacred Scripture, and every human being's mind. The entire human race is interconnected by mental fibers to each other, and to God, and to God's *words*. This is part of creation.

Prophets of all nations and cultures were given to write down God's *Words*, which was dictated to them mentally from God though the intermediary of heavenly societies in the afterlife who are located at the celestial and spiritual levels of consciousness. God's Words passed through the minds of the people who are in the highest human consciousness in the afterlife and are called celestial-rational, as mentioned above. God then connected the mind of these heavenly people to the mind of the chosen and prepared prophets who wrote down what they were inspired to mentally hear in their *natural consciousness*, therefore in the natural language of some culture on earth. The prophets were not aware of any of this and did not know that what they were hearing mentally and writing down was the natural-language correspondences of the spiritual language that is used by the heavenly societies.

Because of this two-phase transmission process of God's Words, the text of *Sacred Scripture* in the heavenly societies is not identical with the text that is written down in a natural language by the prophet. The heavenly text of *Sacred Scripture* is in a spiritual language while the earthly text is in a natural language. The two are distinct and connected by the laws of spiritual-natural correspondences. Spiritual ideas deal with mental things in eternity, while natural ideas deal with things of this world. When a spiritual idea is expressed in a word in spiritual language, its correspondential meaning in the natural language changes to a metaphor or symbolism that describes the mental idea as a bodily physical event.

For example, when God tells us something about "spiritual temptations during regeneration", the words in the natural-historical sense of *Sacred Scripture* appear to discuss "a flood", or "deep waters that cover up and inundate". In some places the literal-historical verse specifies numbers and each time the number 4 is used in some combination (e.g., 40, 400), the actual subject that God is discussing also has to do with spiritual temptation. Similarly, when God actually discusses something about the character of people's selfish loves that must be regenerated, the literal-historical sense appears to refer to dangerous "beasts" such as bears, snakes, and scorpions. These are natural correspondences for hellish loves.

Experiencing Regeneration

You can see that if the natural language verses of our *Sacred Scripture* are actually translations of spiritual language, then we can look at the translation process analytically and discover what the idea was in the spiritual language. This method of *backward translation by correspondence* will be illustrated later in the book. But we can mention here at the outset what the results are when deriving the spiritual meaning by applying correspondences. We know what God is talking about in the natural language of *Sacred Scripture*, namely, the historical details of some people that God formed a relationship with and to which we are cultural descendants. This history also includes the Commandments of life that God gave these people, and therefore to us as well.

Now we can ask what is God talking about in the spiritual language of *Sacred Scripture*?

The answer, as you yourself can confirm later, is that in the spiritual meaning of Sacred Scripture God is giving us anatomy lectures in theistic psychology.

This makes rational sense when you recall that God is leading every individual to experience regeneration by which God can bring everyone into eternal happiness in heaven. This is God's ultimate motive. Theistic psychology is the knowledge of the details of how regeneration takes place anatomically with our mind. Discovering and receiving this spiritual knowledge makes us able to cooperate effectively in our regeneration process. This is the goal that God keeps steadfast before all other goals.

Spiritualizing Everything

Any thing or situation that you think of gets spiritualized when you bring God into it.

God is the only spiritual-in-itself and the only Human-in-itself.

The expression "God is life-in-itself" is used to indicate that life does not exist anywhere else. This means that wherever you see an indication of life being present it must be God's life being active there. It is impossible for God to give life away so that it would no longer be God's life. This is

Experiencing Regeneration

because life is Divine and the Divine cannot belong to anybody but to God. *Wherever life is present or active, God's life is there.* It is the same with "God is love-in-itself" and "God is wisdom-in-itself". Similarly, "God is intelligence-in-itself" and "God is truth-in-itself". Intelligence, like life and love, are Divine and cannot be appropriated by anyone as their own. Instead, we are to think that God's intelligence and love are active in the mind of people.

The expression "God is Human-in-itself" means that we human beings are created in God's own Human anatomy and spiritual organic structure. This means that God is Human just as we are human, except that God's Human is infinite while our human is finite. In a spiritual sense everything God creates is an image or effigy of God as Human, but differing according to the complexity and perfection of a thing. We can experience this "Divine Human" framework even in simple things like a rock or a river or the wind in that they perform *uses* for the human race. All things are created for a specific use in God's running of the universe. The highest of all uses is the human being because we are unique in being born with a spiritual body that contains anatomical organs for receiving the inflow of Divine love and truth, by which we can reciprocate God's love within a reciprocal relationship.

We receive the substance of love into the affective system or the will, while we receive the substance of truth into the cognitive system or the understanding. These two Divine substances are living, infinite, uncreate, and immortal. In creation they originate and flow out from the spiritual sun of the mental world of eternity. *The spiritual sun is the first "proceeding" of God into creation.* God created everything by the spiritual sun, including "the natural sun", which exists in endless numbers of "stars" in the physical universe. God also maintains and manages the universe and all things in it by means of the spiritual sun. Its rays of spiritual heat and spiritual light fill the atmospheres of the two worlds, the mental world first, then the physical world through the mental.

Love-substance and truth-substance are therefore the building blocks of all things that exist.

Spiritual heat is the substance of love, while spiritual light is the substance of intelligence, rationality, wisdom, and truth. All things therefore in the mental world and in the physical world are created out of living Divine

Experiencing Regeneration

Human love and truth, these being spiritual substances that are God's own. *This explains rationally how God as a Divine Human Person can be omnipresent* -- if you remember that God's own mental substances flowing out through the spiritual sun cannot be given away but can only be "adjoined" or borrowed as it were, so that we may thereby have the as-of self ability to perform "uses", that is, whatever is useful to society and self.

You can see that God is present in what is God's own in our mind such as the rationality and loves that appear to us as our own. God wills this appearance on purpose so that we may feel that we are independent human beings. At the same time we must realize and acknowledge that this rationality and love is not our own but God's in us. If we fail to acknowledge this and believe instead that we are really independent and have our own intelligence, loves, and motivation, then we are in a delusional mental state that prevents our regeneration from proceeding.

Be careful to avoid the costly error of *nonduality* which involves thinking that God is physically in things or in human beings. Some people who think this way point to the surrounds and say, This is God, or, That is God. *But it is spiritually insane to point at something and believe that it is God.* We do speak that way by appearance following the literal expression in *Sacred Scripture* where it declares that God is "in" us and that we are "in" God. What is meant here in the spiritual-rational sense is that God is co-Present with each of us through the inflow of God's mental substance of love and intelligence or truth. It is rational to say therefore that we "move in God and God in us" since the inflowing Divine love-substances and Divine truth-substance are the only components and activators of our organs that give us our ability to move or to think.

Our ability to feel and think comes about by using God's own love and intelligence that flow in from God's mind through the spiritual sun of eternity. It is through love-substance and intelligence-substance that God is present in our mind. *God's mental substance is actually present in our thoughts and feelings, making them to exist and light up in our consciousness.* Nothing that is God's own has been "transferred" to us. To clarify this in your mind you can think instead that our organic mental fibers in our spiritual body, which gives us our consciousness, are intertwined with God's organic mental fibers, yet the two never co-mingle but remain adjoined to each other. To be mentally adjoined is to be co-Present. It is this adjunction to God that makes us to be immortal.

93

Experiencing Regeneration

Our finite spiritual consciousness is co-present with God's infinite spiritual consciousness. Thus we can dialog with God and share each other to each other. This was God's purpose in creating the universe and in maintaining it in this order.

Sometimes we experience doubt about the idea that God knows everything we are thinking. You can see now that it is not a question of whether "God knows my thoughts" but God is my thoughts in their first initiation or beginning from where God's thoughts as truth-substance bubble up to our awareness of experiencing. As they descend and externalize into our awareness, God's thoughts and loves are covered over and changed in external appearance by the laws of correspondence.

Hence our thoughts are different from God's thoughts in form and meaning even though there is continuity from beginning to end. If you consider any thought that you have, you can realize that it is an organic mental object made of truth-substance that ties it to its originating root in God's mind.

All your thoughts are anatomically traceable to God's substance of truth that flows into the cognitive system of your spiritual body.
Xxxx continue here
From this you can see again that God "knows" every thought we have because His substance of intelligence or truth-in-itself is forming that thought in your mind. *God directly manages the sequence and content of the thoughts of every individual from birth to endless immortality in the afterlife.* This is once more an image of God's infinity.

But note: despite this Divine "hands-on management style", God's substance of love activates in us the capacity *to feel free as-of self*, which is experienced as voluntary control, mental liberty, and being alone in oneself. And similarly, God's substance of intelligence or truth activates in us the capacity to be intelligent, to think with reasons and to communicate with symbols of meaning, which is experienced as thinking rationally and being affected by conscience. We have these capacities and skills from the inflow of God's love and truth as mental substance, for which our spiritual body was created.

Human beings are more obviously in the "image and likeness" of God than other created objects. *Our very humanity is created through the use of reciprocal conjunction with God.* In *Sacred Scripture* this is discussed as making a "Covenant" with God. Human beings have the ability to mentally acknowledge God's co-Presence and to dialog with Him at any time in any place, and thereby to show humiliation, worship, thankfulness, adoration, and obedience.

This reciprocation on our part creates an anatomical conjunction with God, which makes us immortal beings.

It is little known today that for every human being death is not death but the dying-resuscitation process. This is a two-day anatomical procedure that God performs to separate the physical body from the spiritual body, which were conjoined from birth. *This process of resuscitation from death is described in detail in the Appendix at the end of the book.* Here is a brief summary of it.

Spiritualizing our daily activities raises our consciousness of them from merely natural to spiritual, which is the truly human awareness.

For instance, consider the plate of food in front of you at lunch or dinner. To spiritualize the plate of food and to make it a holy subject you can ask yourself, "How many people did it take to get this plate of food on my table"? A couple of hundred? A couple of thousand? More? Start adding up in an approximate way the *categories of people* involved:

- the supermarket employees,
- the managers and executives of the supermarket chain,
- the truck drivers and service stations they use,
- the farmer production company and its employees in the field,
- the police keeping order on the routes and streets,
- the telephone company taking calls about arrangements to deliver the goods,
- the legislators who enacted the laws to allow such a business,
- the lawyers and judges who restore order in disputes and criminal cases,
- the schools that trained the lawyers,
- the drivers,
- the managers,
- the teachers,

- the janitors,
- the companies that supply the desks and electronics used by students,
- the doctors and nurses,
- the inspectors,
- the international trade agreements for import and export,
- the United nations organization,
- their families,
- their schools,
- their government organizations,
- their supermarket employees,
- the managers and executives of the supermarket chain,
- the soldiers that protect the country from invasion,
- the families of the soldiers,
- the companies that manufacture weapons for the soldiers,
- the teachers in schools where their children are enrolled, ...

Wait! Wait! Do not go on. There is no end to it, is there?

That's correct. No end to it.

God produces every single event by involving the entire human race.

No event can exist that is disconnected from the entire humanity, and further, from the entire universe. In other words, God maintains the universe as one integrated single functional unit, which is that of a human being that is surrounded by objects that are created for human uses.

I may illustrate this point from my background in the specialty field of *ethnomethodology*, a field that was popularized by H. Garfinkel in an influential book by that tile published in 1968. He demonstrates that it is not possible to describe everything that is connected to any assertion or sentence. For instance, if you start with the husband's statement, "*Dana succeeded this morning to put a penny in the parking meter*", and tried to explain everything there is to this story, it would get you involved in a divergent series of explanations that increase with each explanation. As you attempt to explain one thing such as "Dana" in its fullness you would need to explain what is a daughter, what is a husband, what is to grow up, what is parking meter, etc.

Experiencing Regeneration

The ethnomethodological principle is: The more you try to explain, the more there is to be explained.

Another example of this idea is the principle of "the indeterminacy of meaning" which I proposed in a 1974 book on language teaching and bilingualism. This says that the words composing a sentence have a specific definition and meaning while the sentence does not. The meaning of a sentence cannot be defined because it is indeterminate. We can paraphrase a sentence and add various explanations. But after all the explanations are added the sentence can be shown to have meanings that were not listed before. You can see that this idea is closely related to that of Garfinkel.

This indeterminacy of single things in a whole is the character of culture and of the universe. This is the implication of the principle that "everything in the universe is connected". This includes the idea that every human being is connected to all others. Also, that no single thought can be disconnected from all your other thoughts, and all the thoughts of all people. This is the meaning of the principle that "in God infinite things make one". God wills the absolute unity and synchrony of all creation. Another way to say this is that God wills that only what is of some use to human beings can come into existence. In other words, every object and event serves a human use, otherwise it could not come into existence.

Experiencing these spiritual thoughts and how they affect us, is to spiritualize the plate of food. This principle applies to any topic, object, or event that is in front of you or in which you are immersed – watching a TV program, driving the car, shopping for clothes, greeting the neighbor, playing soccer, helping a stray cat, texting a message, or just plain hearing the sounds of birds and insects and enjoying the scents of the field or beach. Everything is spiritualized in your mind when you connect it to God, His omnipotence and love, and His ultimate purpose of populating heaven to eternity with more and more human beings coming into that state every day from the endless number of earths in the constantly expanding physical universe.

To spiritualize is to experience the human use that it has in the scheme of God.

Experiencing Regeneration

God is the original and only Human itself, acting with omnipotence from love with reason. In spiritual consciousness our experiencing of life is through God, our maker, protector, sustainer, and provider. We have an organic image of God's infinite soul within our own finite soul. *We are created to be activated by God, not by ourselves.* God's mercy and love leads Him to will that we are to experience living as-if it were our own, and as if we thought and reasoned from ourselves by ourselves.

The "as-if our own" is necessary because without it we would not like it and would reject heaven, calling it God's idea of happiness, not our own. For this reason God in His love and mercy for us concedes to give us the experiencing of an independent and self-sourced self. And this makes each of us face a life and death issue: Will we acknowledge that the experiencing of an independent self-sourced "self" is actually the experiencing of the "as-of self"? Upon this decision depends our eternity in heaven or hell.

We benefit from the "as-of self" appearance as long as we know and remember that it is an "as-of self" and not a real self.

Even in celestial consciousness, which is above the spiritual, we have the normal feeling of the as-of self, but *simultaneously* we actually perceive the inflow of God's love and wisdom that activate our feeling and thinking moment by moment. This synchronicity between Divine Human inflow and as-of self experiencing provides wisdom and love in spiritual consciousness, which cannot be seen nor believed in natural consciousness.

We can spiritualize our daily activities and thus raise our consciousness of them from natural to spiritual. To do this we need to practice reminding ourselves with each event facing us that nothing can exist or happen without God's direct supervision and management by rational and loving principles and goals. So the first need is to re-affirm our belief in God's omnipotence and to rehearse our understanding of how this principle cannot have exceptions.

It is a spiritual temptation to think that God does not actually have total and absolute control over some person, situation or event.

Experiencing Regeneration

We re-affirm our belief that God is perfect in power, in love and in wisdom. Hence it is irrational of us to think that the event we are facing currently is somehow not totally controlled by God.

We might consider apologizing to God for even entertaining such a doubt in the present situation. Such a feeling of humiliation before God brings us closer to Him, which we can experience as Divine warmth, inner calmness, and full reassurance.

Sometimes people are taught that what is "spiritual" is difficult to explain, like what is love. Actually, both of these are easy to explain when you connect them to God. God is the only spiritual itself from which all human spirituality is received. We are born with the natural and the rational capacities of our mind. We can receive God's spiritual in our rational. You can see now that anything whatsoever that has to do with God is spiritual. And furthermore, is holy, for only God is holy. God is also Divine love itself, and Divine wisdom itself. The reality is that God is present from "firsts to lasts" in all of creation, a presence that is made visible through the human use that every created object has. *All of nature is a framework of spiritual use for human beings.*

Everyone experiences mental problems, which vary in lightness and gravity, and in frequency or generality. The experiencing of a mental problem is initiated when we become aware of our thinking that is immersed in natural consciousness. *You cannot experience neuroses, anxieties, or any other mental problems when your thinking is immersed in spiritual consciousness instead.*

The theistic solution to mental health is to spiritualize all mental problems and thereby see them fall off our personality like crusty scabs.

To spiritualize a mental problem that you are facing you need to pull your consciousness out of its natural immersion zone where it is wallowing in semi-darkness and is thereby giving you the experiencing of this mental problem. *The instant you bring God into the situation you have begun spiritualizing the problem or issue.*

Do some self-witnessing along with talking to God. Share your observations with God. Once you begin this process you are well on your way distancing yourself from the "problem". Further, you are placing

Experiencing Regeneration

yourself in the position of receiving conscious help from God. This is what you didn't have when your awareness was held down in natural consciousness. But God cannot actually be filtered out of any situation. We put on the great illusion that God is not right here in our mind and in our experiencing. This illusion makes us mentally sick and we are left unprotected from wicked attacks originating in the mental world of humanity.

Initiating and maintaining a reciprocal relationship with God through daily dialog shatters this illusion of aloneness.

With that affirmation of realism a new anatomical channel of communication and reception is initiated by God. With this new channel we are able to receive and enjoy a higher thinking protocol called *spiritual-rational* thinking. In this new more interior and more human mode of thinking mental problems cannot take hold. All the former plagues are gone. All the painful crusty scabs on our personality have fallen off, leaving clean, smooth, and young skin.

Spiritual-rational thinking has two phases of execution. The first half of the solution is to work out a role enactment script that brushes away the current problem script that is now running itself off in your natural consciousness, and is giving you these mental health issues to face. Now with God's co-Presence clearly in your focus you do a re-appraisal of your mental situation. You can now remember that God is in full charge, not half-charge, with what is bothering you. So now you can ask God for enlightenment to see why He is facing you with these problems. You also want God's reassurance and love-warmth. The experiencing of this exchange leaves you refreshed and enthusiastic. The feeling of being beaten down has vanished into a past illusion.

But this wonderful solution and feeling does not last. Sooner or later your experiencing places you back in the morass of being weighted down by the same mental problems. This is why you must set up the second half of the solution to make it permanent and real. This step consists in *willing to oppose* the natural thinking and *willing to enact* the spiritual thinking. *The first step in regeneration is thinking; the second step is willing.*

New thinking with new willing together provide the experiencing of new mental skills.

Both steps are necessary, and both are difficult, though the second step is most challenging because it involves struggling against severe spiritual temptations. God fully manages the process of this anatomical change in our spiritual body. God initiates spiritual temptations by connecting us with hellish and heavenly societies simultaneously. *They fight it out with each other using our consciousness as a battlefield.* The evil societies run through our *memory* and find there things we've thought, said, or did with which they accuse us and make us feel guilty, impure, and worthless. Meanwhile the heavenly societies to which God connects us run through our heavenly *feelings and intentions* that we've ever experienced and bring them back to our focus.

Feelings of being good are now battling the thoughts of being bad. The feelings always win -- if we appropriate them. And only then.

We have to want to be good more than we want to be bad.

This heavenly love must be applied to the self-witnessing of our problem role enactment.

Brief Summary of
Death and Resuscitation

(1) Death occurs when the respiration and heartbeat both stop. The physical body in this world is then separated from the spiritual body in the afterlife, which is then left to itself.

(2) Resuscitation means the drawing forth of the spirit from the body, and its introduction into the spiritual world. This is done by God alone. The entire process takes about 30 hours to complete.

(3) Emanuel Swedenborg (1688-1772) observed the process of resuscitation with hundreds of people in the course of several years of observation, and he himself had the actual experience, which he was allowed to undergo, as he says, so "that I might have a complete knowledge of the process".

Experiencing Regeneration

(4) When physical respiration ceases and the heart beat stops one becomes conscious of the inner respiration of the spiritual body. *Thinking and spiritual perception continue without interruption throughout the dying-resuscitation process.*

(5) At one point one becomes conscious of angels at a distance, then close by sitting by one's head. Their feelings and thoughts are communicated and experienced. *The person undergoing resuscitation is not aware of his or her own emotions or concerns.*

(6) For several hours the angels hold the person in the same thoughts as when dying. Afterwards the person is awakened and gradually takes over control, coming into the familiar affections and thoughts that were habitual prior to death.

(7) *The eyes then open.* The person now conscious through the spiritual body walks away from the resuscitation zone and begins a new continuation in eternal life, meeting others who are already in the afterlife and with whom they have interactions and relationships.

(8) In this initial exploratory phase the person is led to experiencing various events and relationships that gradually begin to be directed by one's deeper loves that until then lay hidden in one's personality, and now come out to the surface where the person becomes aware of them.

(9) The person then faces an unavoidable choice in personality make up: to reject selfish love and all its hellish affections, keeping only mutual love and its heavenly affections. Or choosing the reverse: to reject mutual love and all its heavenly affections, keeping only selfish love and its hellish affections. Depending on this choice, the person enters the permanent phase of living either in a hell society or in a heavenly society.

(10) *The choice of heaven or hell is not a judgment that God makes*, nor is it a spiritual punishment or a reward. It is strictly voluntary and self-initiated by preference and choice. This choice is determined solely by what loves and habits the person has developed over the years of living prior to death.

(11) The choice for heaven is made by all who have undergone regeneration. The choice for hell is made by all who have not undergone regeneration and still are unwilling to do so after resuscitation.

Once the physical body is no longer activated by the spiritual body it becomes a corpse and disintegrates. It has served its use, which was that our mind could be active in the physical world and from that experience, develop our natural mind. Through our natural mind we learn to think and to reason, and to perform acts in response to our needs, desires, and conscience.

This natural personality then forms the basis from which spiritual regeneration can take place in adulthood.

Without undergoing the process of regeneration, our selfish loves and irrational ideas make us to be unwilling to tolerate a life in heaven with its conjugial happiness and mutual love by all for all. *Only those can live comfortably in heaven who are in mutual love and love to God.* All others are more comfortable in the hell societies where selfishness and insanity hold sway. You can see from this how critical it is for each of us to undergo regeneration. Through this lifelong process of spiritual struggle against our selfishness we gradually equip our personality with the loves and skills that are needed for living by mutual love and love to God.

You can see that there is much to be understood and learned about the anatomical and mental details of how we are connected to God. This knowledge of "theistic psychology" is useful to clear our minds of the cobwebs of misunderstanding and misinformation about God that we all learn from various spurious sources. The knowledge of theistic psychology gives you the details of reasoning that you will need to spiritualize everything in your life for the sake of your regeneration.

When you spiritualize a topic you are making it holy because it pertains to God.

Are the Contents of This Book Compatible With Science?

Experiencing Regeneration

The answer is Yes. This conclusion needs to be supported rationally.

Rationality is at a higher level of thinking than science. Many people will bluster at this assertion. I think it's because everyone in the past two centuries has been raised and educated in the perspective of scientific materialism. We were taught to feel awe for scientists as people who are superior to others in our society, especially in intelligence and thinking. So now when we consider the assertion that rationality is higher than science, we experience revulsion and deride such an idea with ridicule. But if you realize now that you are dismissing the idea that rationality is higher than science merely because you are role enacting what you've been taught, then you might be willing at this point to grant that it is possible that science is below rationality. Having taken this positive attitude you might wish to proceed with the development of the argument.

We may ask first, from where does science acquire its methods? The history of science and the observation of current practices of scientists give us the information that "normal science" is an activity that is driven by hunches, insight, trial and error experimentation, deductive and inductive logical argumentation, and most importantly, by construction of cause-effect explanations that allow others to replicate or falsify the offered explanations. This is the activity of scientists.

You can see that this standardized activity of scientists must proceed and be guided by a higher mental faculty than the activity of science itself.

Human thinking goes on at various levels of "height" or complexity. You can observe this in yourself since you are an expert at human thinking, having done it 24/7 since your birth. In the professional literature you can find the idea that anyone who spends 10,000 hours doing some particular thing is to be considered an expert at it. This means that you can use your mental skills to monitor your thinking and observe that you are thinking at different levels at different times or in different moods. Your higher-level thinking observes and guides your lower-level thinking.

Soon you will feel confident that your rational level of thinking is higher and superior to your sensorimotor level of thinking. It will be clear then that the work of science is guided and built by rationality or rational thinking.

Experiencing Regeneration

But now we also need to confirm the fact that there are two distinct levels of rationality that may be called "natural-rational thinking" and "spiritual-rational thinking". When scientists either confirm or invalidate a scientific theory they are thinking at the level of natural-rational ideas. All concepts of confirmation or disconfirmation of scientific hypotheses must contain only natural concepts that are definable and measurable. Everything in the contemporary scientific method must come down to a bottom line, which is the physical measurement. This is the status quo in all of the sanctioned materialistic sciences and disciplines. This *modus operandi* is strictly enforced, making it impossible for anyone with the explanatory concepts of dualism or God, to publish or to practice at accredited institutions that receive government funds for research.

Leaving all of this behind and below our sight, we can enter with our thinking into the level of spiritual-rational ideas. First we need to lay out the context and the perspective that is called "scientific dualism" and also "theistic psychology". I have done this in some detail throughout this book everywhere, so there is no need to do it again in this section. Think of all that you have read here about God, how the universe was created and why, the mental world of eternity in the afterlife, the two-day dying-resuscitation process, heaven and hell, and the details of experiencing regeneration. These ideas are meaningless in natural materialism so they are ridiculed or judged delusional.

From this inability of natural consciousness to comprehend spiritual ideas we can conclude that natural-rational thinking is below spiritual-rational thinking in our mind. What is above at a higher level sees more and has more powerful explanations to construct then what is below at a lower level of thinking and understanding.

As you continue developing your spiritual ideas and thinking, you will see that your higher-level spiritual-rational thinking can actualize in your experiencing and in your consciousness only when it "descends" and operates in the lower-level natural-rational thinking. This is not a contradiction. It takes into account the anatomical fact that outer activity in organs must be directed and operated by internal activity, and the internal is always superior in complexity and higher in function than the exterior. People who manage large complex projects know that they need to set up an "inside cadre" of executives who operate with more facts, information, and resources than the outer ring of managers below them who supervise the actual activity of workers. This is also a familiar pattern with the institution of the armed forces in a war zone.

So it is clear that scientific activity is directed and operated by higher order rational activity. There are two possible phases to scientific activity. One is the current situation in materialistic science that is guided exclusively by natural consciousness based on materialistic philosophy or premise. A second phase is scientific activity that is guided by spiritual-rational thinking. This will be discussed next as theistic science or psychology.

Theistic Psychology Is Distinctly Different From Religion

Now with this background we can ask again the question with which we started this section: Is theistic psychology compatible with science? The answer is Yes, because spiritual-rational ideas and principles guide theistic science and its method and content. At the same time we need to separate theistic science from religion, especially since they both focus on the idea and experience of God.

Religion may be defined as the cultural collective worship of God that is based in a particular *Sacred Scripture*. All the major religions to which belong the vast majority of earth's population have their own *Sacred Scripture*. In general, religions do not claim to be scientific. Instead the idea of "faith" or "belief" is used to talk about it. Thus there is no experience of conflict between religion and science as long as this distinction is maintained in the mind. Conflicts arise when the religious perspective is claimed to be scientific. A well-known instance of this conflict may be witnessed if you search the Web for the expression "intelligent design". We need not review any of the details of the arguments on either side of this intellectual battle – as long as we make a distinction between the external literal meaning of *Sacred Scripture* and its internal spiritual meaning. This is the distinction between religion and theistic science, which is based on the internal meaning.

None of theistic science is based in the literal sense and none of religion and intelligent design is based in the internal sense. So there is zero overlap.

106

Experiencing Regeneration

Every idea that is based in the literal sense of *Sacred Scripture* is to be defined as religion.

Every idea that is based in the spiritual sense of *Sacred Scripture* is to be defined as theistic psychology and theistic science. All ideas, facts, and principles in this book are based in the spiritual sense of *Sacred Scripture*.

I said above that "normal science" is an activity that is driven most importantly by the construction of cause-effect explanations that allow others to replicate or falsify the offered explanations. We may wonder whether, or how, "theistic" psychology follows these scientific procedures. When faced with creation proposals called "intelligent design" the concern has been expressed that science must not be coerced into modes of thinking that we find in theology or religious doctrines that prescribe what is to be believed about God and creation. This limitation is the result of applying the literal meaning of *Sacred Scripture* to scientific investigation of issues. Indeed there is a conflict here. But there is no conflict if we focus exclusively on the spiritual sense of Sacred Scripture, as is done in theistic psychology.

This book is an illustration of how scientific thinking can construct cause-effect explanations for the various concepts put forth such as, God, creation of the two worlds out of love-substance and truth-substance, the cause-effect relation between experiencing regeneration and the development of spiritual-rational thinking, the mental anatomy of the spiritual body, the vertical community, heaven and hell, and many other concepts. You will note that all explanations in theistic psychology must be consistent rationally and holistically as well as in detail. All the cause-effect explanations that I offered in this proposal can be theoretically disproven by others who are willing to take the argument to the level of mental anatomy and *Sacred Scripture*. If the investigator in theistic psychology makes a false proposal it can be exposed by others by showing how the spiritual sense of *Sacred Scripture* contradicts that proposal. This process follows deductive and inductive reasoning.

Can you find any assertion or explanation in this book that does not fit with any other assertion or explanation also in this book? You will see when examining all the details offered that they fit together rationally and are coherent holistically. This result is superior to materialistic science in all disciplines because most of normal scientific activity consists of facts and principles that do not agree with each other. When I was in graduate school at McGill university in the early 1960s, my first seminar course was with the illustrious Professor Donald Hebb, founder in 1950 of the highly touted scientific approach known as neurophysiological psychology. It led others to develop modern neuroscience, which is much acclaimed for being the scientific study of the mind and brain.

Hebb impressed a general rule upon all his students, which was that the best scientific theories are those that are disproved within ten years of being proposed. If it survives longer it means it is too vague to allow new experimentation to disprove it. Hence it is not a good scientific theory. I mention this here to show the basic character of normal science, which proceeds by mutually incompatible theories and proposals that are based on restrictive facts or inaccurate observation conditions. People who are unaware of how science proceeds believe that everything in science fits together and is rational. However to believe this is an error.

Theistic psychology makes more rational sense as such contradictions are eliminated and not kept around, as in normal science that contains multiple theories that contradict each other. When you read a textbook in psychology you can see that most of it is made of specialized sub-fields and incompatible theories. There is no coherent integration in most scientific disciplines. This can change in the future when spiritual-rational theories as exemplified in this book "descend" into natural-rational thinking and spiritualize all its concepts. All natural-rational concepts and principles will then "correspond" with all spiritual-rational concepts and principles.

In the following chapters I will continue to show how theistic psychology is a coherent rational body of knowledge that can give people the ability to manage their everyday experience throughout the life process from birth to death to eternity. People need this knowledge to overcome the negative life experiences fostered by materialistic thinking, culture, and science.

Q&A on Theistic Psychology Preview

Experiencing Regeneration

The Q&A Section appears in the last chapter where the answers are also given.

1. *Why do we need to be saved?*
2. *What's so bad about loving yourself?*
3. *What if I don't believe in the afterlife?*
4. *What happens to me then if my personality is selfish?*
5. *Is that so bad that I need to avoid it through salvation?*
6. *How does salvation change that?*
7. *Why is loving God also necessary?*
8. *What if I don't believe in God?*
9. *Can I choose and pick which religion and God I should believe in?*
10. *How do I acquire such a relationship with God?*
11. *Do I have to love all people even if they are dishonest, cruel, and hostile to me?*
12. *What about unconditional love, which is to accept people as they are without wanting to change them as a condition of our love and respect?*
13. *Shouldn't people love their children and their spouse even if they have weaknesses and selfish traits?*
14. *Are we to love our country even if there is corruption and injustice present?*
15. *Should public schools teach about God and salvation?*
16. *How can God be taught in science courses?*
17. *What is theistic science and how can it be justified?*
18. *Why does God allow evil to occur since it could be stopped by Divine omnipotence?*
19. *How do you know these things about God and what God does and wants?*
20. *Aren't these different versions of Sacred Scripture contradictory to each other, and are they not often used to justify dissent and attacks against those with different beliefs.*
21. *Some people have given up on God because it seems wrong to them that God punishes people to eternal hell simply for not*

believing something or for having done something wrong. Can theistic psychology resolve this concern?

22. How is evil defined in theistic psychology, given that similar activities that are allowed in one culture are defined as evil in another: does it not seem relative?

23. How is evil related to our afterlife?

24. What is sin and what is the punishment of evil?

25. Since God intervenes and manages every detail what is the point of praying and asking?

26. Is atheism detrimental to the individual?

27. Can good people be atheists, or are all atheists bad people?

Chapter 2
Experiencing Our Daily Emotional Spin Cycle

The Illusion of Self vs.
the Reality of the As-of-self

The idea of an omnipotent and omniscient God managing every operation in our mind needs to be reconciled with the idea of freedom of self and the feeling of freedom in our own mind by which we can think what we want, like or dislike something, or choose what we prefer.

So the idea that selfhood is an appearance or illusion needs to be examined in the larger context of how the spiritual world and the natural world interact. Within this context one can see that the notion of "self" is based on a broken logic based on merely natural appearances. In order to restore mental health to our civilization we need to see that *psychological explanations based on the notion of self contribute to people's mental health problems*, while the notion of *as-of self* gives people the ability to overcome mental health problems.

You will see that the notion of as-of self is based within a *spiritual*-rational framework that may be called theistic psychology. In contrast, the idea of "self" is based within a *natural*-rational framework that may be called materialistic psychology.

When we are still experiencing life in natural consciousness we do not accept the idea of as-of self.

Experiencing Regeneration

This is a spiritual idea that has no meaning in natural consciousness. Consider that the idea of "self" is not compatible with the idea of God's omnipotence. The normal idea of a person is that one is alone in one's mind and acting freely from self as self. But how can this be true if God is omnipotent? To say that the self acts "from self" means that self has the power from self to act. But this is only an appearance to those who think in natural consciousness.

When we consult our spiritual-rational consciousness we can perceive that "self from self" is to remove God's omnipotence, which of course is impossible. The individual cannot act from self because God has all the power and God's power cannot be given to the individual. This is because God's power is always whole and infinite, and this cannot be divided and given to a finite being. God's infinite power is fully the same in every individual. It is not possible for God to divide this infinite power and to give portions of it to human beings.

Hence we conclude that God's infinite power acting within every person is God's power and none of it belongs to or is part of the individual.

As a result of this it is necessary to say that there is no self but only an as-of self.

God's love is such that He wills and sets up within the individual the appearance that we act from self and thus that we have a self. Since we are born into natural consciousness we would be devastated and unable to grow up were we to think and perceive that we don't have a self for real and that it is God that is acting within our mind. To think this would convince us in natural consciousness that we are not real people but God's organic robots. And this would make us depressed, unhappy, and unwilling to learn and to make plans. Hence we could not be regenerated and live in eternal happiness. This outcome would be contrary to God's love and purpose. Hence God in His infinite goodness provides us with the appearance of a self.

At the same time when we develop mentally into spiritual consciousness we begin to understand that the self is actually an appearance and that we in fact live through an as-of self. This new idea allows us to acknowledge God's omnipotence and presence in our mind. Further, it allows us to be regenerated by experiencing that the evil traits belonging to selfish love

Experiencing Regeneration

occupying our mind are in fact not our self at all. We can stop identifying with these evil traits and begin seeing them as belonging, not to us, but to the spiritual societies to which God connects us when managing our mental growth process. Once we realize that they are not our own we can get rid of them by not holding on to them. As long as we believe that these evil loves and fantasies are from self we cannot reject them and we cannot be regenerated. These evils will therefore actually become our self when we join those spiritual societies in the afterlife.

Prior to regeneration we are anatomically connected to the evil spiritual societies. Their evil loves and spiritually insane thoughts *appear within us and appear to be ours*. For instance, those who deny the existence of God and make it to be an invention of the weak-minded have these negative thoughts and feelings about God flow into their mind from those spiritual societies. This also applies to heavenly feelings and thoughts. For instance, parents who love their children and care for them for the children's sake have these intentions and thoughts from the spiritual societies in heaven to which the parents are connected during parenting.

If we confirm as just and right the evil thoughts and selfish loves that flow into us, then we appropriate them to ourselves and they become part of our personality forever.

After death we are automatically and irresistibly drawn towards those societies, and when we enter them and become part of them the feeling is that of a homecoming. We recognize the people there as friends, brothers, and sisters, having been with them all along while still on earth. Hence we continue our selfish life such as it has been on earth.

If we appropriate the spiritual truths and goods that flow into us from the heavenly societies, we must acknowledge that they are not our goods and truths but theirs, and these are in them not from themselves but from God. However, if instead we appropriate the inflowing spiritual truths and goods to ourselves, making them our own and from ourselves, then we feel our own merit in it, and this is as deadly as selfishness. Meritoriousness and self-justification are called "deadly sins" because they intercept all good and truth from God and turn them in the mind into falsified truths and adulterated goods. For example, to love the work of our employment and to perform it well and sincerely is a "good" if it is done for the sake of others, but an "adulterated good" if it is done for the sake of self only, not actually caring about the benefits it brings to others.

For regeneration to be effective we need to do two things. First, we must acknowledge that "self" is an appearance and has no power, and therefore is to be called an "as-of self", given that all power is God's. Second, we must witness self in daily activity so that we can learn to distinguish between what flows in from heaven and what from hell.

The following sections describe various ways we can get to know our "self", which consists of three discrete functions or systems.

Experiencing Our Threefold-Self

All individuals are socialized in accordance with cultural norms. To be socialized means to acquire particular habits in all three areas of human functioning:

- habits of feeling (anatomically this is the mind's affective system or willing)

- habits of thinking (this is the mind's cognitive system or thinking)

- habits of sensing and acting (this is our sensorimotor system or doing)

Every individual has a threefold-self in which the three mental systems act together, yet each can be distinguished and isolated for observation and self-modification.

Your threefold-self has two life arenas to function in. One is the arena of others and the world; the second is the arena of self (or the private world within). These two life arenas, namely, [others/world] and [self] -- each require their own particular way of functioning. We are required to function in both arenas every hour of every day since we have to deal with others and the world, as well as with ourselves.

Experiencing Regeneration

Our functioning in the two life arenas [*others/world*] and [*self*] can be either negative or positive. For instance, rage is a feeling located in the negative arena of [*others/world*] because it is the feeling of anger against someone or thing. Compassion is in the positive arena of [*others/world*] because it is the feeling of tolerance and caring for someone or thing. Similarly, the negative arena of [*self*] includes depression and self-destructive behavior since these involve negative feelings towards the self. The positive arena of [*self*] includes feelings of self-confidence and enthusiasm since these are positive feelings towards the self.

These four life arenas of our daily life are called "the four options" because it is up to us to choose which of the four life arenas we want to experience in any situation.

Our automatic habits normally determine which option we experience, and in many situations our automatic reactions are negative. Nevertheless, we always have the freedom to switch options from negative to positive. The positive options represent healthy adjustment, happiness, and success, while the negative options represent maladjustment, unhappiness, and failure.

So it makes sense to customize your automatic habits so you end up functioning in the positive arena most of the time, if not always.

The Four Options
of Experiencing Daily Living

The diagram below is called "the four options diagram." It shows the four options that we have for experiencing our daily emotional spin cycle:

The two options in the upper half of the diagram are in the red bridge zone and involve our emotions regarding others and the world (one is negative and the other is positive). The two options in the lower half of the diagram are in the blue bridge zone and involve our emotions regarding [self] (again, one is negative and the other is positive).

115

Experiencing Regeneration

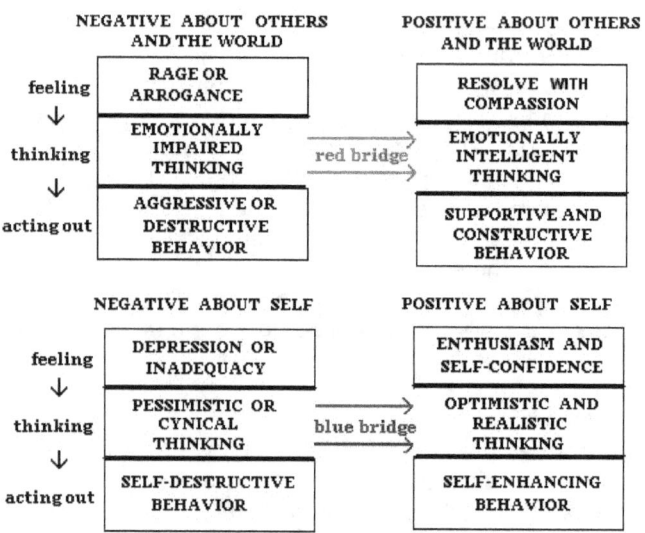

The Four Options
On the Daily Emotional Spin Cycle
And the Two Bridges

Note that each of the four options involves the threefold-self: feeling habits, thinking habits, and acting habits which include sensations in the body that we are aware of but do not show overtly, as well as our body movements and appearance that others can see. The four options are called the "*daily emotional spin cycle*" and they map out the cultural norms of role enactments that we acquire in our socialization or upbringing. To function as socialized individuals our threefold-self must acquire particular habits that run themselves off according to a standard role routine. These socialized habit routines are sometimes called "social scripts" or "schemas".

We all have the impression that when we act we are acting freely from our own feelings and thoughts, not realizing that we are mostly running off the social scripts or behavior routines that we acquired as children and adults. This is shown by the fact that when we compare what people feel, think, and do in specific situations we find that these are very similar and predictable. Some of these behavioral scripts are pan-human (existing in

116

all cultures), while others are specific to a cultural and ethnic sub-group. These demographic similarities or equivalencies in social behavior prove that people's feelings, thoughts, and actions are learned role enactments that are standardized or shared collectively by individuals in a society.

Without this standardization process we would not be able to communicate with strangers and society would not be possible. Communication and cooperation require that people overlap to some extent in their habits of feeling, thinking, and acting in specified situations. These standardized habit routines are performed by our threefold-self and can be categorized into four main types, which are here called "the four options." These are the four types of behavioral routines that are part of our role repertoire. We choose to run one of them off at some particular moment in our daily round of activities. It's up to us which one we choose to experience in any situation.

Focus on your experiencing these routines during your daily activities. See if you can confirm the statement that we normally just react automatically without having the impression that we are choosing our emotional reactions. Nevertheless, these automatic reactions are just old habits that we chose to acquire and reinforce. We can consciously choose to modify them so that the new habits will then become our automatic reactions. These new habits are also standardized but they may suit us better, as for example when we choose to switch from negative to positive zones of experiencing. This switching is indicated on the diagram by the red bridge and the blue bridge.

Self-Witnessing
Our Mental Habit Routines

How well do you know your own daily emotional spin cycle?

There are two methods psychologists use to identify the personality habits of individuals. One approach is indirect and subjective: it is to ask people to respond to various questions. These are called "personality scale items" or just "personality tests". The answers of an individual are compared to other people's answers or to some standards already established. This indirect method has weaknesses regarding its reliability and validity since the data are "subjective" and depend on how accurate people's responses are, or how well the responses represent what people really do. It has been shown that people are not accurate in reporting past events and situations. These are classified as "retrospective reports".

A second approach is more direct and objective. It is classified as "concurrent reports": it consists of having people monitor or observe their feelings, thoughts, and actions as they occur in the course of the day, and make some sort of record at the time for later analysis. In some situations this direct objective approach offers a better promise of being valid and actual. It is the method suitable for self-witnessing our experiencing.

To practice this technique you need to approach it like a project or experiment. The idea in a nutshell is for you to observe your threefold-self at certain challenging times that you select during each day and to observe the negative options that you are spontaneously choosing in that situation. This is called *"baseline observation week."* It will give you objective information about your daily emotional spin cycle. *This information will then allow you to consider choosing other options that might suit you better.* As a result your experiencing of daily life can radically change in quality.

The second part is called *"intervention week"* and consists of your attempt to modify your negative emotional spin cycle when being in that same situation again, by choosing a positive option instead. The change to a positive option is accomplished through the *"bridge technique."* This *involves talking to yourself into switching over from the current option you are using, which is negative, to the positive that is also available to you.*

Look at the Four Options diagram again:

Experiencing Regeneration

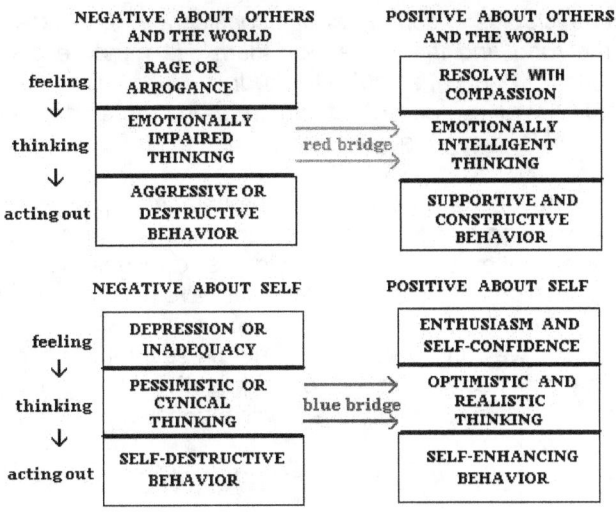

	NEGATIVE ABOUT OTHERS AND THE WORLD		POSITIVE ABOUT OTHERS AND THE WORLD
feeling ↓	RAGE OR ARROGANCE		RESOLVE WITH COMPASSION
thinking ↓	EMOTIONALLY IMPAIRED THINKING	red bridge	EMOTIONALLY INTELLIGENT THINKING
acting out	AGGRESSIVE OR DESTRUCTIVE BEHAVIOR		SUPPORTIVE AND CONSTRUCTIVE BEHAVIOR

	NEGATIVE ABOUT SELF		POSITIVE ABOUT SELF
feeling ↓	DEPRESSION OR INADEQUACY		ENTHUSIASM AND SELF-CONFIDENCE
thinking ↓	PESSIMISTIC OR CYNICAL THINKING	blue bridge	OPTIMISTIC AND REALISTIC THINKING
acting out	SELF-DESTRUCTIVE BEHAVIOR		SELF-ENHANCING BEHAVIOR

The Four Options
On the Daily Emotional Spin Cycle
And the Two Bridges

Notice the option at the top left "*negative about others and the world.*" Here the threefold self is running off the habit routine of rage or arrogance. This feeling seeks and hooks up with a type of cognitive thinking that may be called *emotionally impaired.* In other words, when we are experiencing an enraged or arrogant feeling, there is a compatible cognitive thinking routine that then enters our awareness. This type of thinking is subjective, self-focused, biased, and inaccurate. It is not objective, realistic, or rational but is merely a kind of thinking that is constructed by the mind to be compatible with the negative feeling of rage or arrogance.

For example, a car passes you on the left lane then pulls into your lane ahead of you. After a few seconds the car starts slowing down and proceeds below speed limit. Some drivers, perhaps you too, get enraged at this obnoxious maneuvering. This negative emotion is so intense that it impairs their thinking. To justify and promote their feeling of rage and disapproval of someone, people begin to construct standardized imaginings as to the reasons people have for enacting the behavior that is annoying them.

Experiencing Regeneration

"This driver is stupid, uncaring, and inconsiderate. He hates other people on the road and tries to annoy them. He must be busy with some distractions. I need to honk at this driver to let him know he is doing something wrong. I need to pass him then do the same thing to him. I cannot just let him get away with this kind of stuff."

The negative emotions of rage and disapproval, and the impaired thinking that it fabricates to go along with it, then combine together to produce an overt behavioral routine that is called aggressive or destructive behavior. These are expressions of selfish feelings that have regard only for self.

This is a typical way in which our threefold-self runs off a series of negative habit routines consisting of a negative feeling coupled with impaired thinking and acted out as destructive behavior.

The threefold-self always consists of feeling, thinking, and acting – in that order.

Now notice the option at the top right of the diagram: "*positive about others and the world.*" Here the threefold self is running off the habit routine of resolve-with-compassion. This feeling seeks and hooks up with a type of cognitive thinking routine that may be called emotionally intelligent. When we are in a positive affective state of resolve with compassion, we are highly motivated to do something to solve a problem. Resolve (or determination) needs to be associated with compassion. *This is what makes it different from rage and anger, which are hellish and are devoid of all compassion.*

When we choose the rage option, all sorts of other negative feeling habits will come associated with it, such as cruelty, hatred, and insensitivity. On the other hand the "resolve with compassion" option comes associated with other positive feeling habits such as empathy, fairness, tolerance, and even sympathy. These are feelings of mutual love and they belong to heavenly life.

The positive feeling state seeks out and triggers a compatible cognitive thinking habit. This type of cognitive thinking activity is objective, realistic, and rational. We then understand the realities of the actual situation instead of misunderstanding it and replacing it with the subjective distortions in thinking caused by negative emotions and the impaired

Experiencing Regeneration

thinking that goes with them. Resolve-with-compassion is a positive feeling that seeks out and combines with emotionally intelligent thinking, and together they produce an overt behavioral routine that is called supportive and constructive behavior. In this case the threefold-self runs off a series of positive habits consisting of positive feelings coupled with emotionally intelligent thinking and is acted out as constructive behavior. This pattern belongs to mutual love in heaven.

The "red bridge" (shown in the diagram) connects the negative (left) and positive (right) portions of the upper half of the diagram. The bridge is shown to connect negative *thinking* to positive thinking given that we have voluntary control over our thinking process, and much less control directly over our feelings.

The idea of the bridge technique is that you always retain the ability to voluntarily change your negative thinking into positive thinking.

You enact the bridge technique by talking to yourself in a certain way that helps you turn away from the negative feeling and turn towards the positive.

Then the new positive feeling coupled with the positive thinking together will produce the new overt positive behavior.

At that point you're experiencing the new option and you've been successful in switching over from the negative to the positive option.

You will notice that this change in your mind's turning may not last long. Just a few minutes later a new situation or concern pops into your awareness and you are thrown back into the negative spin cycle.

No worry! Now we can use the bridge technique again and get ourselves moving in the positive spin cycle. Eventually, with daily practice, we will learn to switch to positive as soon as we observe ourselves in negative mode. In this way we change our life and our personality for the better. The bridge technique gives us a choice to customize our options to suit what's best for us and for society.

You use the red bridge to cross from negative thinking to positive thinking, that is, from emotionally impaired thinking to emotionally intelligent thinking. Our ability to use the bridge technique is part of the socialization process that produces all our habits. The red bridge technique consists of talking to ourselves in a certain way so that we stop thinking negatively (with rage) about someone or some situation and start thinking positively (which is resolve-with-compassion). We have the capacity to monitor our thinking and to note that it is emotionally impaired or biased. We can then replace this type of negative thinking routine with more objective and emotionally intelligent thinking routines.

Of course to use the bridge technique we must be motivated to use the positive option that is always available. Without that motivation we keep re-running or re-cycling the negative routines of the threefold-self that we have acquired in the past.

Now look at the third option of routines that is labeled "*negative about the self*" (at the bottom left). A general name for that category of feeling is depression or inadequacy.

These associated negative feelings about ourselves seek out and encourage thinking routines that are called pessimistic or cynical. *Feelings of depression are actually feelings of rage turned towards ourselves.* Similarly, feelings of inadequacy are actually feelings of arrogance turned against ourselves. Rage against others or the world alternates with rage against the self, and vice versa. This *rage-depression spin cycle* and the *arrogance-inadequacy spin cycle* represent two common options many people choose every day. Note that the feelings of depression-inadequacy combine with pessimistic-cynical thinking to produce the behavioral outcome called self-destructive behavior.

If you feel depressed or inadequate it's because you are making yourself feel that way. This may seem like a strange thing to say to one who is suffering from depression and wants to stop feeling that way. Yet it is true even though we are not aware of the many things that go on in our emotions in the layers of our anatomy. These are the complex things in our mind that only God can manage. Depression and feelings of inadequacy are occasioned in our experiencing by the presence of rage against self. Our rage hates everything, including us.

The fourth option is located at the bottom right of the diagram. It is labeled "*positive about self.*" In this mental state we are opting for feelings of

Experiencing Regeneration

enthusiasm and self-confidence which we have available due to our socialization process. These positive feeling states would not last on their own because they need to seek out and be connected with positive thinking habits called optimistic and realistic thinking. The positive feeling states of enthusiasm and self-confidence act together with the positive thinking routines called optimism and realism, to produce the positive outward routines called self-enhancing behavior. The healthy growth of our personality and character depends on our choosing this fourth option. Self-enhancing behavior includes mental health, discipline, orderliness, mastery, and coping. The well-adjusted, happy, and successful individual chooses this option more than the negative counterpart.

Note the "blue bridge" in the bottom half of the four options diagram. It allows us to cross from negative thinking about self to positive. The blue bridge represents our capacity to monitor our own thinking process and to recognize what is pessimistic and cynical in it. We can then question this pessimism or cynicism and substitute positive forms of thinking about self called optimism and realism. But optimism by itself could degenerate into *unrealistic wish-fulfillment*--which is in the negative category. This is why we need to combine optimism-with-realism to insure that we run off only positive thinking routines that correspond with reality.

The blue bridge allows us to talk ourselves out of pessimism or cynicism and switch to more positive and more realistic thinking routines such as optimism-with-realism.

Everyone has the ability to make themselves think and say positive things about themselves. Doing this creates a mental state of reception for positive feelings that we have lying dormant. These will become active as soon as they can act together with positive thinking routines. When we make ourselves think optimistically and realistically we create the conditions for bringing on positive feeling routines such as enthusiasm and self-confidence. Self-enhancing behavior will be the result when positive feelings of enthusiasm and self-confidence combine together with positive thinking called optimism and realism.

The blue bridge may also help you flip-flop in positive zones. Just as rage and depression flip-flop or take turns, in the same way enthusiasm and self-confidence flip-flop with resolve and compassion, keeping us in the positive zones.

Your task in the experiment on your emotional spin cycle will be to monitor the negative options you tend to automatically select in particular recurrent situations every day, and then to use the appropriate bridge technique to switch to a positive zone. You will then observe to what extent the bridge technique worked out or not. Often we seem unable to cross the bridge due to the grip of negative feeling and thinking routines that appear to hold us there captive, and we seem to ourselves unable to get free of them. But at other times we succeed in crossing the bridge and changing the option that our threefold-self is experiencing. Your self-analysis data will indicate when you are more successful and when you are less so. This is the purpose of the experiment.

The Negative Spin Cycle

The diagram below summarizes what was said above about "*the negative spin cycle.*"

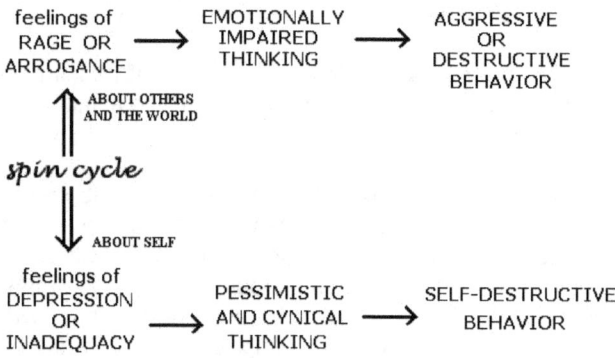

The Negative Spin Cycle

Note the one-way *horizontal* arrows showing the sequence of habits in the threefold-self: the negative feeling states motivate you to select negative thinking sequences, and the two together produce the outward negative behaviors. The two-way *vertical* arrow on the left portrays the negative spin cycle that flip-flops between feelings about [*others/world*], followed by similar feelings about [*self*], and then, recycling both ways keeping you in the negative zones.

Now let's summarize what was said above about "*the positive spin cycle.*"

The Positive Spin Cycle

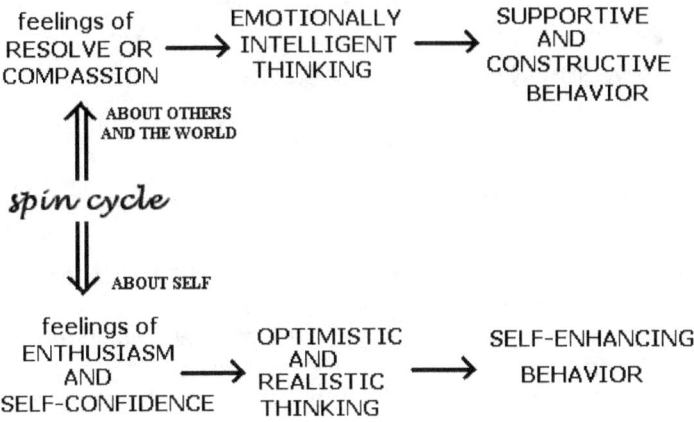

The Positive Spin Cycle

Note what a wonderful life we would have if we kept recycling only between positive feelings towards others (resolve-with-compassion) and positive feelings toward self (enthusiasm and self-confidence). It's our choice.

Here is another view of the negative spin cycle, focusing more specifically on feeling-states and how they connect with each other when we recycle them all day long.

The Others-Self
Negative Spin Cycle

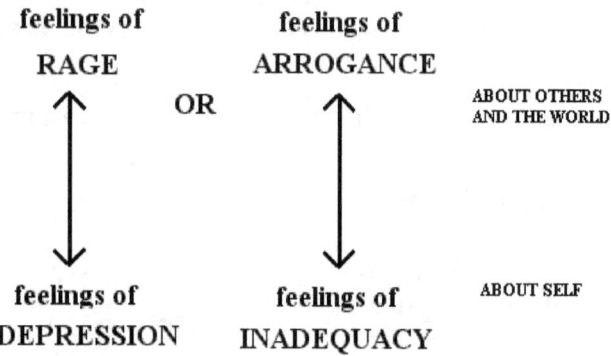

feelings of RAGE

OR

feelings of ARROGANCE

ABOUT OTHERS AND THE WORLD

feelings of DEPRESSION

feelings of INADEQUACY

ABOUT SELF

The OTHERS-SELF Negative Spin Cycle

Note in the diagram above that rage and arrogance are both negative states towards others or the world, and similarly, depression and inadequacy are both negative states towards self. But there is also a specific relation between sub-elements. Feelings of rage flip-flop and are eventually followed by feelings of depression; then, feelings of depression flip-flop and are followed by feelings of rage.

Similarly, feelings of arrogance are followed by feelings of inadequacy. It is the arrogance, when turned inward that produces the feeling of inadequacy. When arrogance is turned outward, others are found to be inadequate in our mind and we want to criticize them and condemn them. When arrogance is turned inward, we make ourselves feel inadequate or flawed in some way. Raging against others eventually is followed by raging against ourselves, which is when we fall into a depressed modality. Then, raging against self is followed again by raging against [others/world].

To avoid repeating this negative spin cycle over and over again we must use the two bridges. If we succeed in crossing one of the two bridges we then enjoy life in the positive spin cycle.

Let's look at a diagram that summarizes what was said before about the positive spin cycle.

The Others-Self Positive Spin Cycle

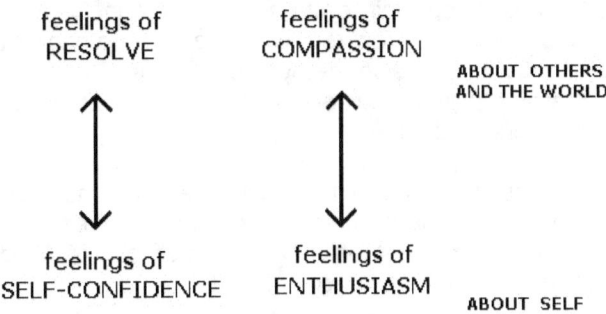

feelings of
RESOLVE

feelings of
COMPASSION

ABOUT OTHERS
AND THE WORLD

feelings of
SELF-CONFIDENCE

feelings of
ENTHUSIASM

ABOUT SELF

The OTHERS-SELF Positive Spin Cycle

The diagram above for the positive spin cycle shows that feelings of resolve towards others and the world can be applied towards the self, in which case we are in the affective state of self-confidence. We cycle between feelings of resolve and feelings of self-confidence; similarly, we flip-flop between feelings of compassion for others with feelings of enthusiasm with one's life. Resolve refers to the determined motivation to do something about a situation. The flip side of this positive feeling is self-confidence, which is a kind of resolve towards our own inner world.

Compassion for others is compatible with resolve. Compassion limits what your resolve is motivated to accomplish. Without compassion resolve turns into rage or arrogance. When compassion is turned toward the self, it is called enthusiasm. The feeling of enthusiasm is the opposite of depression or dissatisfaction. Depression and dissatisfaction indicate the absence of enthusiasm. As soon as you cycle into the enthusiasm habit routine, depression and dissatisfaction vanish into a distant memory.

Now let's take a closer look at the two bridge-techniques.

Experiencing Self-Regulation
Across The Two Bridges

Red is used to represent our spin cycle options involving others and the world. Recall the expression "I saw red" which refers to a negative feeling state of anger or rage. Red is also the symbol of passion and love. Anger is a negative passion towards others while compassion is a positive passion towards others. Both are red.

Now recall the expression "I feel blue" which refers to a negative feeling state of depression or inadequacy. Blue is the symbol for feelings towards the self. Negative blue for depression and feelings of inadequacy, positive blue for enthusiasm and self-confidence.

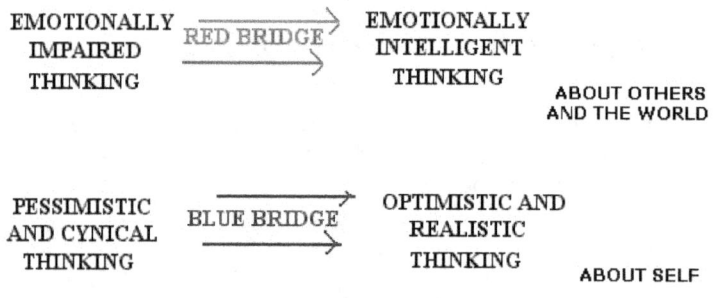

EMOTIONALLY   EMOTIONALLY
IMPAIRED   RED BRIDGE   INTELLIGENT
THINKING   THINKING

ABOUT OTHERS
AND THE WORLD

PESSIMISTIC   OPTIMISTIC AND
AND CYNICAL   BLUE BRIDGE   REALISTIC
THINKING   THINKING

ABOUT SELF

The RED BRIDGE for WORK PRODUCTIVITY
and
The BLUE BRIDGE for EMOTIONAL HEALTH

Note in the diagram above that the bridge techniques is applied to the thinking or cognitive part of the threefold self. This makes sense since we can control our thinking in a direct way while this is not as easy to do with our feeling or affective state. Performing the bridge technique depends on two socialized abilities we all have. First, we are capable of observing or monitoring our thinking process, up to a certain point. Second, if we are motivated, we are able to activate what is in our memory in such a way as to run off new thought sequences that are incompatible with those going on at the time.

For example, when we become aware that we are ridiculing someone in our mind (a form of rage or arrogance--negative red feeling), we can remind ourselves that this is unkind and unjust, and going along with this may corrupt our good character (this is applying the red bridge).

We can also tell ourselves that if we ridicule someone now we are likely to ridicule ourselves later, which hurts, and may lead to depression or feelings of inadequacy and dissatisfaction (negative flip-flop cycle). We can elaborate even further on this emotionally intelligent rationale (red bridge), until we are prepared to accept a new appraisal of the person or situation. This whole event may take just a second or two. Now we no longer feel like ridiculing that individual. We may even experience a flip-flop into the positive blue zone, as we begin to feel good about ourselves, feeling new enthusiasm and renewed self-confidence.

In this way our feeling state changes from negative to positive, and our thinking from emotionally impaired to emotionally intelligent. This is the red bridge. It allows us to change the situation that surrounds us. Rather than conflict with others and waste of opportunity and productivity--which are the outcomes you obtain from emotionally impaired thinking, we can expect instead, initiative, cooperation and productivity--these being the outcomes you obtain from resolve-with-compassion. The red bridge turns conflict into cooperation, and lost opportunity into productivity or success.

The Red Bridge:
From Anger to Resolve

The red bridge promotes productivity and leadership. As the diagram below shows, it consists in bringing up thoughts that are incompatible with emotionally impaired thinking. For example, you might become aware that you're thinking, "*He doesn't deserve my respect. I'm not going to get along with him*" while this person makes a suggestion to you. You're thinking of denigrating things that you can do to him as a way of pursuing your dislike for this individual. But then you decide to apply the red bridge technique to combat your biased and hostile thoughts.

129

Experiencing Regeneration

From your memory you can bring up several favorable things about this person. The moment you convince yourself that you have no data to the contrary and that your hostile attitude is not justified, your feeling state may change from negative to positive, from feeling hatred or anger to feeling resolve-with-compassion. You tell yourself you're going to make the effort and see if this person deserves your compassion and good will rather than just assume he doesn't. Already you might feel better as a result of the flip-flop cycle from positive toward others to positive toward self.

The RED BRIDGE

ABOUT OTHERS AND THE WORLD

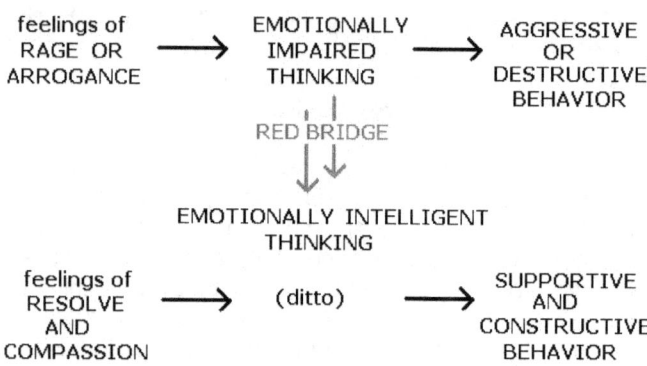

To cross the bridge in your mind you need to say to yourself appropriate *self-regulatory sentences.* You can prepare them ahead of time, write them on a reminder sheet, etc.

Here are some self-regulatory prompts for the red bridge. You can say them to yourself to strengthen your determination to do something constructive (resolve-with-compassion--option 2) rather than to remain in the destructive rage mode (option 1)--consider memorizing and rehearsing these **self-regulatory sentences for the** red bridge *(about others and the world)*:

1. order yourself to stop ruminating, which involves compulsively

    rehearsing the thought of how you're going to get even and retaliate

Experiencing Regeneration

2. question your cold logic or negative conclusion by qualifying it, saying to yourself: "Not necessarily" or "Maybe, maybe not" etc. which help weaken the intensity of your negative persuasion

3. make yourself think of relevant counter-information you've been ignoring so far

4. restore balance by reminding yourself to think of both sides of the issue

5. remind yourself that retaliation hurts people including yourself and it's not good

6. remind yourself that all people have an inherent right to be treated with decency

7. remind yourself that aggressive behavior won't bring you what you want

8. consciously reject any fantasies of revenge as uncivilized and beneath you

9. reject violence as ineffective in bringing about your goal

10. reaffirm the human responsibility you bear to be fair and forgiving

11. think of the consequences you will have to deal with and how much trouble that will be

12. think of alternative options you have available

13. figure out a more effective course of action

14. communicate your ideas to the other person and try for reconciliation or compromise

15. convince yourself it's better for you to forgive and forget insults

16. put yourself in the other's shoes and try to picture their perspective with empathy

17. decide to gather more information before you act

18. decide to consult someone before you act

19. remind yourself that the way you appear in face and tone of voice is a visible message and counts as acting or doing

20. act the opposite of what you feel and say nice things instead of not nice

21. decide you're going to pursue this without anger but with resolve or determination with compassion

22. order yourself to stop

23. etc.

The Blue Bridge:
From Despondency to Enthusiasm

The blue bridge promotes emotional health and objective self-confidence.

As the diagram below shows, it consists in bringing up thoughts that are incompatible with pessimistic and cynical thinking. For example, you might become aware that you're thinking, "*He doesn't like me*" as this person turns down an invitation to lunch with you. You're thinking in a suspicious way about him, telling yourself that he is just giving an excuse for not wanting to be with you. But then you decide to apply the blue bridge technique to combat your pessimistic or suspicious thoughts. From your memory you can bring up several situations when your friend showed signs of liking you. The moment you convince yourself that you have no data to the contrary and that your suspicion is not justified, your feeling state may change from negative to positive, from feeling depressed or dissatisfied to feeling enthusiasm or self-confidence.

Experiencing Regeneration

The BLUE BRIDGE
ABOUT SELF

feelings of DEPRESSION OR INADEQUACY	→	PESSIMISTIC OR CYNICAL THINKING	→	SELF- DESTRUCTIVE BEHAVIOR

| |
BLUE BRIDGE
↓ ↓

OPTIMISTIC AND
REALISTIC THINKING

feelings of ENTHUSIASM AND SELF-CONFIDENCE	→	(ditto)	→	SELF- ENHANCING BEHAVIOR

Notice that you can't directly make yourself feel enthusiastic or self-confident when you're thinking pessimistically or cynically. Pessimistic and cynical thinking are compatible with feelings of depression, dissatisfaction, or inadequacy and are incompatible with feelings of enthusiasm and self-confidence. *You can only feel self-confident or enthusiastic when your thinking is optimistic and realistic.*

The bridge technique works because it depends on your ability to change your thinking, and it does not attempt to change your feelings directly. But once the thinking changes, more compatible feelings are then encouraged.

The blue bridge lets you cross from option 3 (negative blue thinking) to option 4 (positive blue thinking). Negative blue feeling is an emotional state in which you try to persuade yourself that there is something wrong with you and you should feel bad or unhappy about it. This negative role enactment includes depression, generalized anxiety, and a pessimistic or cynical outlook on you as well as on others. Negative blue thinking is activated, supported, and reinforced by negative blue feeling.

To make use of the blue bridge you need to use optimistic self-regulatory sentences that create resistance in your mind to continuing with the pessimistic and cynical thinking. These optimistic self-regulatory sentences move you across to positive blue thinking by creating psychological resistance in your mind against pessimistic or cynical thinking.

Here are examples of **self-regulatory prompts for the** blue bridge (about self) that you can use to create resistance to pessimism or cynicism, and to facilitate the opposite type: optimistic and realistic thoughts.

1. question your assumptions that lead to negative conclusions
2. tell yourself you're catastrophizing in an irrational way
3. tell yourself "Stop it!" when you witness yourself ruminating compulsively
4. do a scenario analysis of the situation, writing down all the versions
5. reject the idea that the worst is going to happen
6. do a re-appraisal of the situation and find some good things about it
7. go over in your mind what others have said to you
8. remind yourself there's a big difference between fantasy and actuality
9. remind yourself there's a big difference between possibility and probability
10. tell yourself you don't want to be known as a cynical person
11. tell yourself you don't want to be known as a pessimist
12. reject any idea that you don't need anyone's support or that you are self-sufficient
13. remind yourself that change is possible
14. reaffirm your belief that you deserve dignity and love
15. tell yourself you want to be civilized and not break things
16. tell yourself you're going to feel better about yourself by switching emotional style

17. tell yourself you're going to be more productive by switching emotional style

18. tell yourself you have the capacity to be successful and your turn has come

19. reassure yourself that you are capable and review your accomplishments

20. question your assumptions that lead to negative conclusions

21. tell yourself you're catastrophizing in an irrational way

22. tell yourself "Stop it!" when you witness yourself ruminating compulsively

23. do a scenario analysis of the situation, writing down all the versions

24. reject the idea that the worst is going to happen

25. do a re-appraisal of the situation and find some good things about it

26. go over in your mind what others have said to you

Now let's take a look at the four options in detail to see how each actually consists of many habits that act together. By studying these lists you will be able to recognize and correctly categorize what your threefold-self is doing in any situation you are observing. See if you can reproduce most of the lists from memory.

Option 1:
Negative Towards Others and the World

Feeling Operations

Negative affect against others can be summarized under the category of rage or arrogance. This refers to a desire or motive to hurt someone or to damage and destroy something. This emotional option includes a large collection of negative feeling habits towards others and the world such as:

Experiencing Regeneration

1. desire to harm or cause injury or loss to someone for the sake of vengeance
2. hatred or the desire to torture or kill someone, or to make them suffer
3. wanting to condemn someone as worthless or useless
4. wanting to discriminate against someone due to your prejudice
5. feeling like throwing something or punching out in blind fury
6. enjoying mocking someone or putting them down
7. wanting to get someone into trouble out of envy or jealousy
8. wanting to insult someone to make them feel bad
9. wanting to hurt someone's reputation
10. wanting to make someone feel dirty or ashamed
11. sabotaging a group activity to get back at someone
12. profiling people negatively on the basis of race, religion, age, or gender
13. being indifferent to how your actions affect others negatively
14. rejecting legitimate authority when you feel like it
15. not caring about others when you expose them to risk
16. allowing yourself to cheat or lie when you feel like it
17. losing your temper but not feeling like apologizing for it later
18. allowing yourself to loaf or not do your duties when you feel like it
19. allowing yourself to miss appointments, phone calls, or be late
20. feeling lack of sympathy for someone who needs your help
21. allowing yourself to misuse things or be careless and negligent
22. etc.

Thinking Operations

Negative cognitions towards others are made of emotionally impaired thinking routines.

This type of thinking process is biased, inaccurate, and irrational. For example, we might assume that someone wanted to insult us when in fact there was no such intention. It's common to make mistakes and exaggerate when we think in this faulty manner. *Emotionally impaired thinking is encouraged or facilitated by anger or arrogance.* When you feel rage or disdain towards someone, you begin to think in an impaired fashion, making the wrong assessment of the situation, losing the sense of reality. Negative feelings and negative thoughts always function together and support each other.

It's common to be aware of our thoughts but most people are less aware of their feelings. This emotional option includes a large collection of negative thinking habits such as those listed below. Take the opportunity of examining each numbered item as applied to yourself. Decide if you have done it or not. If not, why not? Do you have ideas about which ones are done by those you interact with?

1. planning to take revenge or to retaliate no matter what

2. engaging in fantasies of violence or torture

3. thinking about all the things you're going to say to upset or insult someone compulsively

4. going over and over again some past conflict situation or "mental venting"

5. using a biased train of thoughts called self-serving logic

6. conveniently ignoring relevant information

7. exaggerating or being inaccurate in order to justify our rage or arrogance

8. keeping blinders on to maintain one's skewed thinking which serves our selfish intentions

9. interpreting many things as insulting that are not meant that way

10. not considering alternatives or "rigidified thinking"

11. maintaining an attribution bias that favors self and makes others to be always at fault

12. putting things together in a false sequence that supports your side and serves your selfish loves

13. justifying something wrong that we did instead of accepting responsibility for it and resolving not to do it again

14. discriminating against or for someone on the basis of status, family, race, or religion but without admitting this publicly

15. rejecting something because it comes from an authority by rebellion without examining its uses or rationality

16. accepting something uncritically because it fits with one's prejudices

17. thinking in a stereotyped way even if it's irrational and without examining its rationality

18. maintaining views and attitudes without examining their logic, rationality, or consistency

19. being suspicious of people without rational cause

20. thinking badly of people from habit or amusement

21. etc.

Lists like this actually apply to everyone. It represents human nature in natural consciousness. This lower level of experiencing resists its own anatomical undoing. In natural consciousness we do not know nor believe that there is a spiritual consciousness. Hence our automatic, unwitnessed, and unexamined life of emotion is described by such lists. *The items reveal the numberless dimensions of selfish loves.* Each item is a selfish love that is allied to numerous sub-loves that are compatible with selfish experiencing and help promote it in our personality.

Experiencing Regeneration

If you consider item 20 it is clear how this comes from a selfish love. A supporting sub-love might be, "enjoying the feeling of self-aggrandizement that comes from putting everyone down below oneself". Item 18 reveals a selfish sub-love of "being intellectually stubborn and resistive of rational order as a way of feeling superior to others" and also: "... as a way of not exerting mental effort for the sake of feeling special and more deserving".

You'll find that with a little practice you can develop the ability to experience the affective source of many emotions, especially whether self love or mutual love. This is the important element to know because one leads us to heaven, the other to hell.

Doing Operations

Negative sensorimotor behavior or "doing things" does not occur by itself. It is always preceded by negative feeling and thinking.

For instance, if you're feeling anger towards someone (option 1) and you become aware of negative thoughts, you frequently act out your anger by behaving aggressively or destructively, which are selfish loves. But in other situations it's dangerous to express hatred and judgment in overt action such as saying something or making an insulting face or gesture, or throwing something. In that case we inhibit the overt doing and our rage remains private. In either case, whether our rage is overt or private it is spiritually damaging to our personality.

Before you go through the next list make sure you have the main diagram of the four options pictured in your mind. For your convenience, here is the diagram again:

Experiencing Regeneration

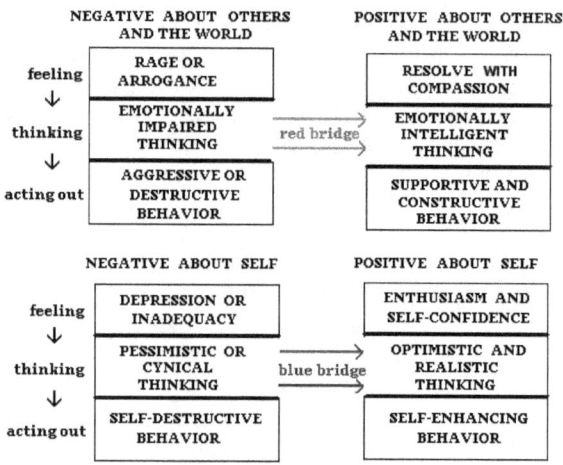

The Four Options
On the Daily Emotional Spin Cycle
And the Two Bridges

Here are examples of negative red doing things or sensorimotor behavior:

1. making your voice loud, shrill, or sarcastic to express your disrespect at someone
2. attacking someone in anger using your body, an object or weapon instead of using legal methods to control that person
3. standing in a hostile or aggressive pose to threaten someone who does not want what you want
4. yelling at people to make them feel bad to satisfy your dislike of them
5. speaking with a sarcastic tone to insult someone whom you think deserves it
6. gesturing insults or using offensive, mocking, or ridiculing language to protest or show disagreement

7. setting your face into menacing expressions to scare someone into submission

8. writing an insulting or hurtful letter or leaving an insulting message to show your disrespect or disdain for someone's position or behavior

9. driving off in a hurry, screeching your tires to show you're mad and without care for risk and inconvenience to others

10. driving fast to take out your anger on something without care for risk and inconvenience to others

11. deliberately playing loud music to annoy someone or just due to lack of caring

12. damaging property to retaliate or get even instead of using legal means available

13. sabotaging something ("throwing a monkey wrench") out of spite

14. breaking your promise or commitment because you're mad

15. etc.

Have you decided which items apply to you? Most likely all of them, or the majority of them. Note that each of the negative doings contain within them the threefold-self of feeling, thinking, and doing. For instance item 14 refers to the selfish sub-love of retaliating when you're mad. Consider what is in your desire to retaliate or take vengeance. Is it the pleasure of contemplating the demise of your opponent? Is it a sense of punitive or retributive justice that you subscribe to? Ask yourself if you apply this logic to you as well when someone else is punishing you for something. Try to uncover as much of your motives and the logic that they support. Do you agree with that logic? Or is the reason you desire to retaliate simply a role enactment you are performing without much thought as to why. Sometimes the sentence comes to mind, "Don't be a wimp. Defend yourself. Don't let them walk all over you." This may help you realize that you are being manipulated and propelled by negative habit routines. Thus you can exercise a new option.

Option 2:
Positive Towards Others and the World

Feeling Operations

Positive red feelings (upper right half of diagram) are perfect substitutes for negative red feelings. All red feelings are "hot" or intense and powerful, but it makes a difference if they are negative hot or positive hot. Negative red-hot feelings are associated with rage or arrogance (option 1). Positive red-hot feelings are associated with resolve and compassion (option 2). Resolve, or determination, is an intense motivation for protecting something valuable to society, like a cause or principle you feel strongly about. For instance, instead of complaining and getting mad, you decide to do something practical to change a situation.

Sometimes the feeling of resolve appears to others as anger, but it's not. For instance, anger (or rage) is the strong desire to punish, destroy or injure by an aggressive act, whereas resolve-with-compassion is the strong desire to protect or support something by democratic or humanitarian means provided by law and conscience. The feeling of compassion has to be added to resolve so that you don't fall back on blind anger. Compassion is a feeling of support for someone who needs help. It is the desire to assist, rescue, and protect what we consider valuable or loved. The feeling of compassion includes the fear to injure someone, and so it is the opposite of anger (the desire to hurt someone). Resolve combined with compassion (option 2) is the perfect antidote to anger and rage (option 1).

Here are examples that can help you better observe and describe your red feelings that fall in option 2, called resolve-with-compassion.

1. rejecting your impulse to be violent or to injure someone or something

2. promoting in yourself the feeling of compassion

3. promoting in yourself the desire for peace or the desire to forget and forgive

4. strengthening the desire to protect or promote something worthwhile

5. honoring your commitment to do something constructive and avoid conflict

6. not taking yourself too seriously when feeling offended

7. seeing the humor of your predicament and laughing at the whole thing

8. feeling sympathy or caring for the other person as a human being

9. wanting to resolve the problem and reconnect when feeling separated

10. not wanting to hurt the relationship by being angry or hostile

11. placing trust in the system and relying on it to work itself out

12. compelling yourself to act according to your higher values and principles

13. giving yourself permission to reconnect by forgetting your pride

14. feeling good about being fair-minded and civilized

15. being ready to be conciliatory for the sake of peace and order

16. feeling relief not to have to be angry any more

17. looking after other people's comfort and safety

18. exerting control over how much force is used when necessary

19. fighting to protect what's yours without hatred or malice

20. refusing to participate in activities that you consider harmful or unjust

21. feeling responsible to carry out our duties and promises

22. etc.

Thinking Operations

Positive red thinking has to be compatible with positive red feeling and the two mutually support and reinforce one another. Positive red thinking is the opposite of negative red thinking and can be used to counteract it. This is called applying the red bridge technique. The negative and positive thinking are incompatible and cannot exist simultaneously in our mind with the same force so that one wins and inhibits or suppresses the other. When the negative thinking is strong or pervasive in our mind, the positive is weakened and stays in the background, rendered ineffective for now. This is called seeing red--which refers to impaired thinking due to negative emotions.

We have the ability, from a higher motivation of self-interest and conscience, to perform positive thinking routines in order to counteract the negative thinking routine we are performing in some particular situation. Emotionally impaired thoughts (option 1) are personal, skewed, inaccurate, and unrealistic, while emotionally intelligent thoughts (option 2) are social, objective, realistic, and accurate. Emotionally intelligent thoughts include stopping your negative thinking routines and making yourself enact positive thinking routines such as considering better alternatives that you have in a situation, and their positive outcomes. These positive thoughts interact and reinforce positive feeling routines.

Doing Operations

Positive red doing is to act in a supportive and constructive manner. This is the sensorimotor outcome of positive feeling and positive thinking acting together. Feelings of resolve-with-compassion seek out and encourage emotionally intelligent thinking routines, and the two together produce constructive and supportive behavior such as cooperation, friendship, and sharing. Examples include:

1. hearing your voice as normal and sociable
2. acting safe and being careful of the safety of others
3. softening your stance or expression so it's not perceived as threatening
4. keeping your voice down and acting with civility
5. speaking with a neutral tone that would not be considered aggressive

6. finding something good to say, counteracting the negative

7. showing patience and being accommodating

8. keeping a pleasant expression on your face

9. removing any insult, sarcasm, or condemnation when writing a letter or note

10. leaving only polite and reasoned messages for others

11. inhibiting any overt show of being mad or acting in anger

12. driving carefully and lawfully even when you're upset

13. postponing making an irate phone call, never making it

14. controlling loud music (etc.) so as not to annoy someone

15. being careful with other people's property

16. cooperating for the greater good even when you feel like sabotaging

17. keeping your promise or commitment even if you're upset

18. etc.

Option 3: Negative Towards Self

Feeling Operations

The blue zone (bottom left) refers to the emotional lifestyle we have towards ourselves.

There is a negative blue zone (bottom left, option 3) and a positive blue zone (bottom right, option 4). Depression or inadequacy groups together various negative feelings towards oneself. Depression or feelings of inadequacy are forms of raging against oneself. It includes dissatisfaction that becomes obsessive. It also includes generalized anxiety and excessive worry. They may not be conscious, but these negative feelings towards the self are ways that we make ourselves suffer, even to the point of destroying our happiness and sanity. Of course this is an irrational state of mind and it engenders irrational thinking routines called pessimism and cynicism.

Pessimism is a type of thinking that involves unrealistic and exaggerated expectations of negative outcomes in our undertakings. Cynicism is a type of thinking that involves automatic suspicions and doubts regarding sincerity, goodness, and truth in ourselves and in people generally. Pessimistic and cynical thinking routines are encouraged and strengthened by negative feelings towards the self such as depression, inadequacy, chronic dissatisfaction, excessive worry, hopelessness, and helplessness.

Negative blue feelings (bottom, left) are experienced in many varieties that include self-hatred ("I hate myself"), desire to punish self ("I'm such fool. I could kick myself"), feeling guilty and punishing yourself ("How could I do such a thing"), being ashamed ("Oh, no, what are they going to think of me"), lack of enthusiasm ("Everything sucks"), and so on.

Here are some examples that can help you better witness and describe your feelings in option 3 (left, bottom) titled **feeling depression and inadequacy**:

1. feeling mad at yourself (calling yourself negative names)

2. feeling compulsively ashamed or guilty and unable to stop

3. wanting to hit or kick yourself (raging against oneself)

4. wanting to punish and denigrate yourself

5. feeling worthless

6. feeling helpless

7. feeling over-anxious or terrified about a normal event

8. feeling that you deserve to be condemned or ridiculed

9. wanting to cut or injure yourself

10. wanting to break something that is of value to you

11. wanting to throw away something that is dear to you

12. wanting to die or disappear

13. feeling totally discouraged and unable to stop

14. feeling desperate and out of control

15. feeling a lack of enthusiasm for everything

16. feeling picked on all the time (without objective evidence)

17. ignoring your conscience and feeling bad about it

18. ignoring health motives, letting yourself go

19. ignoring prudence, showing preference for high risk behaviors

20. maintaining preference for a junky lifestyle

21. choosing to associate with bad friends

22. etc.

Thinking Operations

Negative cognitions about self are characteristically pessimistic or cynical. Pessimistic thinking includes catastrophizing, which is the tendency to expect the worst to happen to us in some situation and to magnify or exaggerate the likely negative consequences. Cynical thinking is a kind of pessimism since it suggests that nothing is fair, noble, or sincere in what we do, or what anyone else is doing. Feeling depressed or obsessively dissatisfied engenders pessimistic and cynical thoughts. The feeling and the thinking agree with each other and end up on the same side, reinforcing one another and strengthening their bond. Together they can produce negative forms of acting out called self-destructive behavior. Here are examples that can help you better witness and describe your **pessimistic and cynical thinking routines**:

1. thinking that the worst is going to happen or catastrophizing

2. exaggerating how bad things are and scaring yourself

3. compulsively thinking about bad things (ruminating)

4. not thinking clearly, being inconsistent

5. blocking out what others are saying or suggesting (skewed thinking)

6. ruminating over something that happened and unwilling to stop thinking or talking about it

7. elaborating on fantasies of doom and gloom

8. thinking pessimistically (the possible becomes the probable)

9. thinking cynically and doubting anything good and true

10. thinking there is no higher authority than your own (cynicism, arrogance)

11. concluding that life just isn't worth all the trouble (suicidal)

12. deciding you don't need anyone for support or approval (alienation)

13. deciding there is nothing you can do about some thing (helplessness)

14. planning to hurt your relationship with someone who loves or supports you

15. thinking you don't deserve better (low self-esteem)

16. etc.

Doing Operations

Self-destructive behavior is the overt outcome of combining negative feeling and negative thinking (bottom left, option 3). The variety of such behaviors is quite large and they are familiar to everyone. They include moving with slowness and difficulty, slowing down of the body, reduced activity and productivity, so that we fail to complete tasks or we deliberately make errors to sabotage the outcome, thus insuring that we lose. We also tend to engage in high-risk behavior that is dangerous and destructive to ourselves. This negative sensorimotor behavior continues as long as the negative feeling and thinking continue to act together. In other words, as long as you continue to feel obsessed with your dissatisfaction and reinforce this feeling with pessimistic or cynical thoughts, you will act out some self-destructive behavior.

Here are examples that to help you better witness and describe self-destructive behavior routines:

1. moving abnormally slow or feeling tired all the time

2. unable to complete tasks

3. sustaining injuries due to carelessness

4. engaging in high risk behaviors due to recklessness

5. looking downcast, unhappy, discouraged, sad sack

6. not taking care of your body

7. overdoing or indulging in harmful substances

8. purging (bulimia syndrome) or gorging

9. doing dangerous and reckless things that are out of control

10. deliberately spoiling your chances and insuring defeat

11. etc.

Option 4:
Positive Towards Self

Feeling Operations

Positive blue feeling towards self typically includes the feeling of self-satisfaction, self-mastery, and the desire to enhance your potential. It's the opposite of negative blue feeling. Positive blue feelings seek out and promote positive blue thinking routines. Positive blue feelings also function to counteract negative blue feelings so you feel less depression or dissatisfaction, if any. Positive feelings towards self include feeling enthusiastic, effective, productive, grateful or appreciative, and feeling more integrated and whole.

1. feeling satisfied with your work

2. feeling confident you'll succeed

3. having a "Can Do" attitude

4. not being afraid to stand up and be counted

5. being motivated to improve yourself

6. being motivated to maintain a healthy lifestyle

7. being committed to uphold your beliefs and values

8. feeling hope or certainty about your future

9. feeling respect for what's good and true in yourself

10. feeling enthusiastic and full of vitality

11. feeling motivated to protect your best interests

12. etc.

Thinking Operations

Positive blue cognitions are optimistic as well as realistic. They are compatible with positive blue feelings such as the feeling of self-mastery and self-confidence. Optimistic thinking counteracts pessimistic thinking, and instead of expecting the worst, one ranks the possible or likely outcomes of any event in terms of their probability or likelihood of happening. Positive thinking is not only optimistic but realistic, objective, and rational. Switching into positive thinking about self is called the blue bridge technique. Some illustrations:

1. thinking about what is likely to happen instead of what one fears

2. giving yourself the benefit of the doubt by thinking you might be right

3. questioning your pessimism and cynicism

4. arguing with your negative position

5. ordering yourself stop thinking about something negative

6. deliberately trying to figure something out instead of jumping to conclusions

7. examining what others are saying about your situation

8. thinking that you deserve respect as a human being

9. thinking that with practice you can achieve your goal

10. etc.

Doing Operations

As always, the doing or acting in the sensorimotor domain is an outcome of the affective (feeling) and the cognitive (thinking) systems acting together. *Positive sensorimotor behaviors* include a variety of self-enhancing routines such as:

1. following regular and lifelong healthy diet and exercise programs

2. acting with discipline leading to your goal

3. maintaining good relations with others

4. doing things that lead to success

5. practicing good time-management techniques

6. maintaining a neat or appropriate appearance

7. exercising appropriate control over your budget

8. making adequate provisions for the future

9. preparing for challenging experiences

10. practicing healthy habits and routines

11. avoiding unnecessary risk

12. acting in a prudent or careful manner

13. taking steps to protect what's yours

14. etc.

Controlling The Emotional Flip-Flop Effect

Why do we want to know in detail what our daily emotional spin cycle is?

The reason is that we can then control it or customize it to our preference and rationality.

When we are coping, happy, and successful we have learned to control the daily emotional spin cycle.

Polls show that the majority of people say they are experiencing anger and depression on a daily basis. This means that they are choosing the negative options many times each day in their activities and interactions.

Thinking about the Four Options diagram, there is a habitual and automatic flip-flop effect between the red option (others, upper half) and blue option (self, lower half), either negative (left side) or positive (right side).

For instance, after choosing the rage against others option (top left), we find ourselves soon after sliding into the rage against self option (bottom left), which is a state of depression or dissatisfaction. The experiencing of this rage-depression flip-flop is a sociogenic habit that we acquire in our socialization without any awareness of the anatomical process.

Similarly, there is a flip-flop effect for the positive options: feelings of resolve with compassion towards others (top right) spin us into feelings of resolve for ourselves, which is called enthusiasm and self-confidence (bottom right). Vice-versa, feelings of enthusiasm and self-confidence (bottom right) flip-flop into feelings of resolve with compassion (top right). Both these habit mechanisms are portrayed in the diagrams you saw above. They will help you understand and memorize the mechanisms involved.

The following is a self-witnessing exercise that many will find beneficial as a way of mapping out objectively some qualities of your experiencing on the daily round of activities.

Designing Your
Self-Witnessing Experiment

Experiencing Regeneration

Note that the procedures for your project are summarized at the end of this section.

Here is just one possible design for your self-witnessing project. As you gain experience you will be able to modify the approach to suit you best. For Week 1 select any activity that occurs daily and in which you are feeling challenged as you try to cope with some event or person. For activity A, observe your experiencing of that activity for three days in a row and then do the same for activity B. On the Four Options diagram, negative red means against others (top left), while negative blue is against self (bottom left).

Here is a schema that shows the set up for your experiment:

Week 1: Baseline observations—merely observing

Sample activity A (top left, negative red):   day 1 || day 2 || day 3
Sample activity B (bottom left, negative blue): day 4 || day 5 || day 6

Week 2: Intervention--practicing the bridge technique

Sample same activity A again   day 1 || day 2 || day 3
Sample same activity B again   day 4 || day 5 || day 6

You can repeat the above experiment with additional weeks and with different sample activities.

The purpose of the experiment is to enable you to map out the negative spin cycle options that you choose to experience in some of your normal and recurrent daily activities.

At the completion of your mere witnessing observations in week 1, you repeat the same observations in week 2, but this time you are consciously making an effort to use the bridge technique in order to help you flip flop from negative (left side) to positive options (right side).

Experiencing Regeneration

You need to select an activity that you do on at least three consecutive days each week, which limits your choices for now. Later you can modify this as needed. Examples of activities for most people include:

- getting up in the morning under various conditions
- doing routine things at home (e.g., cleaning, fixing, cooking, etc.)
- driving or walking to work or school
- performing particular job tasks at work
- going shopping by yourself or with someone
- talking on the phone or communicating in familiar ways
- watching a particular TV program alone or with others
- studying or catching up on your paper work, bills, etc.
- and other such recurrent activities that you do alone or in company.

The activity could be short (just a couple of minutes) or long (several hours), but it should be recurrent or routine *so you have to face the same psychological issues every day.*

At the same time, the activity you select should have elements that fall in the negative category (top and bottom left). In other words there is some feature of it that annoys you or challenges you on a recurrent basis. One sample involves an activity in which you feel, think, or do something negative towards others and the world (top left, negative red). And a second sample should involve something negative towards self (bottom left, negative blue).

So you need to select a daily recurrent activity during which you can observe yourself enact negative routines towards others and self.

It might be useful to take notes of your actual feelings, thoughts, and doings, or use a recorder to dictate them. Your smart phone has a recorder. You can also dictate your notes into your texting app or email.

Method of Self-Witnessing
Your Experiencing

Experiencing Regeneration

Now consider some details about *how to monitor your threefold-self.*

(1) To experience what you are *feeling*

Ask yourself:
(1)*What am I feeling right now?*

and after awhile ask yourself:
(2) What do I feel like doing right now?

You can alternate between these two questions as many times as you wish. You can also add related questions. Usually you get an inkling of what the answer is and then you can describe it: I feel like jumping off the roof; or, I feel like smashing something; or, I feel I'm being denigrated and manipulated; I feel totally hopeless and caged; I'm never going to get over this; etc.

Keep noting the various things that are involved and related to your feeling.

Try to distinguish between what you are feeling and what you are thinking. The two occur together but we need to learn to manage each separately. Look over the lists given above for option 1 (top left) and Option 3 (bottom left) to help you experience the *feelings*.

(2) To experience what you are *thinking*

Make up an approximate transcript of your thinking sequence in the selected situation.

Obviously, we think many sentences in any situation in a brief period of time so the transcript will only give you samples of your thinking. But this is enough.
Look over the lists given above for option 1 (top left) and Option 3 (bottom left) to help you observe your *thinking*.

(3) To experience what your sensorimotor is *doing*

Ask yourself: *What am I sensing in my body?*

Experiencing Regeneration

Sensorimotor routines that are negative include sensations of weakness or tension, pain or unpleasantness, heat or cold, and so on. Look over the lists given above for option 1 (top left) and Option 3 (bottom left) to help you observe your *doing*.

Afterwards ask yourself: *What can others see about me?*

Visible sensorimotor routines that are negative include what others can detect from your voice, choice of words, face, hands, gestures, posture, appearance of your clothing, smell, etc. Look over the lists given above for option 1 (top left) and Option 3 (bottom left) to help you observe your negative *doing*.

When you finish the first day with activity A, you repeat the process for day 2 with the same activity, and finally, the third day.

Then you begin observations with activity B on day 1, and repeat for day 2 and 3.

This is the end of your baseline observations and week 1--two activities observed on three different days each.

Week 2

Now you begin your intervention in week 2, doing the same thing as before. The only difference is that now you are going to apply the bridge technique.

You stick with the same two activities but now you are introducing an intervention that we called the *bridge technique* in the discussions above. You need to make observations on how you use the bridge technique in addition to observing your feeling, thinking, and doing (as you did the first week). Keep track of what you actually said to yourself to move yourself over from the negative (left) to the positive (right) options, either red (top) or blue (bottom).

Consider the consequences of applying the bridge technique: *What was your feeling after the bridge*? *What was your thinking*? *What was your sensing and doing*? These consequences may be immediate or longer lasting. Or, it is possible that the bridge technique may not work out this time or may end up having no visible effect.

In addition to the above, you can also to collect **Global Ratings** once at the end of each day:

_____ 1) What was my overall stress point today: (1=very weak; 10=extreme)

_____ 2) What was my overall level of satisfaction with myself today: (1=very weak; 10=extreme)

_____ 3) What was my overall level of dissatisfaction with others today: (1=very weak; 10=extreme)

_____ 4) What was my overall level of effectiveness or productivity today: (1=very weak; 10=extreme)

_____ 5) What was my overall level of coping successfully with my feelings today: (1=very ineffectual; 10=extremely effective)

_____ 6) What is my current level of hope for the future: (1=little hope or brightness; 10=extremely hopeful and bright)

_____ 7) What was the worst level of negativity or selfishness of some other people around you (1=almost no negativity or selfishness observed; 10=extremely strong negative or selfish behavior observed)

By collecting these 7 numbers at the end of each day you will be able to use a global assessment comparison between the baseline week and the intervention week. You may also find it beneficial to keep these daily numbers even after your self-witnessing experiment is over. You may then inspect the numbers for six months and see how your feeling quality changes over time.

Chapter 3
Experiencing Release From the Daily Plagues

Life is experienced in natural consciousness until the mind is elevated through spiritual "rebirth". This refers to the beginning of experiencing regeneration.

Rebirth and progressive regeneration begins first of all with initiating a reciprocal relationship with God. And afterwards, maintaining that relationship by having a dialog with God on a daily basis.

The individual is to do that as a reciprocal act to God who is standing at the door of awareness ready to pull the individual up into spiritual consciousness. The individual's act of reciprocation is necessary to begin a reciprocal relationship with God. Do we not answer our front door and open it when we heard a knock by a delivery? To open the front door is the act of reciprocation to the person who knocked and makes it possible for a transaction to take place. The act of reciprocation refers to our willingness to have a daily dialog with God as a way of acknowledging God's co-Presence in our mind. Since God's presence in our mind is the actual reality, we gain in rationality by acknowledging that reality, and we remain in spiritual insanity by denying spiritual reality.

The act of reciprocating God in relationship provides the experiencing of humility and appreciation before God. This is called being in a "state of innocence". To not acknowledge God's presence in our mind is the opposite of innocence and is called arrogance. We are all born arrogant by inheritance, and our job here on earth is to divest our self from that inborn arrogance, and thereby to equip our personality with the traits that we need in order to support our immortal consciousness in conjugial heavenly bliss to eternity.

God inflows into our mind with love-substance and truth-substance, and by means of this inflow raises us to a life of spiritual consciousness. But this can be done only after we get rid of our inborn arrogance that stands in the way and blocks the inflow. If we live in spiritual consciousness here on earth we will continue to do so in the afterlife of eternity. This elevated mental state provides us with the experiencing of conjugial love and rational intelligence that increase daily to eternity.

The benefits of elevation of consciousness before God are multiple and significant. Here we are going to discuss the benefits of experiencing release from the daily plagues that make up ordinary life in natural consciousness. We all would like to get rid of the plagues that make our life difficult, unpleasant, and miserable much of the time. Think about your own daily plagues and how they negatively impact your life, your contentment, your productivity and success, and your relaxed happiness and peace.

It is possible to get rid of the daily plagues that assail us in natural consciousness.

To accomplish this, each emotional plague must be observed, marked, isolated, and removed from our personality.

God is our constant companion, guide, teacher, protector, therapist, and loving father. Our reciprocal relationship with God is the source of power that gets rid of our daily plagues.

God's power is received in our effort exerted as-of self, in battling and destroying each plague one at a time.

There is no transfer of power from God to us, as has been explained before. There is only our participation as reciprocation. Reciprocation defines the condition under which God's power will flow into the act of self-change. *The power ceases to flow the instant we think that we are the one defeating the plague by our effort.* The power resumes its flow the instant we acknowledge that we are already defeated in the battle against the plagues, and only God has the power to save us from their tyranny.

159

Experiencing Regeneration

We are thus experiencing the spiritual reality that it is not our own power that produces our "reborn" personality, allowing us to equip our personality for living in the afterlife of eternal conjugial happiness.

In regeneration we are experiencing the stream of Divine Providence carrying us through the healing of our character.

As we engage and do spiritual battle with our selfish and unintelligent thoughts and habits, we are experiencing God's assistive action. We perceive by rational thought that if we stop fighting our plagues, the flow of God's power also stops. *From bad we cannot become good by sitting down on our hands and waiting for God's power to save us.* We understand rationally why this is impossible. God cannot take away our selfish loves and foolish ideas, or else *He would have done so already*, as Divine love desires to do to every human being. But to remove our emotional plagues without our voluntary as-of self-effort would turn everyone into a mere organic robot that is activated by God, and thus we would cease to be human beings.

Hence there is no other way for character change than to exert as-of self-effort in full awareness that God's power activates only through the as-of self effort. God's power flows into the effort. If the person does not exert that effort God's power cannot flow in to make the change. If the person exerts the effort but believes that this effort gets rid of the plagues, the power of God cannot flow in. *We must fight against the plagues thinking that God's power will flow into that effort and make it efficacious.*

The daily plagues that we discuss below are common to everyone living life in natural consciousness, yet there are individual differences in their range, frequency, intensity, and quality. In experiencing regeneration each plague is addressed separately and discussed with God. There is no other effective method. God will first give you rational insight, and then you will be experiencing the will to change, even as God flows in with the power of love-substance, which is actually spiritual heat from the spiritual sun flowing into the spiritual body or mind.

Love-substance inflows into our willpower with spiritual heat, and simultaneously into our thinking with spiritual light or truth-substance. You can experience that "spiritual marriage" in your mind, which is the union between love-substance and truth-substance. This spiritual marriage in your personality provides the experiencing of a new love in your will that may be called resolve, which provides a powerful desire for change and its exciting anticipation.

When you get into the habit of reading *Sacred Scripture* analytically or spiritually you will receive endless forms of enlightenment from God regarding your own regeneration. All of *Sacred Scripture* in its spiritual sense is about the anatomy of the human mind and the developmental process of regeneration and resuscitation. God enlightens your spiritual-rational understanding when you read *Sacred Scripture* with the purpose of receiving spiritual truths about your regeneration.

Sacred Scripture is God talking to your mind through the meaning of the text.

At first we understand *Sacred Scripture* in its literal or historical meaning, which contains only correspondences in natural consciousness. But when you initiate and maintain a reciprocal relationship with God, your spiritual-rational understanding develops and is able to see the analytical or spiritual meaning that is enfolded and hidden in the literal verses.

You begin to realize that *the interior spiritual meaning of all Sacred Scripture constitutes theistic psychology*, which is the study of how the mind develops and is regenerated by God through spiritual temptations. God wants us to study this subject since it obviously helps us to know in detail how we are to cooperate with God in our regeneration process. Such as is our cooperation with God, such is the effectiveness and extent of our regeneration.

The daily emotional plagues that we endure here on earth flow into our mind through inherited anatomical connections to hell societies in the afterlife of eternity.

These anatomical connections are a basic feature of the human mind. The entire human race is anatomically connected together to function synchronously as a whole. Whatever goes on in the mind of one person on some planet in the physical universe affects every other person past and present on the inhabited earths, and in the afterlife of heaven and hell. In this way there is a constant flow of synchrony and correspondence in all human beings. God integrates the whole human race to function as one human being. No one can exist outside this Divine matrix.

When you reflect on this you will experience an awe-filled feeling. Whatever you think and feel moment by moment is not something that comes and goes away. It continues forever and it connects with every other human being that ever lived. This is an awesome feeling, and very holy, as it gives us a peeking image of God's benign infinity.

To God the entire human race is integrated as one Grand Human being. If God gave you a vision of the entire collection of humanity in the afterlife you would actually see one well-formed human being which has all the internal parts that each of us have in the body. In the afterlife everyone rejoins the spiritual society with whom they had been habitually connected in this life, and from there continues immortal life in that society. The ranking love of each society determines in which anatomical part of the Grand Human that society is located.

In our inherited natural consciousness we live our lives slavishly dominated by negative emotions that we accept as being our own, since who else's could it be?

But now you can step away from that anatomical illusion. *They are not our emotions.* They are the emotions of particular spiritual societies with whom God brings our affective system into a more direct communication. *The connection makes us to be the receptors of their ranking emotions.*

God is doing this continually, connecting us and disconnecting us with various other spiritual societies or people who are the source of the individual's emotions, bad and good. The pattern of these connections constitutes our experiencing of the daily plagues, but as well, of our enjoyments of the positive features of living.

This anatomical fact has immense spiritual significance for us and for our salvation.

It means that God cannot blame us or hold it against us as sin, when we are engaged in a negative emotion and outward act that comes from that emotion, such as getting angry and striking someone.

Experiencing Regeneration

It is not *our* anger, but it is *our* deed if we act from that anger, believing that it is our own, and consequently we are guilty of a sin. In our regeneration we have to address such negative emotions that we have made our own by acting upon them. The emotion is not ours to begin with, but merely flows into our mind from the spiritual society to which God connects us. *The emotion becomes our own however when we act on them as if the emotion were our own.*

All our negative emotions and daily plagues belong to the spiritual societies to which God connects and disconnects us to help our regeneration process. God gives us the choice either to reject the negative emotion as "not my own" or to appropriate it as "my own". If it is appropriated to oneself as "my feeling of anger", it becomes our sin and we must suffer the punishment that is built into the experiencing of *negative emotions as being one's own*. For instance, in the afterlife we are unwilling and unable to remove ourselves from that negative emotion. As a result we are bonded more closely to the evil society that is ruled by that negative emotion.

Every negative emotion we can experience originates from some hellish society and flows into our mind where we experience the emotion as our own. We can then appropriate it to our self and make it ours forever, or we can reject it using the power of regeneration, and in that case we are freed from it forever.

Remember that God is perfect in love and therefore is mentally incapable of punishing people on account of their sins or for any reason. The punishment is built into the negative emotion itself and in the inconsiderate act itself. This is obvious when you remember that entering heaven or hell in the afterlife is by choice that we exercise after our resuscitation. No one is forced to choose one or the other. Everyone chooses freely of themselves following their loves and delights. If the resuscitated personality is managed by anger or other negative emotions, the strength of those emotions pulls the individual towards the regions of the hells in our mind where others like ourselves are met and with whom we become consociates.

This is the built-in punishment of sins, namely having to live with others who have the same infernal loves and sins.

163

Experiencing Regeneration

This type of negative life spontaneously devolves and gets progressively worse. You can see that if the people devolve too far too low there is no comeback possible. To come back requires the willingness to return the mind into the order of rationality and mutual love, and then to tolerate that life in heaven.

The process of ridding ourselves from negative emotions is the experiencing of regeneration. It is a joint and reciprocal interaction between you and God.

Experiencing Release from Anger

Anger is perhaps the most common method people use to control each other. The listing below shows you some common occasions when anger is experienced: e.g., having a power struggle or being told unflattering things about oneself. For each occasion there is a particular reaction to anger, as listed. For instance when we are being forced to do something that we don't like to do, the anger we feel prompts us to do a bad job of it, thus to withhold our cooperation.

In spiritual consciousness anger is inner hatred that desires to torture, kill, and annihilate a person. In the literal sense the commandment "Thou shalt not kill" refers to killing the physical body, but in the analytic sense killing signifies hatred that comes from anger, which is desiring to kill all of the person, thus the spirit as well the body.

In speech people make distinctions regarding the intensity or type of anger they are experiencing, as for example: I'm ticked off; I'm annoyed; I'm very irritated' I'm so frustrated; I'm angry; I'm mad; I'm furious; I'm boiling inside; I could squash you; I'm incredibly upset; I could kill him; I wish he was dead; may he explode; may he never arrive; may his children and children's children rot in hell; let the whole thing explode and collapse; etc. These are so many ways in which our love of self when snubbed, longs to retaliate, take revenge, and cruelly put to death.

When we think about anger in this spiritual context we can perceive that all the ways one can experience anger are negative emotions that are tied together in a collection under the title anger. The same devastating and

Experiencing Regeneration

overwhelming anger disguises itself under different forms and appearances, so that the person may think that some anger like, "I'm very irritated" is not as bad as, "I wish he was dead". Psychologically, morally, and legally this may be true, but spiritually all anger is anger, regardless of its outward appearance. And again let us recall that anger is the desire to torture, squash, kill, and annihilate someone.

This may be surprising when you think about it for the first time. It reveals the ugly and brutish character of selfishness, which is to love oneself more than others and more than God. Self becomes the god one serves in total slavishness. *To what or to whom?*

The answer is that anger is our slavishness to hell.

This is literally true. It is not a metaphor or exaggeration. To understand this rationally or scientifically you need to recall a few facts about human anatomy. Our mind and mental operations are not physical but spiritual. Hence we have a spiritual body that works in synchrony with the physical body, so much so, that our mind is fooled by the illusion that we are in the physical body and that if we remove the physical body nothing would be left of the mind. We can remove this wall by thinking of the physical body as temporary and dying, while our mind or spirit continues living in the afterlife by means of our spiritual body. The laws of the spiritual world in the afterlife attract people who are similar and repels those who are dissimilar.

Hence since time immemorial all the people who pass into the afterlife encrusted and tied to selfish traits are incorporated into the immense collection of communities and societies that live together as one large society of hell in the afterlife of eternity. And it is parallel with the people who make up heaven. God creates and maintains this arrangement for the sake of the people themselves. Those who love themselves more than others cannot form a society with the people who love others as much as themselves and God more than anything. The selfish people are angry with the altruistic people for being altruistic. They hate what is good or unselfish, and what is from God. In the afterlife there are no physical restrictions and punishments in relation to justice and law enforcement. Hence the selfish are like wolves that rush upon sheep to devour them, and they cannot be persuaded by anything to live peacefully. Hence God maintains the arrangement of heaven and hell in the human mind to accommodate the needs of all personalities and human loves.

The people in the afterlife who live in the hells and in the heavens of the human mind are anatomically connected to our spiritual body from birth onward. This is because every individual from birth onward has the human heavens and hells in their mind. This is what it means to be human. We all share the same mental world, though this is not apparent to us while still conscious with the physical body attached. But as soon as we are resuscitated into the spiritual body by the two-day dying-resuscitation process, we can see, touch, and communicate with everyone who is already in that state. This convinces us that there is only one mental world and every human being is born into it.

From birth till the dying-resuscitation process God connects our spiritual body with individuals and whole societies that are in heaven and in hell. This is the method God uses to guide and regenerate people by means of their loves and affections. Spiritual societies in heaven and hell are distinguished by their chief love, which subordinates all other loves to agree with it. Some societies specialize in anger so that no other love is held by them more intensely. Or they may specialize in greed, or vengeance, or salaciousness and cheating, or deception and conspiracy, or bullying and mistreating, or dominating and enslaving, or living in insane fantasies, etc.

By connecting us to particular spiritual societies God can evoke or activate our various inherited loves. Simultaneously, God connects our spiritual body with some society in heaven that specializes in a heavenly love that is contrary to the hellish one. This creates a perfect balance in our mind as we are pulled in opposite directions simultaneously. *The result is freedom of choice.* Poised between giving in to our anger and revenge on the one hand, and on the other, giving in to tolerance, compassion, and peace.

It may at first feel shocking to think of God connecting and disconnecting us dozens of times a day with all these societies and people who had also lived on this earth at some time in their history. But this idea becomes comprehensible when we think that God connects all human beings all the time as part of creation. No one lives on their own, just as no branch or leaf can exist apart from the plant or tree. The entire human race is anatomically connected like a giant tree or bush.

Experiencing Regeneration

Now that we know this we can experience emotions in a different mode. We are not the emotion and the emotion does not belong to us. We are merely receptors of emotions that belong to others to whom we are spiritually connected. Once we get into the afterlife and into the society of our chief love, then all other loves and emotions are stripped from us, and then and only then, do we become that emotion. But until then, anatomically the emotions we experience are not ours but are received by our organs.

Experiencing regeneration requires that God connects and disconnects us to various spiritual societies, both heavenly and hellish. When we are connected to a particular spiritual society our spiritual body actually appears there amongst the people and can be seen by them. However there is no direct conversational interaction, only a transfer of specific emotions and corresponding thoughts. The thoughts of the people in the spiritual society are not reproduced in our own awareness, but instead we experience our own thoughts that correspond to theirs. This is why we are not aware of the spiritual societies in which are spiritual body is temporarily located. Since there is no physical space in the mental world, the expression "being located" in some spiritual society actually means to enter into a mental state in our own mind that is in synchrony with the chief mental state of that society. When we do this, we appear in that society and can see, touch, and interact with the people there.

Every spiritual society is formed by the chief love in the personality of those who congregate together in the mental world of the afterlife. Each spiritual society has its own unique chief love that defines the character of the people who are congregated there. An analogous situation can be seen in some large cities where each ethnic group has its own district or street where visitors can come to experience the character of the particular cultural life there.

It's pretty awesome to think about this! Our mind or spiritual body is actually travelling and teleporting to different real spiritual places where there are people in the afterlife of eternity and their cities. And this is done by God in an instant. God knows and maintains the integrity or identity of the specific character of each spiritual society. He then teleports numberless individuals back and forth and around when the chief love of that society is needed in the mind of an individual on earth undergoing regeneration. This is awesome!

From these details you can see that the loves and emotions we experience are not our very own. They are actually the loves and emotions of particular spiritual societies. We identify with those loves and experience them as-if they were our very own. But actually they do not become our own until the final phase when we enter the spiritual society of our home. It is called our "home" because everyone calls home where their love is.

Rejecting Anger From Self

Now you can experience anger as something that is going through you from others and is not you. It is like Wi-Fi. You are in their stream of emission because God connected you to that particular stream. You have the illusion that the anger is yours and not just passing through you. Similarly, the people you have been connected to have the illusion that the reaction you are having to the anger is their own reaction. There is thus a double illusion that God creates here, in each case for the sake of the people involved.

It is similar with the experiencing of altruistic feelings like sympathy, sharing, good will, peacefulness, and usefulness. When we know that these are not our own emotions or affections, then we cannot take credit for them, which would be very bad for our regeneration. Thinking that the good we do is from self is arrogance and meritoriousness, two emotions that opposes all further progress in regeneration, which is based on a reciprocal relationship with God and submission before God in all things, The condition for progress in our regeneration is knowing and remembering in our thinking that all good and all bad that we do is not from us, nor does it belong to us.

Keep all this in mind when you catch yourself angry or irritated at something or someone. Experience the progress of your anger as you rehearse these anatomical secrets in your mind. Observe the change in the negative emotion. And if it suddenly makes you laugh, go ahead, give in to the Divine comedy in which you are made to participate by God, for your own sake. Experience the release from this anger and its many varieties of negativity. Two things happen anatomically as you do this. First, God disconnects you from that particular anger and vengeance society. Second, God connects you to heavenly societies so that you may experience the resolution of anger in the form of positive emotions such as satisfaction, self-confidence, peace,

In the experiencing of the release from a negative emotion do not try to rush the process. Be aware of the full process of the anger or hatred. Examine it analytically as it vibrates through your spiritual body. Do you perceive the hatred? The desire to kill and squash? Do you see the spiritual insanity of it? Do you see how ugly and sub-human it is in its essence?

In the New Testament we find this passage:

Then Peter came and said to Him, "Lord, how often shall my brother sin against me and I forgive him? Up to seven times? Jesus said to him, "I do not say to you, up to seven times, but up to seventy times seven." (Matthew 18:21-22)

Here we need to remind ourselves that the expressions "seventy" and "seven" are used in *Sacred Scripture* in various places, and always referring to what is timeless, endless, eternal, and holy, like the seventh day of the week, which is called the Sabbath of Holiness and represents an "eternal rest". Hence the expression to forgive "seventy times seven" indicates that one ought to forgive endlessly, as often as the person gives offence. Keep in mind that to forgive, to love, to pray for, refer to activities that must appropriately expressed. To forgive the wrong doers means that we ought to refrain from hating them and that we are to respect their human rights. *But the commandment to forgive and to love does not mean to ignore the wrong doing or to put away punishment.* For to do this would be to harm our community and the innocent, and this we must not do. Hence to forgive is to stop hating.

In Matthew 5:22 in the *New Testament* we are warned not to call anyone "Raca", which is a word intended to derogate, denigrate, insult, and offend someone. It applies to all forms of name-calling like calling someone an idiot, moron, imbecile, can-do-nothing, mental case, or other derogatory name. Name-calling, bullying, making fun of someone are hellish

169

pleasures that must be eliminated in order to proceed with regeneration and preparation for a heavenly life. Imagine what would happen if you raised your consciousness to the upper regions of your mind and entered some heavenly community living there. Your pleasure of wanting to make fun of others or berating them would come out and show itself in public. Everyone there would be shocked and chagrined. The feeling of unsuitability or dissimilitude quickly becomes so strong that you are experiencing the explosive departure from those lofty regions in your mind, and finding yourself back in natural consciousness here on earth. And if this visit to heaven occurs in the afterlife you find yourself back in the lowest regions of your mind where there are others with whom you can make a unit.

Some amazing commandments in the *New Testament* that are also related to anger are to turn the other cheek and not to resist evil.

You have heard that it was said, 'an eye for an eye, and a tooth for a tooth'. But I say to you, do not resist an evil person; but whoever slaps you on your right cheek, turn the other to him also. If anyone wants to sue you and take your shirt, let him have your coat also. (Matthew, 5:38-40)

Clearly we must understand these commandments in their spiritual meaning and intent, which is that retaliation or vengeance must be resisted in our mind because they are united to anger and the rest of hell. To turn the cheek does not mean a pacifism that tolerates criminality and brutality. Such tolerance and such forgiveness would be the death of one's family and community, which is a bad thing to do. Our spiritual duty is to defend and cause to prosper our family our community, and the world at large. Chemical poisons must be contained, bacterial infections must be contained, law breakers must be brought to justice, and personal property must be protected from thieves, vandals, and occupiers.

Again the commandment not to resist evil must be understood in the spiritual sense, which explains the intent God has in warning us. God is telling us to resist any desire to be vigilantes and to participate in carrying out summary justice that is outside the due process protected in courts. We are to resist evil in appropriate ways. First, in ourselves and in our mental life, we are to undergo spiritual temptations and regeneration in order to get rid of our evil traits. This is to resist our own evils. But when

Experiencing Regeneration

we observe the evil deeds of others we are to resist personal justice and instead follow due course by involving appropriate authorities whose job it is to apprehend and stop criminal activity.

These passages in the *New Testament* about anger and forgiveness give us the revelation that heaven and hell in our afterlife depends primarily on the mental activities with which we arrive after death and now form our habits of thinking and feeling. *Heaven and hell are not rewards or punishments about what we did in this life on earth.* They are about current choices based on current habits as we begin our new immortal life in the afterlife of eternity.

We ourselves get to choose whether we want the life of heaven or of hell. It would be unloving of God to force people into one or the other.

So we must come to the spiritual realization now that the mental habits we establish are to determine our life in eternity.

I say "now" because regeneration takes a lifetime. No adult person should postpone the start of regeneration, which is called rebirth. We experience rebirth when we fulfill these two conditions: (1) Acknowledge God and begin a reciprocal relationship with Him; (2) Begin to resist as-of self the physical and mental habits that are contrary to heavenly traits.

Our mental life right now is what prepares our mind either for eternal life in heaven or extreme misery in hell.

It has been revealed that calling someone derogatory names in one's own mind is a hell-bound habit, one that must be extinguished in regeneration. There is no other way since we are what we are anatomically and organically, like a paralyzed arm, or a long and involved vine in the field by a river.

All organic reversals must be done organically, hence progressively, step by step, phase by phase, modifying the anatomy and physiology of the spiritual body. One cannot simply reverse the long time devolution of human experiencing into sub-human modes of living called the hells, where mutual insanity and appalling butchery go on continuously as a preferred way of life. It is shocking to experience this new horrifying perspective on anger and its little serving demons like feeling resentment or impatience, being defensive about a sense of self-entitlement or merit, throwing a temper tantrum, feeling offended when not being favored, wanting to insult and hurt, etc. Take a few moments to think about some of the mental habits you have that fall into the general category of anger, irritation, annoyance, disapproval.

Now be prepared for the next time that you are experiencing one of these negative loves and demons that are ruled collectively by the emotion of anger. Experiencing each variety of the negative emotion ties you anatomically or by spiritual Wi-Fi, to some particular society of the hells who love this variety of anger more than any other society of hell. This communal love binds them together spiritually and they live outwardly a life of banding together with those who share the same infernal love. *Think about the fact that your are anatomically or spiritually bound to them as long as you believe that this emotion is yours rather than going through you from them.*

The instant you perceive your experiencing that this anger or resentment is not yours, the Wi-Fi is interrupted, which is the signal that God has disconnected you from that society. *The feeling of resentment (etc.) ceases and is gone into a mere memory.* It is not possible for the emotion of anger or ill will (etc.) to continue in your affective system once God has disconnected you from that spiritual society where it originates. This phase of disruption of the negative input is followed by a phase of spiritual calm and closeness to God. There is now calm confidence in one's ability to handle the negative emotion in the future, which may be a couple of minutes from now or days and weeks later.

Sometimes we might get the wish that God would disconnect us from all societies of hell to which we are bound. Wouldn't that be nice and convenient since we wouldn't have to undergo the pains and suffering of temptations in regeneration? But when we think of this in terms of spiritual-rational consciousness we can perceive that disaster to ourselves would follow if God removed us from the Wi Fi reception of the daily emotions which we call our life. We would suddenly wake up to a day where almost all of our loves, pleasures, and fun in life would be gone. We would be in no mental state to be able to regenerate in such a semi-dead state of life. It is through God's love, compassion, and kindness that He keeps us connected to our hellish loves, meanwhile trying to slowly and progressively guide us out of the web of hell into which our mind is born. It

172

Experiencing Regeneration

takes a slow-motion organic protocol to extract us from the depths of such mental mud.

Each time we experience anger or other negative emotion, we are in a spiritual temptation to either go along with it or to oppose it. *Opposing a negative emotion brings awareness of its spiritual origin.* We now perceive that the anger or resentment is not our own but is something we receive from people in hell to which God is connecting us for as long as we do not oppose the negative emotion.

A recent headline at the Smithsonian web site screamed, *"Our Brains Hate Waiting So We Speed Up Everything Else -- Sidewalk rage, road rage and anger at slow-loading web pages are all part of our evolutionary inheritance"*. The article, which quotes me from an interview, confirmed how people are experiencing anger in many walks of life today. One person is quoted as saying: *"Instead of getting irate at a slow-moving friend, she focused on positive things—her friend's sense of humor and past times together. It worked to calm her sidewalk rage. But as soon as they got to the restaurant, she writes: "I begin quietly raging at the server, the kitchen, the return tram. I'm even raging at my rage; it feels like it's lasting*   *forever."*

Little do we suspect that in such habitual and normalized ways of expressing anger we are chained deeper and deeper to the hells of atrocity. In my 2000 book on *Road Rage* I present a three-step method for overcoming one's anger as a driver or pedestrian. Called the "AWM Method" it involves three steps:

(1) I **A**cknowledge that I have road rage and it is a bad thing;

(2) I **W**itness myself having road rage while I'm driving or walking;

(3) I **M**odify one at a time, trip by trip, the many ways I express road rage,

such as: feeling impatient, feeling furious, tailgating, yelling, gesturing,

insulting, thinking bad things about the other drivers, etc.

Experiencing release from road rage and walking rage elevates our consciousness and strengthens our good will towards the community. *We feel a new sense of wholeness and bonding with the good.*

Objective vs. Subjective Talk

The first speech act or statement is somewhat aggressive. It is a *subjective* judgment of another person who feels somewhat attacked by the statement. There is no need at all to give this impression. It can be entirely eliminated by making *objective* statements about oneself that can inform the other of what you are experiencing.

"You are being testy today" vs. "I experience you as being testy today."
"You're always in a hurry." vs. "I experience you as being always in a hurry."
"You are too critical." vs. "I experience you as being overcritical."
"You are lazy." vs. "I experience you as being as being lazy."
Etc.

If you say to someone, "*You are being overcritical*", the person might respond, "*No, I'm not.*" This deadlocks the situation where it is, offering only repeats of the same thing in different forms. But if you say to the person "*I'm experiencing you as being overcritical*", the person cannot say "*No you're not.*" Then follows a discussion about how the person comes across in your exchanges. You want the person to focus on what feature of his or her behavior that you are finding disturbing.

Note the fundamental difference between speaking subjectively vs. objectively about others. Subjective speech acts about others are hypothetical and judgmental statements, thus prejudicial and offensive, consequently aggressive and hostile to some degree. You are being objective however when your speech act describes how you feel or what you are experiencing in then interaction. We can be objective when discussing ourselves since we can observe ourselves and our experience ourselves, but we cannot observe or experience the other person's feelings. Hence for the sake of peace we are to avoid making categorical statements about the other person's feelings to avoid appearing aggressive.

Experiencing Regeneration

If you say to someone *"Why are you so mad about this?"* or *"You're acting uncooperative."* You are being aggressive by making a subjective judgment of the other person's mental state or intentions. The person is then prompted to disagree with you and the ensuing dialog is an argument, possibly a fight. But if you say *"I'm wondering why I'm experiencing you as being so mad about this?"* or *"I'm wondering why I'm experiencing you as acting uncooperative."* Note that the other person cannot objectively question this statement since you are discussing yourself. They can retaliate by saying *"You're the one who is mad or uncooperative"*, but this type of aggressive subjective judgment is to be handled differently then if it is a reaction to your subjective judgment of them.

There is a confusion in people's minds about what is subjective and objective that is caused by science education in school. Children and adolescents learn that to talk about yourself is subjective while describing what you see others do is objective. So the contrast is between "talking about yourself" as being subjective vs. "describing what you see others do" as being objective. But now you have the opportunity to clarify in your mind what the real distinction is between subjective and objective. Keeping this confusion causes problems in our interaction with others and in our relationships.

Objective has to do with describing observations, while subjective has to do with making personal judgments. You can be objective when you describe the observations you make about others and about yourself. This principle is recognized in all courts of law when judges rule out subjective statements by a witness on the stand. Only objective statements are admitted into evidence, as is shown by the questions asked by the lawyers: "What did you say at that point?" – requires reporting actual speech made and being recalled. "Did you get angry at him for doing that?" – requires reporting and confirming whether or not a particular emotion was experienced in that situation.

But questions such as these are denied: "Were they mad at you for what you did?" requires a subjective judgment about the participants in an event. Or, "Why did they refuse to let you use their phone?, requires a personal judgment about their intention or motivation. This question would have to be rephrased as: "What explanation did they give for not letting you use their phone?" This is admissible because it requires an objective report of what someone said in that situation.

Plan on doing some self-witnessing of yourself while engaged in dialog with someone, or with everyone. Do this privately only in your mind without outward indication. Start by talking to God about it, and perhaps asking Him to enlighten you in your self-witnessing. Of course He would do that without your asking but by asking you will be experiencing a closer contact. Now look at your speech acts in the dialog. Are there a significant number of subjective judgments? Ideally there should be none, and there is never a good reason to depart from the principle that one ought to eliminate them all.

When you cease experiencing the plague of being subjective you will feel liberated from those hellish societies that insinuate themselves or their affections into your affective system without your knowledge or assent.

There are two modalities of being objective, one merely natural, the other spiritual-within-the-natural. Thinking and speaking objectively within mere natural consciousness is experienced as materialistic thoughts and principles that provide for natural-rational consciousness. In this mode of experiencing one feels resistance to eliminating what is here called subjective judgment. When contemplating this possibility the natural mind revolts and feels threatened. If these were eliminated then one would have little to think with or about, given that in our mind we are being constantly judgmental, intolerant, critical, inaccurate, and subjective about what others think, want, expect, or feel.

In the *New Testament* there appears this spiritual warning:

Do not judge, and you will not be judged. Do not condemn, and you will not be condemned. Forgive, and you will be forgiven. (Luke, 6:37)

This must be understood in the spiritual sense, that is, that we must not judge others regarding what they are feeling or intending since this information is not available to us, though it is available to God. Sometimes people experience the confusion of this principle when they want to judge someone's conduct and are held back by the idea that they must not judge anyone. But it is clear that social and community life requires everyone to judge rightly about *outward conduct* that may be immoral, criminal, deceptive, or warlike. Every citizen has the expectation and duty to form such judgments about others. We must condemn those who have been judged by the law or else family and society could not survive on this earth. It would be irresponsible and hellish to remove people's right and duty to judge, to condemn, and not to forgive, that is, to hold the wrong doer responsible. The verse is that passage obviously refers to subjective judgment and subjective condemnation. Hence in another verse it is explained:

Do not judge according to appearance, but judge with righteous judgment. (John, 7:24)

But when it comes to inward things that are outwardly not visible, such judgments are morally and spiritually inappropriate. Our subjective speech acts about others are so many pathways to hell in the afterlife. Hence we are warned to be tolerant, to have good will towards all, to exercise right judgment, to respect the human rights of every person regardless of the situation, and so on. But this must be interpreted to mean that we must not have a policy to let the guilty go unpunished, or to let criminals and terrorists go free where they can continue to threaten and injure innocents. Thus it is our spiritual duty to protect the innocent in our community from being injured by those who would be bad.

In what sense can we interpret the commandment to love one's enemy, as in this passage of the *New Testament*?

But I say to you, love your enemies and bless the one who curses you, and do what is beautiful to the one who hates you, and pray over those who take you by force and persecute you. (Matthew 5:44)

When I first became aware of this and related passages I was astounded. I could not see how I could pray for my enemy. I would be scared to death to do that. And how can I love those who threaten me, my family, and my community with robbery, injury, and death? Clearly this attitude would not be sensible and God who loves us and takes care of us would not allow it as something right or good. We must think therefore in a spiritual-rational sense that these passages have. To love your enemies and to do good to them refer to the experiencing of the cessation of spiritual anger, hatred,

177

and vengeance. It is the cessation of our hatred that must be effected in our regeneration. We cannot regenerate by loving our friends and families while hating those who declare themselves our enemies.

We must not hate since this is a desire to kill and maim. We must not hate our enemies because hate destroys our mind. Hate is an emotion that originates from a particular hell society where hatred is practiced as their chief love, occupation, and pleasure in life. By hating our enemies and wishing them ill we are being bound more strongly to those hellish societies. In the afterlife we remain bound to them, thus not being able to escape, held there by our mental habits and loves.

In what sense are we to take the commandment that we ought to love our enemy? In spiritual consciousness we can perceive that our enemies are human beings and do not lose their human rights because they hate us and choose to harm us. Therefore we need to love them in the appropriate way, which may include ignoring them, neutralizing them, killing them, or defeat them until they are no longer a threat. Once this is done, we are to treat the remnants of the defeated enemy with human dignity as prisoners. And we must not out of vengeance or anger punish those around them, their family and community, who may have been innocent bystanders. This humane attitude is the spiritual meaning of "love your enemies".

The Unreality of Not Talking to God

Establishing a reciprocal relationship with God is an essential condition for benefitting from the practice of experiencing. It is an essential feature of being elevated to spiritual consciousness.

First we need acknowledge that it is bizarre for two people to be roommates, to be travel companions, or teammates on a project, and never talk to each other. That would be either a very strange experiment, thus not real, or it means that they are living in unreality. God is a Divine Human person and is the architect of your moment-by-moment living and experiencing. God constantly connects you and disconnects you from particular heavenly and hellish societies that provide you with all your emotions, positive and negative. In this management of your emotions God also wants a reciprocal relationship with you. Clearly He is very intimately involved, being present and aware in every single emotion, feeling, sensation, or thought that are in your mind and heart. He manages and adjusts the sequence of your moment-by-moment experiencing with a plan and a goal, immediate, distant, and forever.

Before God your entire past, present, and future appears all at once and is so perceived by Him in a unified whole. His purpose is to take your mind into ever higher forms of enlightenment and intelligence, and your feelings into ever higher experiences of love and beauty. This is what God wants. That is God's Love for you as a unique individual person. God created you and continues to create you moment by moment from birth to endless eternity. Can you think of anything or anybody who can be more intimate, closer to you in love, emotion, and thought? God wants this intimate relationship with you to become conscious so that you are constantly aware of God's presence with you. God wants your connection with God to be conscious to you, with awareness, focus, and certainty, so that you may be in the experiencing of God. This is your reciprocation, which is your acknowledgement with awareness and perception, that God is this great thing in your life, actually the biggest. Then at last God can elevate your mind to spiritual life and consciousness, thus to real eternal happiness and intelligence. This is God's desire for you. God cannot make you happy and intelligent in any other way!

Hence you can see that not talking to God is experiencing and living in unreality.

And furthermore, talking to God brings immediate benefits with issues you might be having in experiencing release from this or that mental plague that you desire to be rid of. Talking to God brings elevation of consciousness from unreality to reality. The thoughts are clarified and elevated into the light and understanding of heaven, which is the highest portion of our mental world.

Managing Recurrent Negative Emotions

Our emotional life needs an effective manager. This means self-witnessing our experiencing. Effective management techniques for improving mental health are rarely seen successful in operation. Here is a three-step method of experiencing 12 intervening self-witnessing and self-affirmation steps. The only personally relevant and objective way of finding out if they work for you, is to try out the method. They work for me.

Step 1 is the acknowledgment of the negative emotion without comment, but in clear awareness
Step 2 is the objective self-witnessing through metanoid perception and the making of comments on the experiencing.
Step 3 is the experiencing of release from natural captivity into spiritual freedom. This release is accompanied by emotional relief and intense gratitude to God.

Let's step through the three Steps using an illustration. For example, suppose you are feeling dejected and longing for positive emotional enthusiasm. You can talk to yourself as follows:

Step 1

First make the acknowledgement:

"I am immersed in the inflow of dejection and abulia. I am dejected now that I became dejected again. I feel powerless. A little anxious, but I don't know why. I'm pessimistic about my future. I feel that none of my friends like me. I've got too much credit card debt to pay off. My blood pressure is up again. I feel scared about that. My neighbor's dog barks at night and wakes me up. I didn't get the pair of shoes I wanted. And I gained five pounds. Etc."

Note that going through Step 1 involves your effort to become more clearly aware of how you're feeling. In almost all cases negative emotions are complex and multiple, acting jointly on the victim and pooling their resources. They gather together in emotional gangs or teams and pool their power to upset you.

Your effort in Step 1 is to stick with the focus on the negative emotion and feeling. You can get more insight in five to ten minutes compared to just one or two. Begin to uncover the anatomical fibers and layers of emotions that are entangled with your spiritual body or mind. *Follow up the mental strands that you find in your experiencing. This is your solid rock. Experiencing cannot lie.*

Step 2

Now as you enter Step 2 direct your effort to perceive the deeper layers of your experiencing, namely those that are spiritual. (1) First note what your relationship to God is right now. (2) Comment on it. (3) Then initiate or re-initiate your reciprocal relationship to God by acknowledging the Divine Human's co-Presence in your mind and in all your mental operations. (4) Now consciously rehearse and focus on the idea in your mind that God is co-Present with you individually. (5) Now focus again on the idea that God is personally interested in participating in your experiencing. God wants this with everyone's experiencing.

Now you're halfway there. Already you will be experiencing some welcome and sweet relief. To continue the process: (6) Now have a dialog with God about your negative emotions, dejections, and depressions. (7) Acknowledge that you understand that it is God who keeps you connected to the evil societies that inflow with the negative emotions. (8) Acknowledge that you desire to accept the spiritual principle that God controls all things and uses your negative experiencing to help you undergo the process of regeneration. (9) Repeat again that it is your desire and intention to let God regenerate you through your as-of self cooperation and effort. (10) Repeat again that you understand that it is into this as-of self effort that God provides the power to change your character from selfish love to mutual love and love of God.

Step 3

(11) After this when you are ready to enter Step 3 focus on experiencing the consciousness of your new understanding and new feeling that God has just given you. Become aware of the underlying cessation of anxiety and its replacement with calmness and a positive outlook. (12) Notice that your thoughts now flow in rapidly with enthusiasm and excitement. Your plans and goals now orient towards how you can be useful to others and to society. You feel liberated and blessed.

Congratulations on your effort!

Now over the days and weeks it is likely that your consciousness falls back into the experiencing of despondency, lack of enthusiasm, fear of the future, and distance from God and God's friendly reassuring co-Presence. You may even be wondering if God really, really exists or you just made the whole thing up. This means that you need to enter Step 1 with your current feeling and go on from there as before.

There is a cumulative change and positive growth that will follow this practice of self-witnessing one's experiencing. Make it into a daily habit and you can avoid ups and downs in peace and mood. Then you can at last enjoy your life with the unbroken and unshakable certainty that God is preparing you for a conjugial life in heaven in eternity.

The Enormous Spiritual Cost of Wasting Time

In natural consciousness it seems right that we should consider the weekend and evenings as spending an appropriate time for relaxing, eating, being entertained by the media, and socializing with one or more friends engaged in the effort of having fun together. This is experienced as talking a lot and fast, listening together to music, dancing, laughing frequently, gossiping about people, and making jokes of all types. But viewed in spiritual consciousness these activities are categorized as spiritual waste of time.

You may see this idea more clearly if you consider that everyone has X number of minutes to live on this earth, consequently to change life-course through regeneration, and thereby to prepare the mind for a heavenly life. If we refuse to undergo regeneration we continue to acquire multiple habits of thinking and willing that are marked by loving self more than others, and loving God the least.

To love self more than others is the same as to love self only.

This requires some figuring out because from natural consciousness we see people's personalities as mixed, containing both good and bad traits, or both selfish and altruistic. However in spiritual consciousness we can see this issue anatomically and more realistically. People argue for the mixed selfish-altruistic position because they think of good and bad as a judgment someone makes. This act was good. This intention was bad. Etc. A judgment is subjective and can go either way any time depending on how the person who makes the judgment is involved in the situation. But in spiritual consciousness we make objective determinations based on human anatomy. The explanations we make up must not violate the facts of what we already know about mental anatomy.

To love self more than others is an act that connects us by spiritual love to hellish societies. These involve anatomical fibers of mutual reception of each other's love or pleasure in a situation. This spiritual connection remains in place no matter what is the subject we are thinking of. These spiritual love-connections are maintained by us because we experience pleasure and even a sense of victory and enthusiasm, and we do not want to give this up due to some argument about spiritual consciousness which appears abstract and less than real to natural consciousness.

For example in natural consciousness we argue that sometimes we can love ourselves more than others but at other times we seem to love others more than ourselves. For instance, consider this description: "*We are partying and making quite a bit of noise, but when 10 PM comes around, we stop. Though we would love to continue, we are being considerate of others, hence we love them more than self.*"

The spiritual meaning of "*we are being considerate of others, hence we love them more than self*" is "We want our action of ending the party to count as our loving others more than ourselves". The argument involving "*to count as*" is the experiencing of natural consciousness. It is a subjective judgment or determination, one that benefits the people who decided to stop the party. This is a self-motivated intention as shown by the fact that if the people next door get into a disagreeable interaction with us we no longer feel like being considerate to them. On the other hand, when our motive for being considerate is for the neighbor's sake and comfort, then we continue to show consideration for them even after they stop favoring us. You can apply this kind of thinking to many situations in order to distinguish whether we are doing something good for the sake of ourselves, or for the sake of others.

Because our thinking and willing are activated anatomically by spiritual connections, we tend to be wired from birth with the hellish societies of selfishness and egotism from which follow all our other selfish thoughts and acts. That's why God tells us in *Sacred Scripture* that we must be reborn and regenerated, and this means changing one's character by anatomical reconnection and gradual new growth through daily practice.

You can see now that selfishness can cover itself up in pretty clothes for outward show from a hypocritical and self-serving motive. People sometimes think that giving financial gifts to foundations and hospitals or schools can to some extent count in their favor when their good deeds and bad deeds are lined up to see the preponderance, and consequently to enter either heaven or hell in the afterlife. This is a selfish consideration immersed in natural consciousness, thus in spiritual unreality.

Think instead from an anatomical perspective. No one judges people in the afterlife before they enter either heaven or hell. This idea appears to be reinforced by the literal meaning in the *New Testament* such as in this passage in which Christ says to Peter:

> *I tell you that you are Peter, and on this rock I will build My Church, and the gates of hell will not prevail against it. And I will give you the keys of the kingdom of heaven; and whatever you bind on earth will be bound in heaven, and whatever you loose on earth will be loosed in heaven. Matt. 16:15-19.*

When taken literally in natural consciousness the passage can be used to argue that judgment of heaven and hell on anyone is decided not by God but by a human being. This interpretation leads to all sorts of errors and false conclusions upon which religious practices may be based. However spiritual-rational thinking immediately detects the error of this conclusion since it is clear that a mere human being cannot judge anyone rightly due to limited knowledge of a person and a situation. Such judgment would be a false one. Christ said these words to Peter because the idea was exactly at the level of Peter's thinking and the thinking of others in that generation. Had Christ said something more spiritual, even Peter would have doubted it.

But as in all places where *Sacred Scripture* verses are quoted, there is a hidden spiritual meaning contained within the words of the verses for those who are in a mental state of regeneration and are willing to look beyond the natural-historical meaning, and understand and accept the spiritual meaning. Here the spiritual meaning is that people are saved when they base their connection with God on spiritual truths from Sacred Scripture that they apply to themselves. Peter, a name that means stone or rock, represents unshakable spiritual faith in God, which is faith based on experiencing a reciprocal relationship with God. In many places in Sacred Scripture, this type of rational faith is called "the Church", meaning the inner Church or the Church in our mind. This kind of personal rational faith is solid and eternal. It has the power to "shut the gates of hell" in our mind so nothing evil enters there, and it has the power to "open the gates of heaven" in our mind from where flows in all good and happiness.

The true faith that prevails involves the actual anatomy of our spiritual connections. It is not a judgment that is made by Peter or anyone else including God, for God judges no one to hell but everyone judges themselves through the habits of thinking and willing that they have accumulated in their anatomy. In the afterlife, after the two-day resuscitation process, everyone feels compelled by their own loves and motives to follow a certain path downward towards the spiritual hells, or a path upward towards the spiritual heavens in their mind. For both heaven and hell are located in every individual's mind. It is a matter of mental anatomy.

There is therefore no other task that is as important as the task of regeneration. If any other task is set before it in importance, regeneration ceases and is destroyed. Given this consideration we need to examine how we actually spend our time in the x number of hours and minutes that we available on earth between birth and the dying-resuscitation process. *It makes rational sense to think that wasting of time refers to any minute or hour of any day that is spent for another motive than regeneration.*

It is a spiritual error to think that hard working people "deserve" time off where they can be entertained and not worry about their regeneration. This thinking is a death wish and a death trap, for by "death" in Sacred Scripture is always meant ending up in hell. God doesn't want anyone to end up in their mental states of hell. That's why He calls it "death" because in that mental state we are no longer acting human but sub-human. We can no longer think rationally or observe reality as we are entrapped in fantasies and insanities from which we refuse to exit by denying all truths that could get us out.

God wants to keep us out of that endless misery! Thank you God!

Cleaning Up the Pollution of the "I"

The pollution "of the I" refers to the thoughts that "I have" in my mind on a daily or recurrent basis when these thoughts are polluted by the many things involved in wasting time. The polluted atmosphere of our mind is produced by the pleasures and delights of selfishness that we allow and seek out in our social environment. These enjoyments continuously immerse our mind in that which is non-productive for our regeneration and consequent salvation. That's why they are categorized as a waste of the time we are allocated on earth before the dying-resuscitation process puts a sudden end to all these natural indulgences.

When wasting time people's experiencing moves into a mental zone of being bad. For instance, children and adults spend hours every day watching television and playing videogames. During all this time bad behavior is encouraged by the content and method of what is being displayed, watched, observed, and spiritually consumed. *These are all strategies that are oppose regeneration.* People experience delight in watching portrayals of violence, rape, cruelty, butchery, deception, adultery, profanation, and more. People laugh and feel energized when they witness disrespectful portrayals of ridiculing and persecuting various categories of people. The mental environment of the person is totally polluted by these anti-spiritual experiences. No spiritual truths or consciousness can grow in such a mind. It must be cleaned up for regeneration to begin.

It is similar with the waste of spiritual time that is enacted though partying, reading many books, talking junk on the phone, hanging out with friends, standing on the corner and watching all the girls go by (as the song says), watching sports and being involved in results and statistics, pursuing hobbies that are not productive spiritually, and so on.

It may not be easy for people to agree with this argument when they focus on the external experiencing of wasting time as defined here. Consider therefore the idea that *it is possible to infuse any activity with spiritual consciousness and the motive of regeneration.*

Experiencing Regeneration

The activities listed here as waste of time can be infused with spiritual consciousness as an alternative to stopping them altogether. And when that is done they are no longer in the category of wasting time.

Take for instance your favorite TV show. Chances are it contains portrayals of bad behaviors and spiritually forbidden or harmful pleasures. Refuse to give your mind over to the portrayal. Often people want to "really get into the movie" and pretend that what is being portrayed is real, as this makes the sought for excitement even stronger. This is achieved by suspending all moral and spiritual judgment, and just watching and taking it in. Try to break with this pernicious and dangerous habit.

Do not sell out your mind to entertainment managers who do not care at all about your salvation. Analyze what you see and hear. Label the bad and the good. Disagree with the bad and agree with the good. Take sides for good. If there are children in the room watching with you be sure to comment out loud and expose the bad and why it ought be avoided. Use the movie or the game as an opportunity for practicing being good. Gaming can be a two-edged sword, an opportunity for practicing bad habits, or for pointing them out as bad. If you experience intense competition in gaming or sports you need to work extra hard mentally to counteract your desire to win no matter what, or to reduce your delight when another loses instead of you. Games, shows, and sports are spiritually worse than useless unless they are transformed into opportunities for practicing being good.

A method I used to wean myself from TV and movies was to watch without the sound on. It started with using the director to mute the TV during commercials. Then we switched to headsets so that at least we don't disturb any of our neighbors in the evening. Then I eliminated all sounds. It's an amazing experience to watch TV and movies without a sound for weeks and months. I was making up what didn't show. I started with the character and decided whether this was a good person or bad. Then I tried to determine the relationship between the characters, like spouse, client, boyfriend, detective, lawyer, spy, assassin, etc. After awhile I no longer needed the experience of watching by habit.

I am drawing your attention to a real spiritual danger in your life, which is wasting time and polluting your mind with content that is worthless for your all-important regeneration, which is the reason we all are here on earth. If you accept these things and practice them, happy are you now, and will be even happier in the future of eternity.

Experiencing Release
from Neurotic Mental States

Neurosis is the experiencing of mental disorder.

Everyone lives in a disorderly mental state until rebirth and regeneration. Then the veering into the opposite direction begins internally. It is an anatomical organic process that the spiritual body undergoes, just like the leaf of an indoor plant turns itself toward the ray of sun coming through the window of the room. We are born and raised surrounded by neuroses in every area of life. We learn and acquire our neuroses in the same way that we acquire other negative mental habits like being deceptive, feeling despondent, overeating, criminality, aggressiveness, lack of conscience. These negative modes of experiencing life binds the person ever more securely into natural consciousness. There is no exit but down, which is where the hells are in the human mind.

The cessation of one's neurotic behaviors requires the activation of the will to turn itself into the opposite direction of its ongoing natural consciousness.

What keeps us bound to various neurotic mental states is inner resistance to letting go of the neurosis.

We don't feel like stopping and exiting our neurotic mental state.

This resistance is produced by the infernal marriage in our mind of selfish love that adjoins to itself some suitable falsity as its consort. This is the union between selfish love in the affective organ or the will and some invented false justification in the cognitive organ or the understanding. Various invented explanations are held on to in order to justify not changing. There is no end to this disorderly and spiritually insane internal dialog. It is useless to try to overcome it from one's own willpower or from rational argumentation offered by someone else.

Experiencing Regeneration

Resistance to fundamental mental change is locked into the experiencing of natural consciousness. It is suicidal and there is no human solution. Those who end up at the end of the line of this insanity are in the hell of their mind. In that state one is called "dead" because all reality has left and hardly anything human remains. Thus we need salvation to be freed from such a fate.

Where there is no mere human solution there is nevertheless a Divine solution.

The power to switch and turn upwards towards spiritual consciousness is given instantaneously when we enter the mental state of humiliation and submission before God.

This involves the experiencing of a reciprocal relationship with God.

This is the return to spiritual sanity. Until then we lived in the spiritual insanity of thinking that we power ourselves in the mental world and are alone there. Thinking this way is spiritual arrogance and spiritual meritoriousness because it involves experiencing the denial of God's omnipotence and omnipresence. Anxiety is from worry, and worry is from arrogance and loss of humility. It is the false thinking that God is not in charge, or that God is not in full control, or that God does not know what we really want and need, while we know. This is the source of natural anxiety.

But now in the presence of God we no longer feel the need to resist getting rid of our neurotic mental states. *Everything has suddenly changed.* A new experiencing has begun, free of the cruel tyranny and spiritual insanity of materialism and the denial of God's omnipotence and direct involvement. *This new mental state is the experiencing of Divine love.* It feels totally warm and reassuring. There is the feeling of having arrived at last. There is a lifting of the burdens of life. There is an end to the cruel stabs of anxiety and uncertainty.

Experiencing the end of neuroses opens up the person's creativity and energy. This opening process is built into our experiencing. We don't do anything. We feel carried by the river of Divine Providence looking after our welfare. Life is like a vacation. We are led into situations, positions, and roles that provide a rich arena for experiencing. We are honest outwardly and inwardly because we are no longer alone, doing what we want, as before in the state of spiritual insanity. We are dependable in our responsibilities because we love the idea of doing God's will. We implore God that His will be done not our own. If we are also blessed with a married spouse then we discover the experiencing of spiritual marriage, that is, marriage in spiritual consciousness. And if not so blessed now, then we know with certainty that one's soulmate spouse is to be met in the afterlife for a conjugial love union in eternity, where two are no longer two but one mind.

Uncleanness

Why does the popular idiom say, "cleanliness is next to godliness"? The words "clean" and "cleanliness" have a natural meaning and a spiritual. Everyone knows the natural meaning from parents, teachers, and books. People who study the Bible know that it uses the idea of cleanliness spiritually to refer to moral rectitude. In common parlance people use the expression "dirty cop" and "he is clean" to refer to not being guilty of any crime. In the spiritual sense cleanliness in worship corresponds to external worship in which there is internal worship. Uncleanness is external worship as ritual without any internal acknowledgement or belief. The Bible in the *Old Testament Book of Leviticus* is filled with commandments addressed to the people of Israel, of when someone is ritually unclean and what specifically he or she ought to do to become clean from defilement or touch of something defiled, such as a corpse or another ritually unclean person.

It is obvious that these elaborate procedures for getting rid of uncleanness were not commanded for health reasons, such as having to wash and wait seven days before being clean again. These elaborate rituals were commanded to represent what needs to be done when someone is spiritually unclean, that is, when people are externally religious but internally selfish and hate all who do not favor them or do not favor what their own, such as their reputation, their wealth, their family, their circle of friends. These are religious hypocrites and are designated by the expression spiritually "unclean".

Some might wonder whether a person deserves to go to eternal damnation in hell because they were unclean or less than clean in this life. To gain a spiritual-rational perspective on this question, consider why people are physically unclean as a habit or personality trait. Why are they not attracted to cleanliness and order, such as there is in heaven. Note that being unclean as a habit is a syndrome with other branches like living in a clutter, disorderly closets, junk in the car trunk and garage, unpaid and lost bills, etc. You are looking at the picture of disorder physical and mental. Now what use does this neglect serve for the person, a good use or an evil use? Here you will perceive a deep seated rebellion, stubbornness, and arrogance on the part of that person, that is hidden within the matrix of uncleanliness as a habit.

So it is like external worship of rituals but without the internal worship of commitment to regeneration, that is, without the desire to learn to love others as much as self, and God more than anything. The *Old Testament* says that if a person remains unclean he shall be "cut off from his people", which refers to damnation. Does being unclean deserve hell punishment? Remember that this refers to being spiritually unclean, which means arriving into the afterlife without having undergone regeneration prior to the dying-resuscitation process. As a result the person follows the path to the hell societies and there recognizes with a homecoming joy the people with whom they had been connected spiritually while on earth and promoting in their mind an affection for habits of uncleanliness and disorder to rule their life. But their joy soon turns to suffering when they begin to be victims of their neighbors who gang up and are delighted to make others suffer.

Negative Body Self-Image

Many people suffer from negative body self-image issues that are created by cultural attitudes and norms regarding individuals who are overweight or unattractive looking. Growing up in natural consciousness it is easy to become a target and victim of those who champion approved "looks" and criticize others who don't match up. As a result there is a constant litany of complainings that people enact for each other and for themselves, as indicated by these familiar speech acts relating to body self-image:

"I feel fat" "I feel ugly" "I'm unattractive" "My thighs are too fat" "My waste is too short" "I am old looking" "My arms are too skinny" "My nose is too big" "No one would pick me at a prom dance" "She is so fat" "He is not very attractive looking" "She looks terrific" "Wow, you

Experiencing Regeneration

lost weight!" "His ears stick out funny" "Terrific looking bod" "Like a knock out" "He has even looking teeth" "He is kinda short"

A colleague who was doing research on how people diet, once told me that dieting and other lifestyle issues are not general imperatives for everyone. According to him people need to decide which way they're going to derive greater rewards and be happier living their life. Perhaps they might decide that they derive more rewards from life by eating freely what they want, even if this means being overweight and putting up with some deceases later, and even if it shortens their lives by five years. How do you see this issue?

The things we say about others we also turn against the self, and vice versa as is discussed in chapter 3 on the emotional spin cycle. Being in the habit of criticizing other people's appearance, eventually spins off to criticizing one's own appearance, and vice versa. In spiritual consciousness we begin to realize what is involved in criticizing someone's appearance or body part. There is disapproval of the person being criticized. There is also hurtful gossip with those who discuss with each other people's body and appearance. Ultimately there is hatred in it of the human form, which is the image of God's form. Who would have thought that casually saying to a friend, "He is unattractive", might be sourced in a hatred for God? Criticizing someone's body is to judge the person spiritually. Similarly, living with a negative body self-image is to judge oneself spiritually. This must never be attempted.

Experiencing release from a negative body self-image involves spiritualizing the issue, as discussed in Chapter 2. In spiritual consciousness you can go through knowledge you have acquired about the spiritual aspects of your body. For instance, your body is created in the image of God's Human body. The human body is the most complex object in the universe because it combines all the other properties and relationships in the universe. All things in the universe were created for some use to the human body. The physical body is a material and imperfect copy of the immortal spiritual body, which is perfect in form, health, youth, and vitality. The misshapen imperfections of the physical body, by birth and by injury or illness, leave the spiritual body completely unaffected. It remains perfect in shape and function regardless of what happens to the physical body. Following the two-day dying-resuscitation process we awaken in the spiritual body and the imperfections of the physical body are but a forgotten memory.

All this can convince you that there is no spiritual significance to our body shape and appearance except that which reflects on habit and practice.

Is being overweight a moral issue? Clearly it is when one considers the spiritual meaning of being overweight when this is caused by one's diet management. Experiencing regeneration covers all departments and areas of living and personality, including lifestyle and diet. The three levels of conscience are involved, namely civil, moral, and spiritual. We have a civic duty to take care of our health so that we may not become burdens on society. Schools have recognized this individual responsibility since they started focusing on diet and being overweight as negative outcomes. We also have a moral duty to strengthen our integrity, sincerity, and rationality in the management of our conduct and personal habits. To be overweight means that we need to focus on our diet management practices and to make them more effective. Finally, we have a spiritual duty to undergo regeneration and to elevate our consciousness from the corporeal to the rational and ultimately to the spiritual levels of functioning.

Getting back to my colleague's argument, it would appear that all three types of conscience and duty just discussed oppose the idea of obtaining our rewards and happiness of life by eating what we want. Rational diet management is therefore for the sake of society, for the sake of moral development, and for the sake of spiritual regeneration. These benefits far outweigh the shallow and brief reward of eating what one wants, whether healthy or not. Indeed it is an error to think that this kind of corporeal reward can make one happy in life. The opposite is the case. Being overweight brings hassles that shrink the quality of life.

What is the Fall of Man?

A shocking feature of natural consciousness is that it hates innocence. It loves to make fun of the good. It is entertained by portrayals of cruelty, unchastity, and deception. It questions God as either non-existent or powerless and even evil. Innocence is the humiliation and submission before God. Natural consciousness hates this idea. Within this context natural consciousness hates anything that appears innocent, such as good-hearted people, chaste sexuality, and above all hates infants and children because they bring the experiencing of God. Such hatred is not felt consciously so that it may not interfere with parenting. Such is the devolution of the human mind in unending natural consciousness.

As a result of this psychotic condition, children and women have been molested and abused by men throughout human history after the Fall. The expression "the Fall of Man" or "the Fall of Humankind" refers to the cessation of spiritual consciousness in the human race on this earth due to anatomical devolution of the mental organs brought about by natural consciousness and materialism. Prior to the Fall women and children were loved and appreciated for bringing the experiencing of God into every situation. But after the Fall women and children began to be abused as part of traditional rituals.

Today we read in the News available on the Web from around the world and the practice of child abuse and the abuse of women has increased to epidemic proportions. For example in some countries girls aged eight are married off to men in their seventies. Genital mutilation of girls is a sanctioned practice in various communities. Sexual molestation and abuse of children is commonplace throughout the Western countries. Rape of women, forced sex, and violence against women are common occurrences in most civilized cities today.

Religion itself is not sufficient to stop these human psychoses. Knowledge of God and regular worship and prayer are very common among the people who perpetrate these atrocities against children and women. Religion in natural consciousness is different from religion in spiritual consciousness.

The spiritual solution to social psychoses and community breakdown is the giving up of arrogance and meritoriousness before God and to maintain a reciprocal relationship with Him.

God continually strives to soften and reduce the individual's arrogance and consequent spiritual insanity that prevents the reception of Divine power that we need for changing our selfish and neurotic loves. *God stands by the door of awareness in our experiencing, and knocks, asking to be*

Experiencing Regeneration

admitted into full and conscious co-Presence with the persdon. This is the salvation from the Fall. It is the elevation of our experiencing back into the mode of spiritual consciousness and sanity. It is arriving back home.

We hear about "the Fall of Man" or Humankind but few may know that it refers to the anatomical and evolutionary progression of the mental world of eternity. This is our home both now and in the eternity of afterlife. A radical change was taking place in human mental anatomy when people started migrating down from their spiritual consciousness, which they inherited from birth. The migration was downward to natural consciousness and this is why the ancients called it the "Fall" of Mankind. Later however this origin was no longer known. But now people's experiencing is changing with the new development of theistic psychology that is based on the spiritual sense of *Sacred Scripture.*

Those who have attempted to draw a new science based on the historical and literal meaning of *Sacred Scripture* have not been able construct a successful or believable scientific account of the Book of Genesis and its Creation Story. Now however as spiritual consciousness is returning to humankind on this earth, more people will begin to perceive the correspondential sense everywhere in *Sacred Scripture.* The Creation Story will then be seen as one of God's lectures on theistic psychology that is perceivable by all who look into the correspondences there, and perceive the details of the topic of regeneration. You are reading many of these details in this book.

The details of theistic psychology derived from *Sacred Scripture* are not opposed in any way to religion and its practices in every nation of this earth. They are independent, just as the historical narrative in the Bible is independent of the analytic sense that people may derive from it. To think that theistic psychology is an attack on religion is an error. To think that religion may be a source for theistic psychology is also an error. It is also an error to think that God could have simply given us the language and words of theistic psychology instead of the historical narrative.

Ask yourself who in the world could have received the words and ideas of theistic psychology that is hidden within the Old Testament if God had dictated them to the prophets? The answer is that no one would have received them, understood them, or believed them. And in that case they would have been without religion for all those millennia and centuries. As a result the population on earth would have been doomed forever, destroyed by the deadly virus of inherited selfishness endlessly transmitted to every generation born on earth. "Doomed" is a correct description for it refers to inherited anatomical ties to hellish societies from which no one could get free. All this was the result of coming down from spiritual consciousness and shutting the door. In consequence people were trapped into the experiencing of materialism in science, in culture, in talk. This entrapment is called the Fall.

Religious Neuroses

Until we separate in our mind the idea of God and the idea of religion we are not able to elevate our consciousness to the spiritual level.

We need to see that having a religion is just one of the cultural things that human beings do with God. This relationship to God through religion is expressed in community with others through jointly acted out worship, celebration rituals, and doctrinal rules of life and good conduct. God has always provided for the existence of various religions on earth, each religion being suited for that particular culture. God has also provided for a *Sacred Scripture* to go with each religion. It is clear that what matters spiritually is whether the person of any religion maintains a relationship with God and faithfully obeys the commandments of that religion.

Anyone who does this lives a life of obedience to God, doing no harm to others because God forbids it. Such a person easily undergoes regeneration, either before or after resuscitation. Living this way equips the individual's personality for living in mutual love in heaven. It makes sense to think that there are many heavens, each suitable for the genius of the people who are from the same religion or cultural generation.

But as you can see when thinking about it, people from all religions can also have a reciprocal relationship with God that is not related to religion, culture, family, or community. It's just something personal and private between the individual and God. And in fact God wants this one-on-one and face-to-face relationship with every human being regardless of religion. It is through this intimate and reciprocal relationship that God can give the individual what His Divine Love wants most, namely through that relationship to make that person immortal and happy to eternity.

Experiencing Regeneration

There are people who have a religion but who do not have at the same time this reciprocal relationship with God. They are then vulnerable to the false doctrinal interpretations of the leaders and may become victims of their love of dominion and ruling over others, especially their "souls". Anyone thinking about it would see that what makes one's religion living and valid is contained in one's private relationship to God and not in the cultural religious rituals. What use is it for people to participate in outward physical rituals without inner connection and love to God? If we love God then we are automatically opening up a reciprocal relationship with Him. Love conjoins inwardly and personally, while community ritual only associates people socially and externally, as in a large city where worshippers remain strangers to one another.

Without a reciprocal relationship to God the individual remains vulnerable to false ideas and doctrines that may cause religious neuroses that some therapists refer to as "religious trauma syndrome". This mental malaise includes the following symptoms:

- poor critical thinking ability which is discouraged by religion
- negative beliefs about self from religious teachings
- difficulty with decision making due to religious confusion
- anxiety and depression from religious beliefs and fears
- anger against being dominated by religious leaders
- difficulty with pleasure from religious definitions
- unfamiliarity with secular world due to separation
- sexual difficulty from religious interference and confusion
- suppression of normal child development due to religious interference
- dysfunctional beliefs from religion about society and other people
- being taught that self is not a reliable source
- experiencing use of punishment as discipline
- etc

The causes of these religious neuroses is traced by therapists to "toxic theology" that puts the individual into an emotional and intellectual double bind from which it is impossible to ever be free. For instance, the idea that you can't stop sinning and yet you are punishable for it with eternal damnation. You can never be sure if you are saved or not so you have to keep asking for forgiveness of sins that you cannot stop doing.

Experiencing release from religious neuroses requires that the individual maintain a reciprocal relationship with God through daily dialog and conscious co-Presence. God will then inform the person what is the truth and what is not, or what makes us good and what makes us bad. There is no need to stop having a religion. But there is a need to start having a reciprocal relationship with God independently of religion.

It is not clear what is the source of religious neuroses. As explained by mental health professionals religion is the cause of these neuroses. But it makes more sense to think that *it is the falsified principles of religion that contribute to the creation of these neuroses in the individual's personality*. It is an error to confuse "religion" with "false principles of religion". This can be seen clearly when you see that religious doctrines vary greatly and many appear to contradict each other. People who experience doubt about God or the holiness of *Sacred Scripture* confirm themselves in this error by pointing to all the conflictual religions and being unable to understand how God could allow such a confusing state.

Without distinguishing between true ideas about God and falsified principles, it is not possible to resolve this issue. And in that case all religion and religious ideas are dismissed as promoting neuroses. Meanwhile, prohibiting discussion of God in public schools may also cause various neurotic consequences by cutting off all mental health growth that depends on a healthy relationship with God. Hence it is best to separate religion and God since they are distinct. Prohibiting discussion of religion in schools is understandable in a multi-cultural community, but prohibiting discussion of God is a scientific, educational, and moral blunder that can have negative consequences for society and the mental health of each individual.

Experiencing Release from Swearing

In natural consciousness we make all sorts of excuses trying to justify a habit of swearing in its many varieties. In my own experiencing I had some difficulty confirming that swearing as a spiritual habit is as bad as murder as a spiritual habit. If I had habitually thought of killing others who are in my way, I would have confirmed that it leads me to hell. But swearing didn't seem to me to be serious enough to take one to hell.

But now I can perceive that all swearing seen from within is hatred of God and the desire to kill Him if this were possible, and to take His place and to be god.

What would happen if you arrived into the afterlife with a mental habit of swearing?

A little time after you are resuscitated from the two-day dying-resuscitation process you begin to experience the spiritual laws of association and its mental atmospheres. You feel your chief love slowly emerging from the depths of your personality where it lay silently emitting the desire, love, and pleasure of swearing in different ways in the course of a single day. *Each time you swear you are consummating the love of being disrespectful to God.* This is to hate God. Sometimes we swear against God by making a joke out of some spiritual truth, event, or person mentioned in *Sacred Scripture.* Or we may act disrespectfully towards some other religion whose practitioners seem strange or wrong.

Acting disrespectfully towards anything that relates to God, worship, or *Sacred Scripture* falls into the category of swearing.

A more hidden variety of swearing and hating God is the habit of swearing when something is in our way, or breaking something in anger because it is not working right, or in frustration kicking and hitting the wall or some other object. *These nonverbal forms of anger expressed with the physical body are a form of swearing against God.* We know that ultimately God is responsible for everything that happens. So if that nail got bent instead of going in straight it is easy to think that it is God's fault for making it happen that way, and swearing expresses our anger against Him. Some people try to justify their swearing by modifying the swearword to make it sound innocuous, as for instance, "Gosh" or "Dang" or "Shoot", or even "Fiddlesticks!" Spiritually it does not matter what external expression is being used for anger, whether expressed verbally, by act, or by mere thinking and emoting. In each case there is anatomical bonding of our character to the spiritual society that is into the lust of hating God. After resuscitation this becomes clear and people then feel free to utter abominable hatreds against the Divine and against anything that is good and innocent.

There are even deeper and less visible forms of anger and hatred against God that connect us to the hells until we start opposing their influence on us. An example is the experiencing of being forever idle in luxury and comfort, and not feeling the need or requirement to serve others or to be useful to them in some way. *A fundamental spiritual truth is that everyone is born for others and not for themselves.* This means that we are created primarily to be serviceable to others, and only secondarily as a result of that, to ourselves. To be created in this order means that our anatomical evolution and healthy mental growth is dependent on our opportunities to make ourselves useful in the lives of others, and then to derive contentment from doing that.

To want to be idle in the sense of not wanting any responsibility for others in some way, is therefore a direct attack on reality, on spiritual truth, and hence on God. Love of self always produces hatred of God, while love of others and God always produce love of wanting to be useful to others, to take appropriate responsibility for them, and whenever possible to make them happy from one's own talents, abilities, and effort.

We need to understand the anatomy of negative emotions in our mind and how they get hold of our focus and consciousness, holding us captive in a purely sensuous consciousness. This is the key: Our spiritual consciousness lies in the awareness of our experiencing the negative emotion. It is action by the negative emotion and reaction by our self-witnessing. *We need to make a self-witnessing comment on the situation as we are experiencing it, not sometimes later.* When our two children were growing up in our house swearing was forbidden. When they used a swear word or some substitute we insisted that they "take it back". This may be an important practice with all children given that they often acquire the habit of swearing from each other outside the home and begin to use it without even paying attention to it.

Life with swearing pulls the person down to the lowest level of natural consciousness called "corporeal". Few people care to know or to believe that the entire hells are behind the continuous habit of spewing out swearwords and other ranting against the Divine. People think, "*It's just a*

Experiencing Regeneration

habit, that's all. Why compare it to a murderous bank robber or a child molester?" But the point is that this is not a matter of judgment so that one might be too harsh or severe relative to the offense. It is a matter of mental anatomy and spiritual biology. Any mental habit cannot exist on its own but must be supported by assistive habits that make it possible for something to be a habit.

Swearing as a habit is supported and assisted by connected loves that include anger, disrespect, impatience, retaliation, helplessness, arrogance, and still others. We need to remember that the hells compose numberless societies in the low regions of the human mind. These spiritual societies congregate into sub-groups and larger groups and form a unified infernal congregation acting with one force that no individual on earth can resist if attacked. *The love that binds us to a hell society binds us to the entire hells because that society acts in unison with all the other societies.*

It is the case that all regions of the human mind are arranged by discrete levels of functioning. Therefore the hells are also arranged by levels with the worst hells lower down and the least bad hells in the upper region of that zone. Perhaps some negative loves like swearing or being in a bad mood all the time, may involve the experiencing of a milder hell compared to negative loves like cruelty, hypocrisy, greed, and arrogance. This might mean that after resuscitation when the time comes to decide between a heavenly life and a hellish one, we may be able to give up the negative loves that are mild, and this would allow us to prepare our mind for a heavenly society. But it's not wise to take a chance with your eternal fate. It makes sense to want to get rid of swearing now.

Experience your life with swearing. Monitor how often you swear in a day and on what occasions. Monitor how often others around you swear and what they use for swearing. Notice how much swearing is hidden in the background of your day. It's almost easy to be unaware of it except when it becomes a neurosis for some people who swear every sixth word when they talk. Write down all the swearwords you use and arrange them in an order by frequency or preference of use. Ask yourself why it is considered disrespectful to swear in many social situations and why it is forbidden to swear before authorities and in school.

Experiencing Regeneration

You may then become more aware of the pernicious damage that swearing can cause to children and to other adults, and especially to yourself.

Note also the element of anger and threat that is hidden in swearing. People justify themselves when swearing under duress or emergency situations. For instance you may be cleaning some object when it snaps or breaks. The word related to damnation quickly comes out of the mouth and lips. Whom are you sending to damnation? Yourself? The object? Other words also come to the fore that make allusions to sexual activity and excrements. Is this who you want to be and align yourself with those who delight in such things? It does not make sense, right?

So you need to declare war on your swearing habit because it is bad, gross, disrespectful, and allied to really bad and evil people who hate God, innocence, marriage, children, spiritual good, and spiritual truth.

Use the three-step method to practice getting your life back from the slavishness of the habit of swearing.

Step 1: **Acknowledge** that your swearing is a bad habit, evil, and hateful of God and innocence. Renew your reciprocal relationship to God and confess to Him that you are powerless to get rid of your habit by yourself. Acknowledge that God will get rid of it for you as soon as you agree to cooperate with Him.

Step 2: **Witness** yourself swearing. Monitor the words, the times and the occasions. Experience the underlying anger or rage that triggers the swearing. Experience the feeling of raging against God, blaspheming God, blaming God, blaming authority, blaming fate, blaming people and wanting to destroy them and their belongings.

Step 3: **Modify** your swearing by changing it from within. The instant a swear word escapes your lips do damage control. Don't just let it sit there; don't just let it go. Pursue it. Bring it back to the fore. Expose it. Disagree with it. Judge it. Condemn it. You can say for instance, "*Sorry God. I don't mean that. I take it back.*" Say this every time you swear. If you mean it, God will remove this plague from your mind.

Experiencing Regeneration

You will discover how clean life feels like without any swearing on the lips or in the mind!

Experiencing Release From Fear of Aging, Death and Dying

Fear of aging and fear of death and dying is an experience possible only in natural consciousness, which denies or doubts God and life after death.

Once you are in the experiencing of spiritual consciousness you can look back on your life prior to the start of your regeneration. Quite likely you will remember that you used to have a fear of death and dying. Everything we read seems to reassert the idea that death and God are "mysteries" that are not comprehensible rationally. But thinking this is an error.

In spiritual consciousness we can deal with dying and death on a de-dramatized level. It's just like a medical operation or surgery that we are contemplating for the physical body. It's anxiety provoking at first but eventually as we discover more information we calm down and wait for the day. Such is also the day of our dying when we enter the anatomical surgery that the omnipotent and loving God performs to separate every individual's spiritual body from the physical body with which it was adjoined since birth.

The two-day process of dying and resuscitation ends with awakening and recapturing the personality with which we have lived life on earth. Nothing is lacking or changed in any way. We are fully and totally ourselves. This includes our appearance, face, and voice. We then begin a new exciting social adventure in company with many others who have preceded us into the afterlife and are now living in various mental communities across the vast endless spectrum of human thinking and emotion.

Understanding spiritual reality as God reveals it can be had from the study of theistic psychology that is based solely and exclusively on *Sacred Scripture*. *Extreme care must be taken not to comingle other intellectual sources to theistic psychology*. Nor must one invent or modify what is there. Genuine theistic psychology is *Sacred Scripture* read in the spiritual

Experiencing Regeneration

sense. God speaks theistic psychology when His Word is read in heaven where nothing is known or understood that relates to history on this earth, nor to particular people, nor to geographic places, dates, or numbers, nor to commandments about sacrifices, nor to eternal punishments for sins. These natural details that are found in the literal sense of *Sacred Scripture* are understood only in their spiritual and celestial correspondences.

But it should be known that there are a few places in *Sacred Scripture* where natural-spiritual correspondences are identified and spoken of in the letter or literal sense of those verses. These are called *"naked spiritual truths"*. *This transparency insures that people who never hear or read about correspondences in Sacred Scripture or about theistic psychology, are nevertheless able to obtain the minimum spiritual information that is needed for rebirth and regeneration.* This is true as long as they don't falsify those "naked truths" by fantasy elaborations that are motivated by human foolishness, pedantries, selfishness, and arrogance.

The fear of aging is present even while we are regenerating and even though we fully understand that we are our spiritual body and not our physical body.

The spiritual body does not "age" because there is nothing of physical matter and time-space in it. Our spiritual body is apart from space and time. Its composing substances of spiritual heat and light are immortal, as they originate from the mental sun of eternity. Our spiritual body develops and grows into adulthood in parallel with our mental abilities and maturity. This is because our mind is the spiritual body in its anatomy and structures, thus all that we sense, think, and feel take place in and through our immortal spiritual body.

We will experience anxiety in the aging of the physical body only to the extent that we bring our focus to the physical body without considering the parallel changes occurring in the spiritual body. You can weaken the distress associated with the aging of the physical body by focusing on the spiritual body that is within the physical and is conjoined to it from birth. But at death the conjunction ceases.

An additional way of experiencing release from the fear of aging is to focus on the daily effort of maintaining and enhancing the health and appearance of the physical body. For most people this involves initiating

Experiencing Regeneration

an effective exercise program and planning a gradual change in eating habits to a vegan plant based diet. Such a radical change requires first gathering knowledge about it, which is now made easy with Web search engines. I did this successfully after reviewing Dr. Michael Gerber's brief but data oriented videos at nutritionfacts.org/about (or search for: [Dr. Michael Gerber plant based diet]; but see also others like Dr. McDougall).

The fear of aging is the experiencing of a passive lifestyle, which promotes learned helplessness regarding all things relating to health and medicine. However, additional psychological issues may be involved. Therapists tend to emphasize the importance of maintaining a "healthy body image", especially for those who are experiencing social rejection and family criticisms as a result of being either "too skinny" or "too fat" (being overweight or obese). People then get into various neuroses and compulsions relating to body appearance and functioning. All this emotional trouble and effort can be sidestepped and left behind when undergoing regeneration.

This book teaches how to get ready for undergoing regeneration by giving you information about your immortal spiritual body and about why you would want to initiate a personal and special relationship with God. Every detail of your aging and maturation process is managed by God for both the physical body and the spiritual body. It makes sense therefore for you to reciprocate this involvement by having a dialog about it with God.

With regeneration we ascend in consciousness and see new things and have new abilities. Spiritual consciousness can be infused in our present natural consciousness and enlighten us that we may be able to perceive spiritual-rational truths and principles. We begin to realize that it is our *spiritual body* that is a temple for the co-Presence of God with the individual. The temporary and gross physical body is nothing but a correspondence and image of the real spiritual body, organ-by-organ, gene-by-gene, and even molecule-by-molecule. At birth the form of our spiritual body is infilled with material substances from earth and thereby our physical body comes into being as a temporary and less than perfect "covering" of the real body.

The physical body is rough and crude compared to the spiritual body that is mental and refined. The physical body absorbs and mitigates sensations while in the spiritual body they are pure and intense. We are not human because of our temporary physical body but because of our immortal spiritual body. Upon death, the physical body may be aged or may be young, but the spiritual body is perfect in form, structure, and function regardless of what has happened to the physical body such as aging, injury, birth defect, deformation, malfunction, etc.

Experiencing aging provides the spiritual opportunity of coping with pain. The psychological effects of pain include depression, resentment, and anger. We feel a sense of despondency in pain, a feeling that we are abandoned and alone. No one can experience our pain for us. We are left alone with the experiencing of pain. We feel resentment against our fate, against God, against family members and health professionals, against this miserable world. Such resentment can turn into anger, hostility, harshness, and violence as a desperate search for relief from pain and for the injustice of being singled out. We are tired of feeling tired from pain. We are trapped.

Except for this one reality: We have our relationship with God.

We need to explore with God through daily dialog with Him why He is giving us this pain. And if He is not giving it to us, then why is He allowing it to happen? Why does He just sit there and let it happen to me? Couldn't He just prevail and silence the pain? Why are you not doing it, God? Why? Why, God?

These are the forms of spiritual temptation as we age and cope with a deteriorating physical body. Without the experiencing of aging we would be more entrenched in natural consciousness and would resist the new perceptions and understanding that we receive with spiritual consciousness. Those who wish to have an immortal physical body are wishing for something very dangerous since it would bind the individual to corporeal spiritual societies who do not wish to hear anything rational or spiritual. These people are spiritually insane and are choosing to live in hell, being unwilling to depart from there by adopting spiritual truths in their thinking. *To be tied to them mentally is to experience what they are thinking and feeling as one's own.*

After resuscitation we spontaneously gravitate to them and enter their society. We then feel like it is a homecoming to familiar feeling and

Experiencing Regeneration

thinking, not wishing to hear anything rational or spiritual, consequently being unable to receive any spiritual truths.

Aging of the physical body when viewed spiritually is therefore a useful process to undergo because it helps us avoid the deadly error of identifying ourselves with the physical body and mentally joining those in hell who are in corporeal spirituality. Gradual aging helps us distance ourselves from loving the natural world and its relatively gross pleasures and spiritual insanities. Aging is for our benefit, to encourage us to equip our personality with the traits and abilities that can support heavenly life.

In the afterlife our appearance is entirely according to our inner loves and their associated truths. If these in our mind are genuine from heaven, they make our outward appearance to be well formed, beautiful, youthful, and healthy. But if the loves and ideas in us are not from heaven, but from ourselves, and therefore from hell, they make our appearance to be deformed, repulsive, un-young, and unhealthy. In the mental world of the afterlife what is inside our personality takes over and shows itself outwardly or publicly. Now at last our inner loves and desires can be consummated. We then experience the love's very own pleasure and we delight in it. Now we can join others in spiritual societies who also have these particular loves and desires, which can be positive loves that enhance collective life, or negative lusts that are destructive to community and self.

The positive or negative quality of these inner loves determines the person's final choice in entering permanently into a particular spiritual society.

The spiritual body does not age in heaven but remains in the flower of youth to eternity. Conjugial couples in heaven are strikingly beautiful similitudes of each other, the husband expressing his own unique masculinity in form and intelligence; the wife expressing her unique feminine beauty in form and love. Husband and wife form one conjoined mind, he being her lungs and understanding, and she being his heart and love. The two together are happiness in its own human form.

Chapter 4
Equipping Our Personality For Living In the Afterlife

The purpose of this book is to increase our awareness and understanding of living in the afterlife.

The feeling that we are in charge and there is no time to waste for this great adventure is both exciting and encouraging. Discovering and maintaining a personal daily relationship with God is an exhilarating experience. Knowing and accepting the difference between being bad and being good is half of the battle won. Being good consists of activating the traits in our personality that give us the desire to be considerate of others as much our self. Being bad is to do everything for the sake of self only and what is our own. This includes our children, our estate, and the people who favor us. This topic was discussed fully in Chapter 1.

Many people have difficulty accepting the idea that we need to consciously equip our personality with heavenly habits of feeling and thinking for the sake of being able to live in heavenly and conjugial bliss in eternity. The fact is that after resuscitation from the two-day dying-resuscitation process we undergo an inner physiological change in our personality whereby loves that were deeply rooted and hidden in our earthly life suddenly emerge into our overt personality. After some social experimentation in various directions, the individual's ruling or most powerful love assumes supreme priority and takes over the entire personality. Whatever is compatible with the ruling love is put in place and solidified, and whatever is incompatible with this chief love, is set aside and rendered paralyzed or inactive.

Experiencing Regeneration

The personality now stripped of its opposites emerges fully integrated and consistent.

If the chief love of the individual is doing things for the sake of self only and desiring to rule over all others for the sake of self, then the individual joins one of the hellish spiritual societies that is closest in similarity to that person's selfish love, which can vary endlessly.

Similarly if the ruling love of the individual is doing things for the sake of others not just self and desiring to rule over others for the sake of performing benefits for them, then the individual joins life in eternity in one of the heavenly spiritual societies that is closest in similarity to that person's mutual love, which also varies endlessly.

You can see from this that it is to our critical advantage to equip our personality with heavenly loves if we are to avoid the hellish life in eternity. This is achieved through progressive regeneration during which we must undergo spiritual temptations. Following this process of orderly preparation, our personality is rearranged in the form of heavenly loves.

Life in Heaven and Hell

You may have heard various things about what is heaven and what hell. People imagine many things and assume others. *In theistic psychology, which is based on Sacred Scripture, heaven and hell are defined anatomically.*

There is one mental world into which every human mind is born and where he or she lives an immortal life. The mental world is created by the atmospheres of spiritual heat and light that stream out of the spiritual sun in mental eternity. Spiritual heat is nothing but the Divine mental substance of love and good, and spiritual light is nothing else than the Divine mental substance of truth and intelligence. Hence the spiritual world of eternity is constructed out of these two Divine Human *mental* substances that exist in God. Love and truth are mental atmospheres and states. They are also called spiritual atmospheres and states since what is of the "spirit" is of the mind.

209

Experiencing Regeneration

Hence the spiritual world of eternity, which is our afterlife, is the mental world, and each of us is born into that world and live in it forever.

There is nothing physical in the mind or pertaining to the mind. Hence there are no physical spaces or objects in the mind. Since there are no actual spaces or times in the mental world it is called the mental world of eternity. Eternity means that it is apart from physical time and space. *Since there is only one mental world in the human race, every human being is born in that same mental world.*

This means that the mind of each individual overlaps with the mind of every other individual and this overlaps with humanity's collective mental world, which may be called the *collective mind of the human race.*

The mental world is made out of the atmospheres and substances that surround the spiritual sun and fill everything in the created universe. Since these atmospheres and substances are spiritual and living it follows that the entire mental world is spiritual and living. Everything that exists in the mental world is organic and has an anatomical form, structure, and function. *You can see from this that the overall shape of the mental world is not round or spherical but is in the shape of the human body.*

The shape of the human mind is that of the human body. The outward body is an image in form of the mind that is within.

Therefore the mental world is in itself a complex of mental organs whose location relative to each other make a full human anatomy with all its external limbs and inner organs. *The mental world of the afterlife in eternity is in the form of the human body.*

In other words, the physical body that we see is a model or image of the spiritual body which is our mind. And since the individual mind is in the form of the human body it follows that the entire mental world is shaped in the form of a human, which may be called the Grand Human. In the perception of God the entire human race is integrated into one and is united by Him in this one Grand Human. God sees human beings not just as a collection of individuals but also as a "correspondence" or functional connection to the familiar anatomy of the human body. All spiritual societies in the afterlife are located relative to each other in some specific organ-location of the Grand Human, such as in the province of the brain, or the chest, or the skin, or the abdomen and its various parts.

If you know the anatomical or physiological functions of a body part you can deduce from those properties the mental character of the people in some spiritual society whose location you know. In the afterlife each of us feels pulled and attracted to seek and find a spiritual society to join where people share with us the same particular chief love that is in the personality. *A chief love is one that dominates all other loves in our personality structure.* Prior to regeneration people's chief loves in their endless variety originate and are sourced in self-love. This is due to mental inheritance of traits, or more accurately, of inherited connections with particular spiritual societies.

If we do not undergo regeneration we spend all of our life on earth reinforcing and deepening those selfish inherited loves. But if we undergo regeneration those hellish loves are silenced and replaced by a new will that contains spiritual loves such as mutual love, love of others as much as self, love of uses, love of good and truth for their own sake, and love of God more than anything.

After resuscitation we can all see other people's mind as their spiritual body. So whether you say "the mind" or "the spiritual body", it is the same.

The geographic map of the spiritual world of eternity is therefore an anatomical map of the individual mind.

The upper regions of the human mind are known as the heavens, while the lower regions are known as the hells. *Both heaven and hell are in every person's mind by anatomical construction and necessity.* While we still live on earth with a physical body we can experience living in alternation between heaven and hell when at one moment we are happy and peaceful and relaxed and in a good mood, and then something unexpected and bad happens or is heard, and all of a sudden we are in fear, anxiety, depression. Being in heaven is experiencing consciousness in the upper regions of the human mind, while being in hell is experiencing consciousness in the lower regions of the mind. This alternation ceases and becomes impossible after the two-day dying-resuscitation process that separates our spiritual body from our physical body, and as a result of which we become conscious in the afterlife of eternity. At that point we are spontaneously drawn by our chief love permanently into the heavenly or the hellish mental state. This will determine how our life will be experienced in eternity.

All people in the afterlife of eternity congregate into permanent spiritual communities formed on the basis of similarities of personality and especially of the chief love. If we arrive in the afterlife having undergone regeneration we are prepared to let go of any love that we still have that is not in harmony with our heavenly loves. All loves are organized into a physiological hierarchy that is arranged by the chief love and by which it manages all the sub-loves and their affections. Any love that is not compatible or harmonious with the chief love is silenced and deactivated from the personality. Heavenly loves are those that depend on loving others as much as self and loving God more than anything. Hellish loves are those that depend on loving self only, and loving others only for the sake of self. These are all selfish loves or varieties of the love of self. Loves that are not selfish cannot exist in this hierarchy where self is loved only. All bad traits in the human race originate in selfish love, which is to love self only.

This is an anatomical fact: *Those who are not learning and practicing to love others as much as self, and God more than anything, then it is not possible for them to be regenerated either in this life or the afterlife.*

Since we are born with the inherited tendency to love self more than others it is necessary that we undergo regeneration, an anatomical process by which this inherited evil is discarded and replaced by the love of others as much as self and the love of God more than self.

The process of regeneration must be voluntary and gradual since it is an organic physiological growth process that consists in changing our loves, which is a process that involves innumerable actions acting together. From birth till adulthood and through old age our mind goes through various growth stages that we experience as changes in consciousness. Prior to beginning regeneration we are immersed in natural consciousness that provides us with materialistic principles and ideas about the mind and the universe. But at rebirth when regeneration begins, our reasoning process begins to be based in ideas that are spiritual-natural and spiritual-rational, thus what belongs to the mind apart from the physical body and world. We then enter into a life of spiritual consciousness called heavenly life.

Experiencing Regeneration

There are three levels or regions of heavenly life in the upper zones of the human mind. Hence when we undergo regeneration, our awareness is elevated through these three stages of experiencing. The more we experience the intensity of love for others relative to self, the higher we rise in consciousness and functioning.

To love others as much as self is called *mutual love* or *spiritual love*. It involves being considerate of their needs and comforts more than of our own needs and comforts. This heavenly principle of interacting with others takes innumerable forms in our daily life in society, as for instance how we talk to people, whether with anger and intolerance, or with disrespect, deceit and the intent to exploit. Or whether we ridicule them mentally and esteem them lower than us. Or whether we destroy their reputation with gossip or whether we remain unaffected when they need our help and ask for support. Mutual love is to be affected by people's discomfort and suffering in such a way as to want to help them out. Mutual love also involves being happy for the good fortune of others and to always wish them well in our mind.

Moreover, mutual love and love of others must be enacted through spiritual principles. We do not love everyone the same way, which would not create a heavenly society. *We cannot and must not love the evil of others, but only whatever good that is in them.* To love only the good and the truth in anyone is to love God since all good and truth is from God and is God in the individual.

There are innumerable societies of people living in the heavenly zones of the afterlife. Each society specializes in a particular heavenly sub-love or affection that its inhabitants love more than any other society. Hence heaven is composed of as many societies as there are varieties of good loves, and this is endless. It is similar with the hells. To every heavenly society there is a hellish society that is its counterpart by correspondence and is the specific opposite in love and truth. Each spiritual society is shaped and integrated in the form of the human body. Since each love is unique, each society appears unique and distinct from all other societies. The people in each society therefore look like one another in the face and one can recognize a person's society from the face.

Experiencing Regeneration

People have voiced a distaste for the idea that *"if you believe in God you go to heaven after death and if you don't believe in God you go to hell"*. They object to this idea as unjust or unjustified and arbitrary. Why should it matter so much whether someone said "I believe" or not? Isn't the person more relevant? Some people are good and some are wicked. So if you say that the good go to heaven and the wicked to hell, that makes some sense. But to believe or not to believe, or to profess faith or be neutral, that should not be counted for either heaven or hell. This is an argument from natural consciousness.

This logic is the experiencing of natural consciousness, which does not see anything that is above itself, like the rational, the spiritual, the celestial, and the Divine. So to believe or not to believe seems not so much of importance to them as to be good vs. wicked. Now when we ascend to spiritual-rational consciousness we begin experiencing an entirely different perspective on what is *to believe*. There isn't just one kind of belief. There is spurious belief, which is to believe in something other than God, as for instance to pray to the "universe" and to believe that the universe is God. There is a false belief about God, which is to invent various interpretations of *Sacred Scripture* that are falsified truths. There is a true belief, also called *faith*, which is to believe what is true about God. The *New Testament* in the Bible specifies that a true belief is possible only to those are being regenerated by God. This means that they have acquired from *Sacred Scripture* or "*the Word*", spiritual truths about God and are using them to fight their old selfishness and arrogance by which they hated God.

Spiritual salvation is going from a doubt or hate of God in natural consciousness to a certainty and love of God in spiritual consciousness. The second is discretely higher which means that the highest of natural consciousness can never attain to the lowest of spiritual consciousness. There is zero overlap and no bridge in between. Only a radical change can bring about the spiritual ascension, as for instance a 180-degree turn from facing West to facing East, and from facing downward to facing upward. Think of how different your life would be if you always faced downward physically. You would be unaware of the visual life that everyone enjoys in interactions. You wouldn't see people's faces and expressions, and you wouldn't know what a house looks like, or a mountain, or the sun and moon. You wouldn't be able to talk about these things like everyone else does. Thus you would not be a normal or complete human being if you always looked downward.

Experiencing Regeneration

In natural consciousness we face downward to physicality, materialism, measurement, quantity. There is no sense of cause and end of any of these things and events around us. They are one-dimensional observations, effects correlated with other effects not knowing why. In spiritual consciousness there is a perception and understanding of the why of things, thus of cause and end within the effect.

Spiritual consciousness provides the experiencing of rational faith, which is theistic psychology. This provides the life of mutual love and social uses in collective community living.

You can now see how it is meant to say that believing in God gives eternal life. True belief or rational faith is meant. There is no salvation for anyone without undergoing regeneration of character from selfish to mutual love. Passive belief in truths, or verbal declarations of loyalty to them, do not provide anyone the ability to be regenerated. *But true belief in which there is determination to live accordingly does enable regeneration, thus salvation and a life in heaven.*

Note: An eyewitness report of life in heaven and hell is presented in the Appendix at the end of the book.

Living in a Spiritual Society in the Afterlife

Living in the afterlife is more fully *collective* than what we are used to here on earth.

This makes sense when you consider that the afterlife is a mental world and therefore can be shared with others more fully than living in the physical world.

First, only similitudes can live together as a community and society. This means that the individuals are affected in the same way by specific conditions. God inflows fully and in the same way into every human being and into every spiritual society. But it is the uniqueness of the individual and of the society that determines how the Divine inflow will be anatomically received and processed, and therefore how the people involved respond, react, and are affected.

Second, there is a full sharing *directly* of all affections and their thoughts, which does not occur in earthly societies. Here we share by communication, either face-to-face or online. *But in the afterlife world we are online with each other all the time and everywhere.* This is due to the anatomical spreading of the substance of people's thoughts and emotions outward from the individual's spiritual body to the surrounding atmosphere. This living mental substance is then received from inflow by all who are mentally near to each other in that society. Everyone there is affected or influenced by this reception. *There is therefore a constant renewal of sharing of thoughts and affections moment by moment when you live in a spiritual society.*

Third, there is a synchrony and harmony of breathing in all spiritual societies of the afterlife. Every individual's breathing pattern spontaneously matches everyone else's in that society. Our breathing pattern relates to the experiencing of thoughts and ideas.

Fourth, there is the instantiation of surroundings in appearance due to being similitudes. In the mental world whatever is felt or thought shows outwardly following the laws of correspondence that is built in from creation between inner and outer things. Similar thoughts and reactions results in the appearance of collective living surroundings coming spontaneously into existence, such as mountains, fields, streets, houses and their contents. These are real appearances in that the objects are solid and endure as long as similar thoughts and feelings persist in the individuals of a society.

After resuscitation people are spontaneously drawn to follow certain roads and paths that no one can see except those who are directed to their own permanent society. When they enter their city and society they meet the inhabitants and they feel like it is a homecoming. *At last everyone is like oneself in feeling, thought, and act.* There is a perfect compatibility and the harmony that follows feels like a sudden mental enrichment. Everyone's memories and experiences are mutually shared so that each person is greatly enriched by all the others. Furthermore, emotions and moods ripple through the community back and forth so that the inhabitants' mood and happiness is greatly enhanced by the contentment and happiness of all others.

The chief love that is shared by all heavenly societies is conjugial love.

Every heavenly society is populated by conjugial couples only.

This agrees with the ultimate goal God has in creating the universe and the human race, which is that there be an endless increase in the population of heaven where each individual is kept in maximum happiness all the time. Conjugial love flows out of the spiritual sun into the entire universe, first in the mental world of eternity where are heaven and hell, and after that into the physical world of planets and stars. In human minds conjugial love flows into the feelings of couples and activates them to love each other, to become parents, to love their children, to raise them and protect them until they become adults ready to be regenerated and to enter heaven in the afterlife. This sphere of outgoing conjugial love affects all animals and activates them to engage in reproduction and the preservation of their species as created. The sphere of conjugial love also affects plants and gives them the power to grow and reproduce.

People may wonder about their conjugial spouse in heaven. Do we meet here on earth or in the afterlife? What if my current spouse and I don't get along or even get divorced. Will we have to be together in the afterlife? What if I've been married to more than one spouse? Etc. All these questions can be answered by gaining more knowledge about the afterlife. For now, know that marriages on earth are either natural or spiritual. Couples in which both partners are regenerating form a spiritual marriage and gradually grow into one mind. From two minds they each will to become one mind by enmeshing their lives in every way and removing from themselves disagreements and competitions. These partners will be together in heaven regardless of when each passes on.

Couples remain natural when the partners are not each undergoing their regeneration. When they pass on they will not be conjugial partners in heaven. The partner who is willing to undergo or continue regeneration does this independently of the other and when ready, meets another partner who is mentally compatible. They fall in love and form a permanent conjugial couple in one of the many eternal heavens. But the partner who is unwilling to undergo or continue regeneration, undergoes continued physiological preparation for life in one of the infernal societies of the lower regions of the mental world called the hells. Everyone there loves themselves more than others and despises God. They are compelled to live as couples in infernal "concubinnage" in which the partners loathe each other.

Unless we live in some spiritual society we have no life at all. Since your birth your spiritual body has lived among other people in the afterlife who are no longer connected to their physical body. This anatomical connection to them is absolutely necessary without which we cannot have one thought, or one sensation. *This is a universal fact of the creation of the human race, namely that we are all interconnected by anatomical fibers by which we share our lives.*

Every unique individual is born not for self but for others in this web of human beings. Every individual's unique characteristics contribute some special use to all other societies and individuals in the afterlife. *Every thought, reasoning, idea, emotion, feeling, intention, pleasure – in short, what makes our daily lives, is communicated by these anatomical fibers to everyone else in the human race.*

This may be better understood if you think of how our physical body is completely integrated as one integral functioning unit. If I eat something the digested nutritious components are extracted and delivered everywhere as they are needed in organs, cells, and fibers. If any part of this integral system is malfunctioning and is separated from the rest, it immediately devolves and is expelled from the body, no longer a part of it. No individual body part can exist unless it is connected to the whole. Similarly no thought or feeling can exist in a person if cut off or separated from the rest of humanity. *No one can feel, think, or act except from others.*

Thus it is that your thinking and feeling moment-by-moment is the result of the activation of your spiritual body by this shared communication and connection with all others in a society.

Which spiritual societies in heaven and hell that we are connected to moment-by-moment is determined entirely by God. During every moment of our life on earth God is arranging events in our daily activities in such a way that each event may be an opportunity for regeneration for that

Experiencing Regeneration

person. We are regenerated by mental activity, when we reject in our mind our desire to love self more than others in everything that we feel, think, plan, and intend. To succeed in this lifelong progressive daily effort, we need God to show us the hidden love from which we make the effort, whether love of self or love of others. By maintaining an active daily reciprocal relationship with God we are enlightened by Him as to when we act from love of self and when from love of others.

If we try to do this by ourselves, without God, working on ourselves to become a better person, we will continue to experience the daily plagues of humankind such as anger, resentment, anxiety, self-justification, discontentment, unhealth, unlove, cruelty and deceit. Despite being born with this basic selfish nature human beings are maintained by God in a mental equilibrium of evil that is balanced by good in our mind. Each moment God connects us with particular heavenly societies that love the opposite of the hellish societies to which we are also connected.

Consider the case where you suddenly have the desire to cheat in some competitive or restrictive situation. You might be tempted to explain and define the situation in such a way that you are justified to cheat. Since you possess the love of *winning-even-by-cheating*, you feel compelled to do so in this situation as long as you think that you can get away with it. You cannot exercise your free will. God therefore instantly connects you to a society of heaven where there is a strong love for being honest and straight in this kind of human situation and dilemma. Now you are in freedom because your willpower is in equilibrium being pulled equally in two directions.

This technique of Divine psychotherapy works only to the extent that we maintain a love for doing the right thing because it is what God commands and desires from us. This is the situation in experiencing regeneration. God brings us into some spiritual temptation by arranging the events of our day, and makes sure that we stay in affective equilibrium while we are being tempted. Then He waits for us to make the decision. The instant we decide, He supplies the willpower behind it. If we decide in favor of others, we gain another positive trait in our personality arsenal. If we decide for self, we are tied closer to a selfish habit. In one case we climb closer to heaven, in the other we slide closer to hell. Our final decision will not be made until after the two-day dying-resuscitation process. *But that decision cannot be any other than the habits we've practiced until then.*

Life in one of the hellish societies consists of a continuous non-stop devolution of the human mind. The longer people live there the deeper they sink anatomically into cruel excesses and insane fantasies. *You should know that it is possible for anyone in hell to exit from that state at any time they wish.* Hence we cannot think of this as God's awful punishment for people's sins. They are free to go up to the heavenly regions in their mind where they can join all the other inhabitants already there. God gives them this power, and also constantly urges them to use it. But they constantly refuse.

This is because their entire life has consisted of hellish loves and pleasures. If you removed their hellish loves, which is required for raising the mind to heaven, they would feel nothing living left in them, and would experience themselves as dead, which is a worse hell than before. This is why God does not force them to leave hell but arranges things there to reduce their misery as much as they are willing, and to mitigate and reduce the ferociousness of the savagery with which they treat one another.

About Sin, Confession, and Repentance

The expressions sin, confession, and repentance are religious ideas. These terms are not used in theistic psychology because they are defined in different ways according to the doctrines of each religion. Theistic psychology is based on anatomical and universal concepts rather cultural and local. *Sacred Scripture* in the historical-religious sense defines sin as thinking and acting contrary to God and God's order. Many things are identified that are contrary to God, all of which originate in loving self-alone in our interactions with others. This negative mental state leads to the breaking of all the Commandments of God and of all the laws of the land.

It's important to understand how loving self more than others is the same as loving self-alone.

Loving is an anatomical operation or activity that is going on in our spiritual body. Anatomical fibers are actually extended and interlaced with what is being loved. If we love others as much as self we are anatomically

220

Experiencing Regeneration

intertwined, and as a love-group we receive additional goods or spiritual heat that we can share and thereby enrich each other's experiencing. *Hence by loving others we are mentally enriched with new intelligence and new loves or motives.* But if we love self only we are not connected by love to others and we do not form a love-group with them. We receive nothing from God that can nourish our intellect and emotional maturity.

This mental impoverishment from loving self only is called "sin" in *Sacred Scripture* and we are warned that sin leads to death, by which is meant the inability to progress in love and intelligence, thus in humanity. In the afterlife, this inability relegates the experiencing of the individual to the lowest regions of the human mind, which is called hell. Hence God warns us in many places in the historical narrative of *Sacred Scripture* that we must "repent", which refers to the experiencing of regeneration.

Repentance is a change of heart motivated by our spiritual conscience.

In this new or "reborn" mental state we are able to receive from God the as-of self power to follow through the change of heart by suppressing the self-love that rears its head in all our interactions with others.

When we stop loving our self more than others we move on to loving others as much as self.

This is a totally new mental state, with new powers and truths that are now received through the new anatomical fibers that binds each of us to our love-group.

To love self some of the time, and to show consideration for others at other times, is not yet to love others as much as self.

The issue is independent of the proportion or statistical ratio involved between our good deeds and our bad or selfish acts and thoughts. This is because our acts of apparent consideration towards others are not done for their sake but for the sake of self. We can show consideration for others when we see in it some benefit to self. Still we do not cross the line of loving others as much as self. This love for others must be in everything we do with others. *We cannot make exceptions, for then what we do is never done for the love of others.*

221

"Confession" is also a religious idea, like sin. In theistic psychology there is the process of acknowledging to self one's selfish motive in some act or intention. This involves self-witnessing and the awareness of experiencing through metanoid self-observation. *We need to witness ourselves being selfish and react against it by spiritual conscience.* This is the anatomical operation that is involved in confession and repentance. Acknowledgment or confession without self-witnessing is abstract and ineffective, also called "confessing with the lips only", so that no new power to change is received from God. Hence the selfishness continues and devolves to worse and worse levels of operation, binding the person more and more deeply to the hell societies from which it will be very difficult to give up afterwards in the afterlife.

Experiencing Our Daydreams and Interior Dialog

Daydreaming and interior dialoging are useful windows to the soul, as it were, that God provides in our experiencing, so that we may come to know the hierarchy of our inner loves.

Our personality is an organized and integrated anatomical structure that gives coherence to each person's daily living and biography. Our personality structure adds to itself all new perceptions and meanings that we take in, minute by minute every day and night. The personality of the individual is an organized organic hierarchical structure that contains three types of function, use, or operation. These are:

(1) the *sensations* that we experience with the *sensorimotor* anatomical system of our spiritual body;
(2) the *thoughts* and images that come into our *cognitive* anatomical system of which we become aware and store in our memory;
(3) the *feelings* and perceptions that are activated in our *affective* anatomical system by the inflow of spiritual substances from God's mind.

The changes in our personality that take place in experiencing regeneration must therefore occur simultaneously in all three anatomical systems.

Experiencing Regeneration

Without this joint physiological action, regeneration cannot progress. For instance, if I learn or perceive a new spiritual truth that is not incorporated into my personality, then there is a gain in my memory and knowledge but not in my regeneration. First as always, we must learn or perceive the new spiritual information. Once we do, the immediate next step is to practice that new spiritual truth with our threefold self on the daily round of activities. This "doing" now stamps-in the spiritual truth, which means that it becomes permanently attached to a spiritual good or love. Now it is an integral part of our personality.

There are two categories of "doing", namely external and internal. Doing externally is a social act witnessed by others. Doing internally is private act that is invisible to witnesses and bystanders. For example, saying to someone "*Hi, fancy meeting you here. I'm glad to see you. How have you been?*" may be accompanied in our interior dialog by "*Oh, no! Here is that guy again. I hate having to talk to him. I don't like him.*" The exterior and interior talk is contrastive and incompatible.

Monitor your interior dialog while you are engaged in some routine activity, or while you are in the company of certain people.

If your thinking were to be broadcast publicly around the room would you be embarrassed, ashamed, annoyed, proud? Would the others be surprised, scandalized, reproving? What we are saying to ourselves in interior dialog is an inner speech act and all speech acts by definition constitute "doing". For instance, an overt behavioral speech act would be to say to someone in a conversation, "*I don't agree with your idea.*" This is called disagreeing with someone, which is an overt act or doing. It has various social consequences. On the other hand you would be performing an interior mental speech act when you say to yourself, "*I love the way that looks*" or "*I'm sick and tired of this.*"

By saying things to yourself you are actually consummating an inner love through a mental speech act.

Loves can be consummated by either an overt act or an interior act. For instance, if I am pleased that someone sent me a greeting card, I am consummating a love for being acknowledged by particular others. This is an inner love that is not always visible to the person. Instead it may be recognized in the act of consummation of that love, either as a mental interior act or a social external one.

When a love is consummated it is appropriated, that is, integrated permanently into our personality. It will be there in the afterlife.

Our daydreams are actually interior acts or performances of dramatic imaginings that can be of short or long duration, in which we picture scenes that express some inner involvement or love. This picturing is plastic or organic: not just a flat television screen with superb audio, but also with the smells, feelings, tastes, pleasures, fears, etc., that lie in the entertainment that we enjoy and experience in daydreaming. Daydreams and dreams differ only in wakefulness of conscious thought: dreams feel like real; daydreams feel like short trips to another mental state, another part of ourselves that is equally real and conscious.

Unlike dreams, daydreams don't need to be analyzed symbolically since we are witnessing daydreams live and can see consciously into them. In daydreams there is no veiled over symbolism to hide the obviousness of our selfishness, our unchastity, our immorality, our grossness, and so on. *While dreams are covered up, daydreams are naked.*

In daydreams we can see in clear light what is the content of our hidden affections.
Knowing the content of our affections offers a high vantage point on ourselves. We are in the position to judge. As for instance when we say to ourselves privately some of these things:

This was not nice. That was selfish. This is meritorious. That is unfair. This is lazy. That is fatalistic. This is a cop out. That is a hidden striving for revenge. This is the right thing to do. That is the good thing to do. This is what generosity dictates That is the guide of righteousness. This is most wonderful. That is holy.

And so on; we make judgments on our daydreams, our flashbacks, our flash-forwards, our expectations, our planning, our interpretations, our justifications, presentations, role enactments, and so on. *In self-witnessing we want to judge them all as to the affections contained in them, whether or not they are in keeping with heavenly loves.*

Experiencing Regeneration

All this self-judging activity is the experiencing of regeneration. This is what activates the growth of our spiritual consciousness. It consists of the effort of shunning our own evils because they are contrary to life in heaven and contrary to God's love. Judging ourselves is the process of salvation that equips our personality for living in the afterlife.

When we examine the nature of our daydreams for the purpose of judging them, we gain a new beneficial perspective on ourselves and on society. We notice that every daydream has an external surface content and an inner motive. The external content is dramatic: things happen, feelings and emotions are experienced. In this external content, the daydream is like a TV docudrama, or an autobiographical book. Historical and personal events, opinions, and emotions occur. People are characters in our daydreams, outcomes are altered, and alternatives happen.

In the internal of the daydream we can notice what's behind the events that we are imagining, namely why are they occur. By considering the issue we can understand rationally why we are putting that particular content into the daydream. Consequently we can get a good look at our longings, our strivings, our loves, our real purposes, our intimate affections, the delights of our enjoyments, in short, the real character of our spiritual state.

By seeing and perceiving our loves in our daydreams we are presented with our temptations, and hence opportunities for spiritual growth.

The spiritual societies in the afterlife are closely involved with our daydreams. They are sub-consciously affected by the content and affect of our daydreams. When our daydream is contrary to the mutual love and conjugial chastity of heaven, our spiritual self is being in communication with evil societies who, not knowing why, suddenly experience a new freedom and delight for their evil machinations and pleasures. This new delight is from our daydream. They do not see us; or even know of us; they live in their own fantasies and hells, yet unbeknownst to them, the daydreams *we* have correspond to momentous events in their lives and environment.

As we contemplate or enact in our daydreams such things as hatred, revenge, untruth, or unchastity, thus is their fate suddenly aggrandized;

thus do they experience a new field for their endeavors; thus are they empowered to enjoy themselves in selfish and hurtful ways. Unbeknownst to us, and unbeknownst to them, our daydreams and their daily experiencing are interconnected. It is the *vertical community* to which our daydreams are windows, and in which we can see the concreteness of spiritual life. Spiritual life is here now, real, concrete, immortal, eternal, holy.

When we are experiencing sincerity and innocence in our attitude toward the holiness of *Sacred Scripture*, the societies of heaven draw near our mind and see, in the spiritual sense of the verses that we read, all sorts of marvelous secrets that delight them. In turn, they can communicate their delight and wisdom to us through our rational ideas and the deep delight we feel when seeing clearly rational truths and principles. Those are states of spiritual vision, understanding, perception and feeling. By reading *Sacred Scripture* and applying its spiritual order to our daily social transactions and to our daydreams, we enter into regular conjunction and communication with the people of heaven who are within the affectional sphere of our spiritual body. Thereupon we experience a new life, a new creativity, a new opportunity.

Daydreams change in content and motive in accordance with the level of our consciousness. In natural consciousness daydreams reveal our natural temptations. In spiritual consciousness daydreams reveal our spiritual temptations.

Daydreaming is a type of spiritual flashback in our biography.

It is our will that composes and directs all scenes by means of our intelligence and knowledge. Motives get expressed through events in the daydream to which we react. In this sequence we can trace back the motive, the love associated with the intention behind the daydream and which gets fulfilled in it. In the fulfillment of our loves in the events of the daydream we experience the emotional and sensuous delights of fulfilled strivings, of consummated desires finding their end and resting point in the events of the daydream. There is peace in the resolution of a daydream -- either genuine peace or adulterated peace.

Discourse-Thinking
and Talking to Yourself

Mental life is our life. We have no other life.

There is nothing living in the physical body, which is incapable of sensing and feeling. Many people believe that when they experience the sensation of being touched that it is the physical body through which they sense the touch. This is only an outward appearance and not what is actually happening. The sensation of the touch is experienced through our spiritual body, which is made of the same substance as the sensation, namely mental substance.

Mental substance is more suitable than physical matter for the experiencing of sensations. Nevertheless, the physical body does play an influence on the sensation that we are experiencing in the spiritual body. The effect is to greatly dampen, constrict, and reduce the sensation in which it is involved. This is because the information of the sensory input is in the form of electro-chemical impulses. These are material and what is material is gross and imperfect in comparison to what is mental or spiritual. As a result, after resuscitation we for the first time, can experience being touched without the intermediary of the physical body so that no feature of the sensation is being absorbed and constricted. You will then be able to confirm by experience how superior and greater is the pleasure of being touched in the spiritual body.

Everything in the spiritual body is superior to the physical body by a discrete degree, which means that the best sensation and delight that we can have through the physical body does not even come close to the least of a sensation in the spiritual body. This is awesome to contemplate! It applies to both pleasant and unpleasant sensations, so that pain and hurt are as much intensified as are and pleasure and ecstasy.

The truth is that all of our life is in the spiritual body and nothing of our life is in the physical body.

When you practice daily self-witnessing one of the first things you notice is that our life is mental. Everything of our life and love that seems to involve physical things, like eating food, driving a car, talking to a friend, playing a

Experiencing Regeneration

game, listening to music, looking at the sunrise, etc., is not at all in the physical objects but in the mental activity in which we are while we use those physical objects. *Human life is mental life from beginning to end.*

Our mental life is always active, rich in happenings, and plays a critical role in our experiencing regeneration. Self-witnessing our mental surrounds instructs us concerning the character of our threefold-self. Monitoring our thoughts provides us with a window into the hidden feelings that trigger and direct those thoughts. *These hidden feelings are our actual loves in which our very life consists.*

Every single thought, idea, and image in our thinking is brought into existence by some hidden love deep in our personality. That love is in charge of what we are thinking or not thinking. This relationship is built into the anatomy of our spiritual body. You can see this primacy of love over thinking by considering the corresponding relationship between the heart and the lungs in the body. The heart through its vast circulatory system spreads out the blood throughout the body and pumps it into every organ, nourishing its cells. The heart nourishes the lungs and its system extending into the throat and mouth cavities. The functioning and health of our breathing system is dependent on the quality of the action of the heart and its circulatory operations. You can see from this actual correspondence that the affective system of the spiritual body is primary and initiates and directs our cognitive operations.

The blood circulation system of the physical body corresponds to the affective system of the spiritual body, and its respiratory system corresponds to the cognitive. These two systems must work together and be in synchrony.

Our loves reside and have their life in the affective system of the spiritual body. In other words, the will is primary in the mind and is our very life. We love what we will and we will what we love. The loves in our will are to be regenerated because from inheritance they are anatomically connected to the societies that live in the lower regions of our mind, which overlaps with the mental world of every individual. The mental world is not in space or place, but in states. Those who are in compatible mental states overlap with each other and are actually mentally together. We do not see this communal collective environment until we are separated from the physical body. Until then our consciousness is restricted to the material things that

228

are in time and space, and prevents us from seeing what is not in time and place.

Everyone has the ability from birth to ascend in consciousness from that inherited lower region to the upper region of the mental world. The lower regions of the mind are immersed in the anatomical sphere of natural consciousness, and this is the experiencing of hell. The upper regions of the mind are immersed in the anatomical sphere of spiritual consciousness, and this is the experiencing of heaven. Experiencing regeneration brings us to this ascension in consciousness and the consequent elevation in our loves and thoughts.

Viewed anatomically loves do not actually reside in our mind but in the mind of the spiritual societies to which God connects us throughout our regeneration process. When we speak of "inherited loves" we actually mean "inherited connections" to particular spiritual societies. By connecting and disconnecting our mind to this or that spiritual society, God is managing the inflow of the type of love that is active in our will, from where it directs our thoughts and actions. These inherited connections are made inoperative by our victories in spiritual temptations during regeneration. This makes room in our will for new loves, new thoughts, and a new life that is heavenly and spiritual.

Our ability to become aware of our loves develops at a slower pace than our ability to be aware of our thoughts. The primary factors that move us in all our activities in life remain hidden in the background and unreached by our self-observations.
This is why it is important to monitor our thoughts for the purpose of discovering the loves that create and maintain them.

In general our thinking goes on in several types of discourse that you can observe. The most commonly occurring types of discourse thinking are (a) monologue; (b) dialog; (c) rehearsals; and (d) venting. Perhaps you can discover new types through the self-observations of your experiencing.

Mental Monologues

We use interior monologing when we are debunking a subject that concerns us. It is a kind of role-play enactment in which we talk as if to an audience and explain the situation in all its details, attempting to clarify and explain the reasons why this is happening. The stream of discourse thought is in regular language and expression. It seems to issue spontaneously and enter into our awareness. As we become aware of what the stream of thought is saying we react to it. This is the critical point. In other words, we are instructed and enlightened in our understanding of the subject that our stream of thought spontaneously produces.

This is surprising because ordinarily we think of the stream of thought as issuing from our understanding, and this could perhaps instruct or enlighten others but us. But it is clear that the facts indicate otherwise. We are enlightened and instructed by the content of spontaneous thinking. In actuality this is probably how we learn almost anything. Remember that the stream of our discourse thinking in mental monologue is created, initiated, activated, and directed by our hidden loves.

Our loves have the power and wisdom from God to create discourse thinking that enlightens our spiritual understanding.

This observation has far reaching implications in many departments of living. Perhaps it can form the basis of a new approach to instruction in schools.

Interior Dialog

When experiencing mental dialog we gain an understanding of a subject or concern by processing the meaning through alternating dialectical points. We may express this dialog out loud as well. In that case, one of its forms is the familiar "He says, She says" alternating pattern when reporting a dialog with someone else. We use this alternating pattern frequently when engaged in self-dialog or arguing with oneself what to conclude about something. We are enlightened from this type of mental discourse because the dialectic of alternating turns at talk produces spontaneous statements that contain new information that we have not considered before. Self-witnessing our interior dialog not only improves our understanding but may also reveal the activity of hidden loves.

A type of interior dialog that is of critical importance to our regeneration is dialog with God. When we take our turn and talk to God we engage in the usual types of speech acts, which include expressing appreciation and thankfulness, voicing questions and dilemmas, asking for advice, or reminiscing and sharing. There is no overt voicing of God's talking-turns in these dialogues with Him. There is the experiencing of direct enlightenment regarding the issue. This may be sudden or gradual.

Dialog with God is holy and is always accompanied by inner relief, reassurance, and calm, even peace.

Some people may think of dialog with God as "meditation", reflection, or contemplation. In the *New Testament* there is an instruction or commandment stating this: "*When you pray, go into your inner chamber, close your door and pray to your Father who is in secret, and your Father who sees what is done in secret will reward you*" (*Matthew* 6:6).

When viewed anatomically our mind may be compared to a "chamber" which has an inner or upper part and a lower or outer part. What is inner or higher is always more advanced in perfection than what is lower and outward. "*When you pray*" refers to dialog with God. "*Go into your inner chamber*" refers to ascending to spiritual consciousness. In other words, when we dialog with God we are elevated in consciousness. "*Close your door*" refers to excluding from dialog with God all our self-collected treasures from natural consciousness that we value highly prior to experiencing regeneration. "*To pray in secret*" refers to maintaining a reciprocal relationship with God. "*Your Father will reward you*" refers to the reception and increase of spiritual consciousness with its heavenly happiness and intelligence.

Rehearsals

Mental rehearsals involve replaying a single event several times in an attempt to improve it.

For instance you might be contemplating asking a woman for a date. You can go over many times in your mind what you're going to say and how. Or you might be in the process of writing an email to someone. You write it mentally over and over again changing the wording many times before you feel it is ready for typing. A common type of mental rehearsal involves scheduling things, making and changing plans, or having mental conversations with someone not present.

Self-witnessing your daily rehearsals will give you information about the loves that direct your rehearsals. Why are you trying to improve the wording of this or that? What is it you are trying to achieve or avoid? What makes you alter a previous plan? By inquiring into the reasons for which you are doing the rehearsal you can become more aware of the loves that sub-consciously or automatically activate you in daily living.

In general, becoming more aware of our daily mental activity facilitates the progress of our regeneration.

Venting

Mental venting refers to the activity of building a case against someone for being guilty by offending you.

Self-witness your mental activity while you are driving in traffic and a near-miss incident happens with another car. For minutes afterward, and sometimes for hours and even days, there is a strong desire or love for venting your emotions against that other driver. Examine these emotions and the thoughts that go with them. In many cases these are negative or hellish. Drivers who do intense mental venting think all sorts of derogatory and disrespectful things about the other drivers. Some even fantasize violence and mayhem to make the other pay for his "stupidity" and inconsiderateness. There is also the feeling of wanting to let him know how you feel. You can vent about it privately in your mind or publicly with all who would listen.

You recognize the situation where someone indignantly says, *"How dare they be so disrespectful to me."* This is the beginning of the venting process. Observe your thoughts and emotions next few times you are doing *the venting enactment*, either private or public. What are the loves that impel you to feel indignant and to want to retaliate and even punish? Do you approve of such loves? Can you give them up as useless and harmful, bringing you nothing that's good?

To enact feeling offended by someone's insult or inconsiderate act is a pattern of conduct that we acquire in childhood. When deciding to stop using that mode of enactment you can begin to perceive that "feeling offended" is a hellish mental state. It is good to be caring and trying not to offend anyone, but if someone's behavior offends us, we cannot consummate that hellish love by legitimizing in our mind that the offense was personal against you. The person enacting the "offending conduct" against you, is not in fact acting against you but against themselves. They are playing the monkey, and so they are a monkey. It is an illusion to think that there is an offense against you, your ego, your face, your reputation, your honor.

But these considerations change when the offense is in the category of doing physical damage, such as vandalizing your property or passing around libelous information against you or your business. In that case it is justified for you to use all the legal means to redress your losses.

The Unregenerate Natural Mind Rejects Spiritual Truths

If we read this book mostly or entirely in natural consciousness one experiences not only resistance and rejection but also anger and disparagement.

This is because prior to regeneration our consciousness faces downwards or outward towards the world. The natural mind is not only born selfish from parental inheritance but also acquires its own collection of selfish traits and enjoyments, all of which will be inherited by the mind of one's offspring. Put it all together and you can see that the natural mind is immersed in thinking and doing things for the sake of self only. Sometimes people justify this self-focused attitude as necessary for "survival". In that case our entire life as we know it is therefore threatened when we hear about spiritual truths such as those discussed in this book. The experience involves feeling that the joy of life is being withdrawn for the sake of some fantasy idea.

This is why it is necessary to initiate and maintain a reciprocal relationship with God. One can do this simply by realizing rationally that the life of selfishness is not required by survival in a competitive world with scarce resources. It is a false argument. The contrary is clearly the case. If you remove selfishness you remove negative competitiveness. Consider a society of mutual love in which people consider the needs and rights of others as much as their own. This society survives and provides its members with confidence, safety, justice, and peace.

Experiencing Regeneration

This positive actuality is not seen by the natural mind. Real actuality is above natural consciousness. In matters of consciousness, from a higher level you can look down in the mind and see what is going on there, but when you look up from below you only see darkness. To natural consciousness the truths of spiritual consciousness are dark or non-existent.

Selfish love will not allow the consciousness of spiritual truths. This is an anatomical effect.

And yet it is possible for natural consciousness to be partially enlightened, and thus to be gradually enlightened more and more, so that the spiritual mind can have immediate communication with the natural mind. In that mental state we enjoy spiritual consciousness in daily life. This is the spiritually infilled natural mind that has successfully undergone the beginnings of regeneration. It is our life of heaven on earth, which gives us inner contentment, peace of mind, and full confidence in God.

Experiencing this inner heavenly mental state is continuous and is independent of the ups and downs of the external events that befall us in our day-to-day living.

The Spiritually Infilled Natural Mind

Our higher spiritual mind can "descend" and be active within our natural mind.

This anatomical event results in the greater enlightenment of the natural mind. We are conscious of new perceptions and realizations around us and in our lives. Anatomically there takes place a reversal in the direction of coiling of the fibers in the spiritual body from clockwise twists to counter-clockwise. Practicing selfish loves and thoughts create spiritual fibers that coil from right to left and downward thus making up tight resistive bundles in the spiritual body. But when the spiritual mind becomes directly involved in the management of the natural mind, our experiencing is that of mental pain and distress. There is much mental pain attendant to reshaping of the anatomical fibers from selfish love to mutual love.

Few people want to do this and to endure all this mental distress for the sake of some supposed future life. Within the natural mind there is resistance to the activity of the spiritual mind. And yet mutual love must replace selfish love for the sake of avoiding an afterlife of hell and for the sake of gaining eternal happiness in heaven. As soon as our rational thinking sees this, and agrees with it, a massive mental clean up takes place in the natural mind. It is only possible to achieve this within the context of a reciprocal relationship with God who provides for the removal and deactivation of all our loves that we obtained prior to our regeneration.

All regeneration progresses by enduring temptations, first natural temptations and then spiritual temptations.

Why We Must Engage in Spiritual Combat and Temptations

All mental life is organic and anatomical.

This is a definition to which we need to come back again and again in our focus. It contains the secret to many spiritual truths that puzzle people.

Growth and maturity of organic structures like cells and fibers in the body, take place gradually and by various intermediate stages of development. The substances and molecules that are needed in the spiritual body for mental growth are present plentifully in the atmosphere of the mental world, from which they flow into the receptors of the spiritual body. This is similar to the way in which heat and light from the natural sun flow into the receptors of plants on earth, nourish them and provide them with energy. Mental substances from the spiritual sun in the mental world flow into our organs of the will (affective system) and understanding (cognitive system) and give these organ-systems what they need for operation, survival and growth.

Mental food is acquired by our mind from the surrounding atmospheres in the mental world. These are then incorporated by the organs of our spiritual body when the affective system (or the will) acts together with the cognitive system (or the understanding). Doing something from the will and the understanding together is the condition for appropriation or ingestion of mental food. No human being can survive without mental food coming to us as a continuous moment-by-moment supply-line, just like the physical body cannot survive without oxygen in the lungs (corresponding to the cognitive system) and a heartbeat (corresponding to the affective system).

Everyone experiences hunger through our connection to the physical body, which when it is fed, replaces the unpleasant and painful hunger sensations with pleasure, satisfaction, and contentment. Hence it makes sense to think of the spiritual body as also experiencing hunger, which is satisfied when some new knowledge, feeling, or sensation enters our awareness. There is pleasure and longing in this life for hearing "news" about our friends and the world, and in acquiring information and knowledge about many subjects. This pleasure and longing is greatly magnified in the afterlife where the need and longing for mental food become more acute, and consequently also its pleasure in ingestion or appropriation and subsequent use in one's life and personality.

Regeneration begins in adult life when the individual begins to think independently about what kind of life is desired or wanted for oneself. This includes what to believe about God and the afterlife, what lifestyle to practice, what things to avoid, what things to strive for, whom to respect. In general the easiest road and the one that seems to be filled with more interest and enjoyment is to continue practicing what was inherited from family and learned in upbringing and interaction with friends and the culture of peers.

This results in the mind being immersed in natural consciousness and the selfish unloving society.

This personality phase of early unregenerate adulthood combines with the preceding years to construct a personality that is filled with selfish, self-centered, and hypocritical routines of thinking and intending involving other people.

For instance, we get angry and revengeful against people who fail to favor us over others. We enjoy cruel gossip about others whom we don't like, which hurts their reputation without true cause. We promise things that we know we will not do or feel. We take unfair advantage of others when we can justify it. We hate what is different from us and what we consider our own. We desire to discriminate unjustly on that basis. We fake outward sincerity in religion in order to impress, though we reject it in our own thinking and intending.

These negative affective and cognitive activities operate in the spiritual body through the construction of anatomical fibers that grow from right to left and downward, thus gyrating counterclockwise. Their practice and repetition produce tight bundles of these fibers running down counterclockwise. Now in order to learn new habits of sincerity, compassion, considerateness, justice, and forgiveness, new fibers need to be laid down from left to right going upwards in a clockwise direction. This can be done only to the extent that the counterclockwise downward fibers are first suppressed and rendered inactive in the personality.

The only way that this anatomical suppression can succeed is through victory in spiritual temptations.

Spiritual combat or warfare refers to the experiencing of spiritual temptations.

God brings spiritual temptations to the individual only when the person has gathered enough spiritual truths in the understanding and spiritual goods in the will to be able to overcome the temptation in victory. One's spiritual conscience has to be already active before spiritual temptations can be experienced. Until then God restricts the individual to natural temptations that require the growth of a natural conscience. This includes learning and understanding what is immoral, what is rational, what is fair, what is compassionate. To the extent that these are practiced in daily thinking and doing, to that extent the natural conscience grows and deepens, providing a beacon of guidance to everyday interactions.

God brings temptations by connecting the individual to spiritual societies from both the hellish and the heavenly regions of the mental world.

This ambivalence achieves a balance in the person's willing and thinking so that there is complete freedom as to whether to follow the falsities of the evil societies or the truths of the heavenly societies. The individual wanting to undergo regeneration must therefore already possess some spiritual goods and truths by which one can be conjoined to the heavenly societies.

The first and foremost of all spiritual truths is contained in the daily reciprocal relationship that we initiate and maintain with God.

In spiritual temptations there is a battle to the death between natural consciousness and spiritual consciousness, each wanting to gain dominion over the other.

Our natural consciousness acts to resist the developing spiritual consciousness because our natural mind is bound by inheritance to the hell societies while our spiritual mind is bound to heavenly societies, bonds that may also have been inherited. This conflict between the societies from above and below is experienced as spiritual temptation.

Those who allow themselves to be prepared for regeneration and ultimately heaven experience victory in temptation. This means that our spiritual consciousness has achieved dominion over our natural consciousness. But for those who do not allow themselves to be regenerated by God it is the spiritual consciousness that loses and the natural consciousness that obtains dominion over the person's awareness of experiencing.

Spiritual temptations are experienced within one's spiritual conscience where a battle seems to be taking place. This situation is experienced as anxiety and despair from an unknown cause. The experiencing of the anxiety and distress is acute and that is what we are most aware of. But if we allow our awareness to focus at a deeper experiencing we can become aware that the desire to be good flowing in from God into our will seeks out what spiritual truths we may know that would align themselves with that desire for being good in that situation. These truths provide justifications for avoiding the bad and following the good.

In all spiritual warfare only the spiritual consciousness knows that what we are experiencing flows in from the evil societies. To our natural consciousness there is only the awareness that all our feelings and thoughts originate from our own mind, and it rejects the spiritual truth that they flow in from other minds in the afterlife. Instruction from theistic psychology and *Sacred Scripture* brings awareness of spiritual things to our spiritual consciousness. This is not available to our natural consciousness. People who remain in natural consciousness are not capable of believing or understanding that our mental life originates and is activated by our associations with spiritual societies in the afterlife.

To remain in natural consciousness is to be deprived of freedom to entertain what the senses cannot detect. It is to be stuck in the misleading appearances of materialistic thinking.

If we are not regenerated through temptations we cannot be separated from falsified truths that we have come to believe in our natural consciousness. Truth by itself is not capable of seeing whether it is genuine truth or falsified. But when good flows in it gives life and light to truth so that we can tell from conscience whether some truth is genuine or false. When inflowing good draws near to falsities in our mind we experience anxiety, fear, distress, and torment. We desire to root out these falsities in our mind. They can be removed by God only through the experiencing of temptations by which we reject as-of self the falsities in our mind. When we reject them, God can remove them.

Prior to beginning our regeneration God brings natural temptations to us in order that we might strengthen our natural conscience. For instance, we might be tempted in our loyalty to the Ten Commandments by being exposed to situations where we can be dishonest, adulterous, or envious. Our natural conscience fights against these "lapses" and attempts to keep us within the bounds of the commandments through fears of punishment or retaliation from those who are victimized by our dishonesty, cheating, or bad will towards others. These are external threats that come to us from other people or the law of the land. They threaten our physical welfare, safety, comfort, wealth, rights, honor, and reputation. When we resist in these temptations in natural consciousness we are motivated by the safety and gain to self.

Spiritual consciousness on the other hand is aware that the commandments have an inner spiritual significance, not merely natural. This means that they also apply to our spiritual conscience, which is not concerned with physical safety and rewards but with spiritual gain in our understanding and feeling.

Don't Let Your Dog Poop
on the Neighbor's Lawn

Here are examples of how the *three-step technique* with the threefold-self can assist you in managing the many spiritual temptations that will come your way when undergoing regeneration.

Consider as one example the common situation of walking your dog every day. Consider what might be a spiritually proper way of handling the situation. In terms of natural conscience the practice is accepted everywhere that you are to pick up immediately after your dog poops on the street or on the grass of someone's front lawn. Dog walkers are seen to carry home the plastic bags containing what was picked up. Millions of people in most neighborhoods follow this procedure. There are more than 50 million dogs in US households.

When you are regenerating and undergoing spiritual temptations this practice is felt immediately as inadequate. One is struck by the thought: *"What gives me the right to trespass on a neighbor's lawn and property by allowing my dog to walk on it and to smear it with urine and feces. Even if picked up the smear on the grass brings flies and it's disgusting when owners want to sit on their front lawn."*

Step 1: I *acknowledge* that it's spiritually wrong to allow my dog to poop on a neighbor's lawn, even if I pick it up immediately.

Feeling: It's an awful thing to do even if it is allowed by common practice. I don't like it when a dog comes on my lawn. So I feel bad allowing myself to do this to others. I don't want to be a hypocrite.

Step 2: I *witness* what I do and how it happens.

Thinking: What are my options? I can wait till the dog goes in my back yard then take him for the walk. This however will not eliminate urinating or "marking". I can walk the dog on the street rather than on the sidewalk. The leash will restrict the dog to the public pavement where few pedestrians walk and fewer still want to sit on. I can still pick up and it won't be affecting the neighbors directly.

Step 3: I *modify* my behavior accordingly.

Doing: I walk the dog on a leash restricting him to the street and avoiding people's private lawns.

Use Headphones
When Watching Television

Millions of people watch television daily for several hours. You have experienced yourself what it's like to be annoyed, inconvenienced, and disturbed by other people's television sounds coming to your ear in your own apartment or house. Natural conscience sets some limits on how loud you can make it, especially in the evening after most neighbors go to bed. But within these limits TV noise from a neighbor or family member in one's own house must be endured and is acceptable according to normal practice in the community.

But in spiritual consciousness our moral dictates are different. Even though we stay within normative bounds of loudness we are still imposing on neighbors.

Step 1: I *acknowledge* that it's spiritually wrong for me to be uncaring and to ignore my neighbor's distress due to the noise I am making.

Feeling: I cannot remain uncaring to the perception that they are bothered by the TV noise. How can I love myself only and not love them also? I feel terrible. Guilty. I cannot just go on.

Step 2: I *witness* what I do and how it happens.

Thinking: I don't need to stop watching TV. I do have an option, which is to use headphones. Good ones cost a chunk of money but it's well worth it given that they help me solve this deep spiritual problem.

Step 3: I *modify* my behavior accordingly.

Experiencing Regeneration

Doing: I buy suitable headphones and wear them all the time when I watch TV.

This process of overcoming spiritual temptations is to be applied to other situations where I create noise when others are affected by it. For example, using my cell phone in public or in waiting rooms. As well, I do not allow gardeners and handy workers to use their noisy machines on my property before 8 AM or after 5 PM. Similarly when our children or grandchildren are playing in the pool or on the lawn, I monitor their noise making which tends to be excessive and bothersome to neighbors.

Born Into Eternity

Not many people know that human beings are born with two bodies, one physical and the other spiritual.

The two bodies are necessary because our mind and its mental states of feelings and thoughts cannot exist and function in a physical body. Mental operations such as sensations, emotions, thoughts, feelings, and loves must have a mental body within which to exist, operate, and develop. *This mental body is also called the spiritual body.* On the third day after the death of the physical body we awaken in our spiritual body.

We then realize that our mind is immortal and that death was only a separation of our mind from the physical world.

At this point we make an amazing discovery: that there are other people present in their spiritual body and we can interact with each other, talk and touch, and have social relationships as before. The spiritual body looks exactly like the physical body so that people who knew us on earth before they died can recognize us and we them.

Every human being is born into dual citizenship in two distinct worlds. Our mind with its mental activity such as emotions, feelings, sensations, and thoughts, operates solely in the spiritual body. There can be no feelings or thoughts in the physical body, which contains only things that are material, chemical, and electrical and there is nothing material in mental sensations, feelings and thoughts. At birth our spiritual body and our physical body cooperate and function together seamlessly and unconsciously. *However,*

Experiencing Regeneration

our mental development and personality goes on solely in our spiritual body. When we die, the physical body is separated and becomes a decomposing corpse, but our spiritual body containing our mind and personality is immortal and continues to develop in the afterlife of eternity.

You might question or doubt these assertions and anatomical descriptions of our two bodies and of our mental immortality in the afterlife. This doubt comes from the experiencing of *natural consciousness* in which we are raised and enculturated. This perspective reduces and flattens mental states into physical space, chemistry and electricity. It denies the existence of mind as "real". In natural consciousness we are trained to reject the idea of "dualism" or two worlds, as well as the ideas of heaven, hell, and God. Even when we accept God and the afterlife when we are in natural consciousness we do so through a naturalistic perspective that defines spiritual ideas in a natural context. For instance, instead of an afterlife in a separate world of eternity with an immortal spiritual body, natural consciousness fabricates a materialistic afterlife on earth with our physical bodies. It regards the idea of heaven and hell as a decision God makes on the basis of favoritism, special status, merit, compensation, covenant, etc. These are all mentioned in the historical sense of *Sacred Scripture*.

Experiencing spiritual ideas of dualism in spiritual consciousness is different from experiencing them in natural consciousness alone. This higher experiencing is received within the natural consciousness, which thus is greatly enriched and our life goes from natural to spiritual. In spiritual consciousness we can perceive the truth of these assertions about God and the afterlife, and we can easily assent to them with joy and gladness. For now you may want to put the doubt in your mind to some comfortable distance so that you give yourself the opportunity to hear more of the reasons and explanations about spiritual reality and the potential benefits you can derive from them. For now let us continue to explore these spiritual ideas.

One type of experiencing is natural and another type is spiritual. Hence we have a natural consciousness and a spiritual consciousness, just like we have a natural conscience and a spiritual conscience. Each depends on influx or inflow but of a different type. Our natural consciousness is produced by the awareness of physical influx or stimulation and the physical body's reaction or adaptation to the influx. For instance, when a

243

hot object is brought in proximity to our skin, the organ of the skin reacts to the heat and we become aware of this purely physical reaction and its movement. Our natural consciousness allows us to notice and monitor the physical body's operation, as well as to think and reason about these physical stimuli. This natural consciousness allows us to function and survive in the physical environment. *We thus have two types of rational thinking, one that is natural-rational and the other that is spiritual-rational.*

In order to function in the mental environment of our spiritual body we need the operation of our spiritual-rational consciousness, which gives us awareness and reasoning ability of the kind that allows us to survive in the spiritual environment of the afterlife. For example, in our spiritual environment we need to make decisions about what is right vs. wrong, good vs. evil, moral vs. immoral, selfish vs. other-directed. These decisions require spiritual influx into our spiritual conscience. This influx is constantly present and inflowing.

Spiritual influx consists of spiritual heat and spiritual light flowing in from the spiritual and mental environment and atmospheres that are present around the spiritual body. This spiritual influx activates in our spiritual body the mental organ called conscience, which reacts to the spiritual influx. We are aware of this mental reaction and this awareness provides our spiritual-rational consciousness. For instance, when people borrow a neighbor's tool it often happens that they don't return it right away. When reflecting upon this situation our natural conscience detects an influx that produces a "conscience pang" or emotional pain of regret. At the same time a spiritual-rational understanding is also aroused by which we can see that it is wrong to not return the borrowed tool even if the neighbor forgot about it, or at least, never mentions it. The same applies with borrowing money from a friend who never asks for it back.

And there are many more common everyday examples of such things where we become aware of the operation of our conscience. The experiencing of conscience is unique to human beings and defines our species. Through conscience we can regenerate and be conjoined to God. This conjunction provides us with immortality and eternal happiness.

And so getting back to the question asked at the outset, what makes us truly human, we can see that it is our spiritual consciousness that is produced by conscience in response to spiritual influx of what is good and right, and what is spiritually true vs. false. These ideas will be encountered again and again later in the book so that they will become familiar and easy to you.

If the method of spiritual experiencing works for you, it will change your life for the better. The power to switch from feeling bad and being bad to that of feeling good and being good is available to you.

What is the relationship between "feeling good" and "being positive"? Similarly, what is the relationship between "feeling bad" and "being negative"?

Most human beings in this and previous generations on this earth seem to have suffered more than they were happy. Suffering, pain, and a hard life seem much more common than happiness and creativity, which seem difficult to attain. At the same time being bad seems much easier than being good. If we just let ourselves go where our emotions take us we become a menace to all around us. This is called being bad. In general doing bad things involves the experiencing of selfishness in all our interactions. When we love only ourselves the reserve of bad traits and emotions gush to the fore and take over our personality. People will then experience us as angry, resentful, rude, deceitful, dishonest, uncooperative, dangerous, violent, and internally we are spiritually insane and full of excesses and fantasies.

This is the person we all are – to begin with. We are born animalistic but with the possibility of becoming truly human. This is the state of being good. It involves loving others as much as self and God more than anything. In that state others will experience us kind, generous, compassionate, harmless, cooperative, helpful, respectful of God, and full of good will. In this state we are prosocial, altruistic, and useful to specific others and to society as a whole. We can become good through the process of regeneration, which is the as-of self effort of repressing the bad in oneself and practicing the good that is offered to us by God.

You will notice a connection between being good and feeling positive on the one hand, and being bad and feeling negative on the other. Being bad refers to what we think and what we do to others that harms them and harms community life and survival. Being bad includes being harmful to self and one's ability to be healthy and successful. In natural

245

consciousness we have been taught to be skeptics and relativists regarding what is good and bad. Materialist science courses in our education have infused into our thinking the idea that good and bad are relative as indicated by the fact that different people and cultures define these differently. One kind of behavior that is openly practiced in one society is taboo in another. Further, the confusion between religion and God gives teachers and leaders license to extinguish in people the idea of God-defined good and bad. So now when you hear that good people go to heaven and bad people to hell you might feel skeptical and the idea may occur in your mind that truth and good are relative hence how can you decide who is good and going to heaven vs. who is bad and going to hell.

But when you extricate yourself from the morass of materialist thinking you can clearly perceive that God created all things into an order of truth and good, and therefore anything that departs from this order is in disorder, and therefore hellish. Further, you would realize that since God's goal in creation is to promote a universal heaven out of the human race, everything that is in order promotes this goal and is therefore good, and anything that does not promote it is in disorder and is therefore bad. If you adopt a relativist position on good and bad you are in fact rejecting the idea of God and the order of reality. You are then in a mental state called spiritual insanity. In that case the consequences for you are serious and tragic. This book will help you avoid that eternal trap and its suffering.

From a rational perspective you can confirm that relativism in what is good promotes the destruction of the human race. Why this is so needs to be understood rationally before it can be believed. Take for instance the case of people who are neglectful of their oral hygiene and do not compel themselves to floss their teeth and gums each day. This is a problem I have been struggling with over the years. Does this make me a bad person and will I be going to hell for this crime? Let us look more closely at the issue. What exactly is the crime or the bad behavior in this instance? There is of course negligence involved in not taking appropriate care of what is my duty in keeping healthy. My teeth will suffer, and so will I as a result. *But the spiritual problem is more specific and mental, namely, that I condone this negligence.*

This is the bad behavior: to condone one's negligence. In point of fact, since I can remember I have always struggled to overcome my negligence in oral care. I have not condoned it. Therefore my negligence and my struggle against it is part of my experiencing regeneration.

Now take another example. Since most people are raised in a climate of religious practice, they are faced as they become adults with the decision to obey these practices or not. Are they being bad for breaking the religious rules of conduct that they have been taught? For instance, I've been raised in a Jewish orthodox family and I was taught that I am a Godless and wicked person if I deliberately break the rules of the Sabbath that forbid engaging in weekly work activities, and this includes other observances such as the requirement to fast on the Day of Atonement. The *Old Testament* of the Bible specifies that such a person shall be cut off from his people and should be stoned to death. Am I really going to hell for breaking the Sabbath?

Everyone must make this type of decision on their own terms and understanding. Simply adhering to a practice without being convinced of its being right and good, is not effective in our regeneration, which depends on voluntary decision according to one's rational understanding. Here I have to figure out whether working on the Sabbath is something that I do for the sake of myself only or for the sake of others as well as myself. The primary principle to keep in mind is that being bad or good is not a determination made on the basis of breaking or following some cultural or religious rules. The absolute and universal definition of good and bad ought to be used since this applies to all from God. And this is that good is anything that is compatible with heavenly life and in general this involves loving others as much as self and God more than anything. And bad is defined as loving self only. *All decisions about being good or bad must follow from this one basic rule or principle.*

Hence I conclude that my working on the Sabbath is for the sake of accomplishing things that are useful to others and society and therefore it must be good. Similarly, if I don't work on the Sabbath because of the religious rule, it does not make it to be something good since I may be observant for a the sake of myself only, that I may obtain the rewards thereof, and this constitutes meritoriousness, which is evil.

Spiritual Consciousness
Requires Being Good

It is not possible to be enlightened by God when we are in the experiencing of being bad, like getting angry with someone who does not properly honor us or favor us, or intending to defraud someone or some government agency. *Being bad is the experiencing of natural consciousness.* Can our consciousness be raised when we are overweight or fail to properly floss every day? If we fail to floss or exercise properly because we are being irrational about health style consequences, then we are locked into natural consciousness. *Being bad always locks us into the lowest form of human consciousness.*

Consciousness is the awareness of experiencing. Therefore such as is the quality of our awareness, such is our consciousness.

It is important to realize that the issue of what constitutes good and bad is basically an anatomical issue. Being bad involves actual connectivity to some hell societies in the afterlife, and being good involves being connected to heavenly societies. Not-flossing, not-exercising, or overeating, are bad habits that become possible only if our spiritual body is connected by God with some particular hellish society that specializes in self-indulgence even if it harms our ability to be useful to others. God waits at the door of our mind until we are ready to commit to resist this self-indulgent love on account of it being contrary to our regeneration, contrary to heaven, and contrary to God.

Elevation of our consciousness from natural to spiritual is done by God. To effect this anatomical change God waits until we are ready to do it as-of self for the sake of others, consequently for the sake of being good. *Consciousness raising depends on being good.* We cannot have our consciousness elevated while we are being bad. I have often wondered when I see acclaimed leaders in politics, science, and business mess up their private lives through adultery, promiscuity, alcoholism, being overweight and leading a health poor lifestyle. How can they appear so inventive, productive, intelligent, and patriotic, I asked myself, and still be bad in so many departments of personal life? Today I can see that their usefulness to others and society does not come from their own efforts and intentions but from God who is managing every person's actions and thoughts to bring out uses for society.

Sometimes people want to "balance" the bad things done through good things done. One might think: Well, he is not so bad since he also does a lot of good, so his bad should not be able to condemn him, given all the good he also does. This type of thinking is immersed in natural consciousness. Again it is necessary to think of the issue anatomically. *If one is tied to both hell and heaven one is neither in heaven nor in hell.* But such an ambivalent state cannot last. Sooner or later the person must give up one or the other connection or else all the positive is destroyed and all the negative remains. If a person has been practicing negative habits along with the positive, the negative must be given up as-of self, and this no one can do without experiencing regeneration.

The universal psychological principle therefore is this: If you want to feel good, be positive. If you want to stop feeling bad, stop being negative.

Does this mean that people who suffer from some neurosis connected to past abuse are being bad people? The answer is that feeling negative and being selfish involve the experiencing of being anatomically connected to hell societies in the afterlife. We can exit from this immersion in hell only by regeneration in accordance with the orderly and prescribed anatomical procedures that this involves, as will be explained throughout this book.

What about people who are good and have a tragic accident or are attacked? Does that mean that they did something bad and that's why the accident or attack befell them? The answer is, No. Bad things can happen to good people because being good is a spiritual activity while being attacked or having an accident is a natural event. Experiencing regeneration does not automatically protect us from having to face tragic events in our natural life on earth. It's different after resuscitation when we live in the afterlife of eternity where nothing bad can ever happen to people who are good, and they remain happy forever in heaven. But people who are bad in the afterlife encounter all sorts of further tragic events in their spiritual community in hell.

Feeling good is a spiritual activity. Being good is a spiritual activity. The two are connected as spiritual activities. Similarly, feeling bad is a spiritual activity. Being bad is a spiritual activity. The two are connected as spiritual activities.

This book will clarify for you what you need to do in order to feel good and to be good. The method of experiencing is based on the anatomical facts of theistic psychology, which have been extracted from *Sacred Scripture*. Your mind is an organ like a plant, actually connected by fibers to the organs of those who are already in heaven and in hell in the afterlife. God maintains us in this equilibrium in the inflowing loves in order to allow us to make free choices in our daily lives, rejecting the bad as of self and adopting the good. This process of anatomical regeneration is completely effective and allows us to prepare our mind for the afterlife. The choice will be ours, to choose a happy conjugial life in heaven with like-minded others, or an unhappy infernal life in hell with like-minded others.

Now is the time when this all-important choice can be secured forever. Let the spiritual adventure begin!

The Anatomical Definition of Good and Bad

This book challenges you with many new ideas that come to the mind only when we are elevated to a higher mental functioning called spiritual consciousness. As you find out about these spiritual ideas you can experience the resistance that your natural consciousness puts up against them. Natural consciousness opposes and hates spiritual consciousness because the higher mode of mental functioning puts an end to the lower mode of functioning. As your ideas become more and more spiritual, the natural ideas will vanish into the background and may even disappear from your view. This is the cause of the resistance you may be experiencing. However this resistance will move away from your focus as long as you love the new spiritual ideas. Without this love the resistance will stay.

To love the new spiritual ideas means that they affect you in some way. You hear it, and you feel delighted. That is an affection. Or, you hear it and you feel intrigued, wondering, wanting to hear more. That too counts as being affected.

With this in mind let us review how we define good and truth and in what way are these "anatomical" definitions rather than being someone's judgment or opinion. Is there really a basis for a universal definition of good and truth that applies to all human beings given that it is an "anatomical definition"? We will consider good and truth together for reason to be seen presently.

We need to explain what is "good" or "truth" and how they apply to a person's feeling, thinking, or doing. A natural idea of what is "good" or "true" focuses on a judgment someone makes, e.g., *"This is a good corkscrew"* or *"They are liars and no truth comes out of their mouths."* Good and true appear to be judgments that someone makes about someone else or thing. Going above this level of thinking requires that we acknowledge that there are two realms, one natural and the other spiritual. For example, the physical body is natural or material, but the spiritual body or mind is non-material or mental.

So we need to add this new idea that some real things are not material. For instance, your thoughts are not material. They are mental. So are your sensations, your feelings, and your awareness. *Now if these mental things are real they exist on their own independently of the physical things.* This also means that real mental things must exist in a real mental world since they cannot exist in a physical world. Hence we conclude that there is a mental world as there is a physical world.

Going further, if there is a real mental world in which our mind lives then we must have a body in that world that allows us to see and hear, talk and interact, walk and build. Our body in the mental world is called the spiritual body. You can also call it the mental body, but this strikes many people as odd. So we will stick to the expression our spiritual body.

So when we are born we acquire a permanent spiritual body, which is our mind, and a temporary physical body that allows our mind to walk around and act in the physical world. At death the two-day dying-resuscitation process separates the two bodies and we awaken fully conscious in the immortal spiritual body with which we can explore and live in the mental world forever.

Experiencing Regeneration

So far these new definitions sound abstract because we need to introduce the idea of "*mental substance*" as the material that composes our spiritual body and all that is in it. This becomes clear when you realize that the mental world is created by the spiritual sun that shines there. Our natural sun created planet earth from the materials that are in the sun or star. These hot materials stream out of any star in all directions and create gravity, motion, space or ether, stardust, heat, and light. All materials on our planet are built from this dust, heat and light. The "heat" of the natural sun is actually made of hundreds of chemical elements like oxygen, nitrogen, or mercury.

Picture then the spiritual sun of the mental world in a corresponding manner to see it more clearly. What is that sun and where is it from? The fact is that the spiritual sun is the foundation of all creation and supplies all the building materials for the two worlds. The idea that God created the two worlds out of nothing is not rational since out of nothing, nothing can be created. The rational idea takes into account the fact that before creation went into effect there was only God, and therefore God had to supply the materials from Himself by which to build the two worlds. *The spiritual sun of the mental world of eternity is the initiation of creation and is God's first presence and exteriorizing appearance in the created universe.* Spiritual heat and spiritual light that are in the spiritual sun in infinite variety stream out into all directions and create suitable atmospheres that are filled with the substances needed to build things, whether galaxies of stars, planets with mountains, oceans, animals, or human minds.

So we have arrived at this so far: God creates the spiritual sun, which streams forth and fills the atmospheres and materials out of which the two worlds are built.

Now comes a more difficult idea to comprehend with natural reasoning, but is easy to understand with spiritual reasoning.

Spiritual heat from the spiritual sun is actually Divine Love-substance and spiritual light is actually Divine Truth-substance.

Everything in God is living, eternal, infinite, uncreate substance. If it flows out of the spiritual sun from God into creation, then that Divine substance

Experiencing Regeneration

is now in the created world, composing its space or atmospheres within which all objects exist in the two worlds. The first world to be created is the mental world of humankind. This mental world consists of the substances and atmospheres from the spiritual sun. In other words, the mental world of the human race is composed of Divine love or good, and Divine truth or intelligence. These are *living substances* because they are from God and therefore part of God. Whatever is part of God's substance remains God's and cannot be given away to human beings so that they may be theirs. But God's substance can inflow into human beings where it provides the powers of feeling, thinking, and sensing.

Once the mental world was created, the living substances of that world were "materialized" which means transformed into physical space, atmospheres, time, and matter. These objects of the physical world are not living but they are capable of responding to or being acted upon by living things. This means that the "dead" physical world is shaped and managed by the living mental world. Without this connection there would be chaos and no world. Everything in the natural world is created and managed or directed by what is in the mental world. God manages the physical world through the laws of correspondences that He built into creation. Mental principles, rules, order, and goals are therefore the directing intelligence of all planetary and plant evolution. God's intelligent purposes create and direct all things that occur in the physical world. He does this by the mediation of cause-effect laws built into the laws of correspondence between the mental and the physical.

The shape of the physical world is a sphere, but the shape of the mental world is that of the human body or anatomy. When we are born our spiritual body contains all our mental activity. This activity exists in the mental world that is shaped like the human body. In other words, our spiritual body is a miniature of the entire mental body. Your individual mind or spiritual body is born into the same mental world as mine or anybody else's. There is only one mental world created around the spiritual sun. Hence all individual minds are in the same mental world. But while we are still attached to the physical body our natural consciousness and the experiencing of its conscious awareness is restricted to the natural mind. This is the mind of our every day life and it is based on natural ideas, materialized thinking, not at all like the thinking of our spiritual mind, of which we are not conscious until after death.

Experiencing Regeneration

And so our consciousness while apparently living in this world is a purely natural consciousness composed of material ideas based on time, place, quantity, and measurement. We are not aware of our spiritual rational consciousness that is based on ideas of the mental world and not at all on the contingencies of the physical world. Hence from thinking naturally you are now in this book being challenged to think spiritually.

You can already see from all of the above that good and truth are living substances from the spiritual sun that stream into the mental atmospheres and fill every human mind that has already been born. But the quality and purity with which good and truth are received by any individual mind varies depending on the level of consciousness maintained by that individual's chosen loves. For instance, people who choose and are affected by mutual love and the love of God, experience a consciousness that has risen in the atmospheres of the mental world high into the region of the chest, neck, and head. In this spiritual heat and spiritual light they enjoy pure spiritual consciousness, which is far above the functioning of anything we can achieve in natural consciousness.

But if we choose loves that are selfish and self-oriented, therefore rejecting the love of others and God, then our consciousness sinks into the lower regions of the abdomen, legs, feet, and buttocks. As spiritual heat and light stream into the mind at that level there is a filtering and transforming of good and truth into what is their opposites. Thus, what is bad and false fills the mind and the experience. This is within our natural consciousness in which we are incapable of forming true judgments of what is true and good. At this lower level of functioning we call good what we love, and true what we believe.

Now it might make more sense to you when we discuss good and truth as anatomical substances that form our mind and consciousness, our thoughts, sensations, and all our feelings and personality. To love self only is mad and bad as it is in inverted order from actual reality. It brings misery to self and to others, creating hell in the human mind. But to love others as oneself and God more than anything is according to the rational order of the universe. Good with its truth makes us evolve and progress to ever greater experiencing, but when turned into what is bad and false we devolve and sicken ourselves with fantasy, insanity, cruelty, and hatred for all, and especially God.

Experiencing Regeneration

You can see that good and truth are objective anatomical constructs, not subjective or judgmental. If you fall through ice in a lake someone will have to pull you out or you quickly freeze to death. It's simply a matter of anatomy. It is the same with being good and being bad. God has created an anatomical order based on His own mental substances. This order brings health and progressive evolution for mind who stay within that order. But those who invert that order are destroyed by the built in order of the anatomical substances.

You can also see rationally that if God had not built this order into creation it would not have been possible, or it would have gone into disorder and consequent destruction soon after being created.

At this point the thought might occur to you that most people love themselves, but they also love others not just themselves. For instance parents love their children even if they are selfish and love themselves. Couples in love show evidence that they love each other even if they are also selfish. To this idea we need to add a new notion, namely, that parents who love their children, or citizens who love their country, may do so for the sake of self instead of for the sake of the children or the other citizens.

What makes any love selfish is that it has itself in regard, and everything else only in relation to self. Some people donate to charities for the sake of feeling righteous and merit, hoping for a reward of some sort or benefit to self. Sometimes people will inhibit bad behavior because they are protecting themselves from the consequences of being caught. If they believe that they can get away with it, people will stop donating to charities or to respect other people's belongings. If I do a good job hoping for a raise I'm doing it for my own sake and not for the sake of my boss. Doing this for oneself is not a bad thing, since maintaining a job is a good thing. But not doing my job when I can get away with it is a bad thing since I break trust and create disorder.

You can see that we need to examine what we do by looking at our threefold-self: what we are feeling as love or goal, what we are thinking as plan or reasoning, and what we are doing as act. In everything we do these three are always activated together. Outward act can proceed either from a selfish or an altruistic love or goal. Two people may act outwardly in comparable manner but one is acting from a selfish love or goal while the other is acting from an altruistic love or goal.

For instance, people may act justly and honestly with others in a situation because they are protecting their reputation and honor. Or, they may be looking for some reward or feeling of merit and worth. Or, they may be acting hypocritically in order to deceive. The outward deed of acting honestly and sincerely appears good but in fact is evil because it comes from a selfish love and goal. When self-gain or the danger of detection are removed the same people then act dishonestly and disrespectfully. This shows that all along they were acting selfishly, hence bad.

Those who act good may also do it for various good reasons. For instance they act honestly and justly with a companion from a love of being honest and just. This is not a selfish love. Others act honestly and sincerely because they are aware that God commands it in *Sacred Scripture*. This is not a selfish love. When an act is inwardly good, that is, done from the motive of mutual love and love of God, then it is good both outwardly and inwardly.

The Kingdom of God Is Within You:
Seven Words That Shook Up the Universe

Nothing is known about God in the science of psychology. The current position in all the sub-fields of psychology is that God cannot be used as a causative factor in psychological explanations of behavioral events. This stricture has been intensely enforced so that if you search the conventional literature in the currently recognized sciences the word God does not appear in any proposed theory or explanation. Some researchers report on what people think or believe about God and God's role in events. These are not studies of God but of people's religious attitudes and behaviors.

There is no method in psychology for studying God. The filed of psychology is sense-bound so that all its concepts and theories must apply to something overt that can be measured by observation or instrument. This has been psychology's position since it has considered itself as an objective science, which is about 100 years. God cannot be a theoretical or explanatory concept in psychology as long as psychology denies and rejects *dualism* because it is unscientific.

God and dualism cannot be researched in psychology because these imply that there are two worlds, the natural and the spiritual worlds. Since these two worlds are distinct and discrete it is not possible to mingle them or to go from one to the other. Precisely the same argument prevents psychology from researching the anatomy of the human mind. If you reject dualism then the word "anatomy" necessarily implies something physical. But if you think within dualism you are implying that the mind is a real object, not merely an "epiphenomenon" or "emergent activity" that is based in the physical body. With the mind being acknowledged as a "real thing" it is necessary to construct an anatomy of the mind in order to discuss it objectively and as it is.

Within dualism or dualist psychology, human beings are born with a physical body on earth and a spiritual body in the afterlife of eternity. The anatomy of the mind is the anatomy of the spiritual body. Spiritual anatomy explains that the mental world is anatomical and that every person exists in that collective anatomy. Further, that anatomy is connected to the anatomy of God. If you free psychologists from materialistic strictures they can construct a radically new psychology of self and its dependence and relationship to God. I expect dualist psychology to effective in ameliorating the lives of people on earth and in the afterlife. This book is an early instance of the new modern
theistic psychology.

Historically we can place the beginning of theistic psychology two thousand years ago. In the *New Testament* of the *Bible* there is the following amazing declaration:

"*Neither shall they say, Lo here! or, lo there! for, behold, the kingdom of God is within you.*" (Luke 17:21)

To appreciate the immense significance of this totally new scientific revelation we need to understand what it is actually referring to.

In the context of the verse and chapter it is made clear that "the kingdom of God" refers to heaven and the afterlife. Because people ordinarily think of heaven as a place, it is being specified here that it is not correct to think that heaven is "here" or "there" in some place that can be pointed to and seen. Rather, heaven is "within you". Other translations say "amidst of you".

In other words heaven is a mental state.

This is the beginning of theistic psychology. It puts forth the observation that there is an actual anatomical interlacing between God and every human being. God is not a distant Being who created the universe and human beings as disconnected objects from Himself. God is an integral or anatomical part of our mind, our body, and our world. If God were to withdraw Himself, or His anatomical parts from human beings and the world, nothing will be left standing or alive. This gives you an indication of how closely God's anatomical connection is to human beings. Personality development in an individual cannot occur by itself but must be activated, managed, and participated in by God. The psychology of self and personality that ignores this anatomical bond between our mind and God's mind, cannot come up with effective solutions to human and societal problems and dysfunction.

The new theistic psychology of self explicitly seeks to integrate what we know about the anatomy of God's mind and that of our mind. We know facts about God's mental anatomy from two sources: *Sacred Scripture* and our direct dialog with God. Both these approaches are applied in this book. The new theistic psychology of self and personality has one central focus, which is experiencing regeneration. Every individual's personality must be equipped with traits that are consistent with living in a heavenly community of mutual love and love to God. You can no doubt list the common psychological problems today: neuroticism, violence, depression, lack of energy and vitality, overweight, addiction, rebellion, criminality, dishonesty, combativeness, lack of motivation and focus, etc.

Non-theistic psychology has had limited success with these common problems. The new theistic psychology now has an opportunity to attack these problems in a new way by providing people with mental tools to fight these problems in oneself. People will now be able to take into account their future in afterlife as well as their condition now. This changes everything.

Experiencing Regeneration

As the *New Testament* verse quoted above declares, the expression "to go to heaven" is not a going to some place but a change in one's mental state, that is, in personality and in what we think, feel, say, and do. How do we get to heaven? By changing our mental state. There is a mental state that is called heaven and any human being can experience that mental state. It follows that "going to hell" is also getting into certain mental states. Heaven and hell are therefore certain types of mental states that actually exist in our mental world. The new theistic psychology begins with this anatomical fact.

This discovery has amazing consequences for our understanding of human beings and the created universe. *Since heaven and hell are in the afterlife it follows that the afterlife is a mental state!* Which finally brings us to the conclusion that human beings are immortal since they spend the afterlife in heaven or hell.

Another amazing conclusion is that the minds of people overlap within the same mental world, which may be called the mental world of eternity. This conclusion follows from the fact that heaven and hell in eternity are mental states in every person. *Since people congregate in heaven and hell it is clear that all human beings are in the same mental world.* It follows that after death each of us has interactional access to every other human being that ever lived since everyone comes into the same mental afterlife upon death.

These are awesome and amazing revelations that will shake up the world of science and psychology, once they are discovered and not automatically discarded as worthless for science. Since the anatomical revelation was made two thousand years ago, you can see what fantastic resistance there is in natural consciousness to considering spiritual facts, truths, and ideas. This resistance is reinforced and maintained by the cultural practice of teaching only materialistic science in public education and the complete elimination from discussion of God as a concept in school taught subjects. The result is this resistance to paying attention and legitimizing the spiritual truths of theistic science.

The justification for making God a taboo word in education and science is that by discussing God in school teachers may be tempted to express and even teach their religious views, which is forbidden by the Constitution of the United States. The authors of the Constitution were intent on the principle of separation of Church and State in order to make sure that government will never pass laws that interfere with religious freedom of expression and belief. There is no evidence that the Constitution framers intended to eliminate God from state and public schools. In fact all the evidence is to the contrary as God is mentioned in various places and on various occasions of official government business such as in Congress and in the judicial courts. To eliminate God from all discussion in science and in schools has deleterious consequences in putting pressure on the individual to stick with natural consciousness and give allegiance to materialistic science.

The new theistic psychology can help people realize the scientific nature of God and see God as quite independent of religion. This may have tremendous beneficial consequences for improving relationships among people across the world by weakening the focus on an exclusive cultural religious expression of God in favor of an inclusive universal scientific idea of God as being active in daily events and the individual's thoughts.

Choosing Between Heaven and Hell in Our Mind

From the perspective of mental anatomy, our chief loves and desires fall into two categories, one bad, selfish, evil, or hellish, and the other good, altruistic, and heavenly. These two types are love for the sake of self alone vs. love for the sake of self and others:

(A) love of anything for the sake of self alone

e.g., being selfish, egotistical, self-centered, disloyal, cruel, lacking compassion, domineering, hateful of God, of marriage, of children, and of heaven, deceptive, disruptive, inconsiderate, a danger to others, being cynical, pessimistic, avaricious, envious, deceitful, wanting to possess what belongs to others, being disrespectful of human rights, corrupting marriage and children, disruptive of law and order, discriminating against other groups, etc. This negative love and all its sub-loves create hell in the human mind.

Experiencing Regeneration

(B) love of anything <u>for the sake of others</u>

e.g., wanting to be effective, successful, useful, helpful, positive, popular, knowledgeable, happy, liked, considerate, loyal, sincere, supportive of law and order, wanting power in order to be of service to others and country, being frugal, powerful, rich, compassionate, generous, loyal, respectful of human rights, sincere, avoiding deception, protecting marriage and children, considerate towards strangers, supportive of a just and fair law and order, etc. This positive love and all its sub-loves create heaven in the human mind.

While we are still connected to the physical body we are practicing a mixture of both categories every day of our lives. People like to specialize in one of these categories, adopting its related traits as a daily personality habit. All our inherited tendencies are hard wired into our natural body, and the natural mind that is based on it.

Some people say that sex outside marriage is an "evil" of society. Others say that using drugs is evil. Some people say that you go to hell unless you pray and worship according to the instituted rules of a particular religion. Some people say that "looking out for your family no matter what" means that you are justified morally to hurt others who are in the way or get caught in the way. Some people believe that the ends justify the means, which includes hurting innocents. Some say that overeating and inconsiderate habits are cancelled out by good habits such as being loyal or hard working. Some think that if they don't act out their anger or lust or fantasy, they are not doing anything that is bad or evil. What about being lazy, or forgetful, or enjoying teasing others, or driving aggressively, or telling and laughing at salacious or "dirty" jokes? By whose authority or conviction are we to conduct ourselves? This is something that is critically relevant to you, to me, and to everybody on the globe.

The answer given here is to let the anatomy be the judge! A poisonous chemical substance will hurt your physical body, and a selfish mental substance will hurt your spiritual body. With spiritual consciousness you can acquire a rational understanding of how this process works, that is, the process of the growth, development, and health of our mental organs, with which we have life, experience, consciousness, rationality, and immortality. You can also understand the process of mental sickness that expresses itself in sub-human conduct destroying people and community, hence detrimental to survival. To call something we do or think "selfish" is not just name calling, or feeling guilty, or making a moral judgment. When we point to something selfish in what we do or think we are noting the injury it causes to our own mental future and that of others.

Many young adults begin to examine their socialized philosophy and approach to morality and lifestyle. All along as they were growing up they felt uncomfortable with many rules and regulations they did not believe in as good or right. Now as adults at last, they feel a new sense of choice.

People can look close or far, but sooner or later they begin to realize (1) that there is a God; and (2) that their own conscience and *Sacred Scripture* are two available guides to understanding what is good or evil, heavenly or hellish. A rational and consistent approach to understanding God in *Sacred Scripture* and in one's conscience provides us with the experiencing of God in dialogue any time any place. *This means developing a reciprocal relationship with God that acknowledges His continuous co-Presence in our mind.* The benefits of this approach are of incalculable value to us because they include happiness, love, and wisdom in this life, and the same greatly magnified, in the afterlife of eternity.

This may sound like a 'fairy tale', but you will decide whether it is that, or whether it is the amazing reality.

It should be noted that there is a sub-category for the love of self and world for the sake of self. Some loves are not good in themselves but they can serve a good function when temporarily active. For instance, you may love to fulfill your religious duty by giving ten percent of your income to charity, what some people call "tithing". This idea is based on the historical sense of *Sacred Scripture* where tithing is commanded. This kind of giving for charity because it is a religious duty is in itself not good since it is done for the sake of self or spiritual merit. Nevertheless it is compatible with the love of helping others because we are affected or moved by their need, which is a good love because it is for the sake of others.

At this point review in your mind what you already know and believe, namely that certain selfish traits cause the break up of relationships and of community life. These obviously selfish traits include murder or assault for gain, theft by deception, lying under oath or in a contract, molesting children, having an extra-marital affair, sex with minors, cruelty to animals, libelous talk, indecent exposure, conspiracy, etc. These are ordinary things people do for the sake of self. This is why every community or society must have a specified and expected external law and order governing people's overt behaviors and interactions with each other. This public order is enforced by police and security forces in order to prevent some people from dominating everybody else and turning them into their slaves or victims. What we do for the sake of self is destructive of community life and of family, victimizing innocents, unjust in treatment, irrational in reasoning -- in short, it is "hell." Doing things for the sake of self actually leads to the creation of a life in hell. This is the anatomical definition.

The cause of hell is the love of self for the sake of self, and the love of the world for the sake of self. Hell is the outcome of our depraved self. The self is depraved when it becomes the center of an individual's love. God creates and maintains the mental world of heaven in every person by giving the person a new self that is not depraved. This process of acquiring a new self or personality that is heavenly is called regeneration. Much of this book is about experiencing regeneration because it is the anatomical process of human growth and evolution.

What about heroes: can they be selfish? Heroes should receive honor and social acknowledgement for their heroism regardless of whether their patriotic acts were motivated selfishly or altruistically. This is true of all public offices and community officials. An individual's motive for doing what is commendable is not ordinarily questioned. The person who saved a child from being crushed by a falling object deserves the recognition and thankfulness of others even if the motive for saving the child was selfish.

Motives determine good and bad, yet they are in comparative obscurity of awareness. Hence *Sacred Scripture* declares that people are not to "judge" each other as to motives for only God knows the actual motive behind anything we do or say.

In the afterlife no one is punished for the evils done in this world.

However if evils were done by habit in this life they will also be done in the afterlife, unless the individual underwent regeneration. None of the evils done in this life are counted against those who are regenerated since they have repented and changed their life, ceasing to do those evils. But there

Experiencing Regeneration

is no repentance and amendment of life without undergoing regeneration and victory in spiritual temptations. *Without repentance and regeneration the evils done in this life are also done in the afterlife.* This is what gets punished. The punishment of evil is built into the doing of the evil. When the evils are done in the afterlife the punishment of evil follows and cannot be avoided. The punishment of evil is never far from the evil done and cannot be avoided except by repentance and regeneration.

Everyone is received into heaven after the two-day dying-resuscitation process. Some are able to advance all the way into one of the heavenly societies. Others are able to get to the threshold of one of the heavenly societies, but upon entering it, the sphere of life in that heaven penetrates the sphere of life of the individual creating a clash in the inmost of the person's mind and personality. To be unregenerate and in evils cause the spiritual body to grow its anatomical fibers counterclockwise and downward, which is the opposite of the fibers in a regenerated mind. This inner incompatibility is experienced by the person as being torn asunder with accompanying loss of all sensory input and awareness. When the visitors are experiencing this inner torture they instantly cast themselves headlong into the lower regions of the mental world where the hells are in their mind. Here they feel revived by the stench atmospheres of hell societies, and they continue life in that state without ever wanting to experience heaven again. But should they ever want to, the ability is given them to visit heaven again. *Hence entrance into heavenly life is never prohibited to anyone in the afterlife.*

For an unregenerate person to come near a heavenly society would be comparatively like throwing the gear in reverse while your car is cruising at 50 mph. Or it would be like a leaf falling into a dish that is filled with black engine oil. Or again, it would be like a moth flying near to a flame. You can see why those in hell remain there forever and do not venture out. This is not a cruel punishment by God but the reality of what happens when two things operating in opposition to each other come into contact. God in His mercy and compassion provides that these two human types in the afterlife, namely regenerate and unregenerate, be kept separate from each other and each living in their own compatible anatomical element. This Divine law reduces the misery of those in hell and protects the happiness of those in heaven.

Experiencing Regeneration

The misery of those in hell is not produced by God but by the people in that mental state. God continually is present in the inmost of their mind or soul, and supervises and manages every little detail of the events in their mind and in their daily lives with each other. It is not God who keeps them in hell forever. God did not invent the idea of an "eternal hell" which so many people attribute to God. People sometimes argue that, "*If God is omnipotent and loving He would be able to prevent the tragedy of people who are stuck in hell forever. God would find a way of getting them out.*" But thinking this way is a form of spiritual insanity.

In actuality, as a result of God's merciful management of the hells, the suffering of the people who choose to live in hell is mitigated and reduced, and they are constantly being held back by God from devolving even further and worsening in their cruelty and insanity. God does not anesthetize or take away completely all the evil and selfish loves that consume them, because this would be equivalent to removing their life altogether. This is because *our life is in our loves and to remove our loves is to remove our life.* Hence it is out of Divine Human mercy that God provides the unregenerate with habitations in hell and granting them to have a social life with each other, as otherwise they would have no life.

An example of this merciful administration is that the inhabitants of hell seem to each other to be in normal human appearance so that they may not get repulsed of each other and prevent social relationships. But when some light of heaven is allowed to shine into their habitations, their monstrous and deformed appearance becomes visible. Hence it is that in hell things are always in semi-darkness such as one gets from a fire of coal in a grotto.

This is the sense in which one can say that people's evils keep them out of heaven and not some punishing God, and also that in the afterlife no one gets punished for the evils they did in this life.

Another instance of God's awesome mercy and love for us is making our former pets on earth available to us in heaven! Since animals do not have mental structures such as we do, they are incapable of forming an idea of God and of having a reciprocal relationship with God. Hence their mind or spirit does not survive like ours after the death of the physical body. But God has provided that the laws of the mental world in heaven are such that our loves are empowered to re-create our pets in substantial or spiritual form. They are therefore real, touchable, and active. We can hug them and we can recognize their face, their voice, and their personality. Thus we are supremely delighted. These substantial pets are now forever with us since now there is nothing physical, material, or temporary about them.

This is actually a better solution than it would be if our pets survived and lived with us after our resuscitation. Our pets in that state would not be perfect and suitable for entering heaven with us. Think of your pets. They were wonderful and lovable and yet they did have traits we did not appreciate. Dogs bark when we don't want them to, disturbing us and our neighbors. They can have really gross habits of lack of hygiene. Cats pick fights with other cats, tear up carpets and furniture, and sometimes scratch their owners. We would not want our former natural pets with us in heaven. So when we enter heaven we would have to leave them behind outside, and what would then become of them. So God in His mercy and love for us has arranged that we may have our pets in heaven with us by removing from them all the hellish traits they had on earth.

Our Spiritual Enemy:
Doing Things For the Sake of Self Only

Suppose you work hard in school to get good grades so that you can get a good job and earn a decent income. Even though you are doing this for your benefit, you are not doing it for the sake of self only, but for the sake of others as well as for the sake of self. Your motive to earn a decent income does not benefit solely you. You perform skills that your employer needs. You earn a salary that you pay taxes on, and you spend your earnings on things you need or want, and this allows many others to have a business and a job. So working hard in order to get a good job to earn a decent income is a heavenly activity because it is useful to others, and not just to self. Contrast this with the situation in which you just want the income without having to put up the effort to gain the skills for that job. You are thinking of only yourself so you don't value the uses to others that come to them from your work skills. Or, if you get the job, you are not motivated to perform sufficiently well to benefit your employer and you pretend to do the minimum in order to not get fired. This is doing things for the sake of self only. It is an orientation received from the hell societies in our mind.

Experiencing Regeneration

When you take care of your health you are not doing something just for the sake of self but for the sake of self and others. As a healthy person you can benefit your partner, your family, your country. This is why when you neglect your own health you are acting selfishly and irresponsibly. It is from hell.

When you're nice to people for the sake of self only, you stop respecting them if they no longer favor you, cater to you, and honor you, becoming their enemy and wanting to bring injury to them or their reputation. But when you're nice to people for the sake of others as well as for self, then you will continue to respect them even when they don't favor you any more.

If you are using beaches and parks for the sake of self only, you will leave your empty cans and bags lying there when you depart, but if you are using these public facilities in a way that is for the sake of self as well as others, you will clean up after yourself when you leave.

Our inborn attachment to the love of self for the sake of self only is so enrooted that society has been unsuccessful in motivating people to stop acting selfishly, that is, doing things for the sake of self only. Hence come all the societal and personal problems that so many people have and are plagued by.

You need to examine yourself in your daily life settings to observe the kinds of thoughts and feelings with which you carry on routine activities. In natural consciousness there is an attraction for cultural and moral relativity so that there is disagreement about what is good vs. evil, or even, if evil really exists. But in spiritual consciousness, which is acquired from *Sacred Scripture* and from *conscience*, there is a clear-cut and specific definition of good vs. evil, namely, that good traits in your personality are those that give you the ability to live in heavenly societies, while evil traits are not compatible with living in heaven, but require you to live in of the hell societies. This is an objective and anatomical definition that is free from subjective evaluation systems and opinions. You can also call it a medical definition of good and evil. Personality traits that are compatible with heavenly living are those that support mutual love and love to God. We can enter such a society after death if we are willing to value mutual love and love to God as higher than self-love.

Experiencing Regeneration

But you can see that if we did not acquire heavenly compatible traits through habits of interacting with others on earth, we would not choose to enter a heavenly society since that type of life would not make us happy. The loves we have acquired as habit here on earth are the loves that will direct us to either a heavenly or a hellish society in the afterlife of eternity. We come into this eternity with our spiritual body on the third day after it is separated from the physical body.

When we are resuscitated and we awaken in our spiritual body in the afterlife, we lay off and discard any cultural and personality traits that we put on out of necessity to achieve social and economic success. We lay aside what can no longer serve us in the mental world of eternity, namely, our culture, our languages, our circle of friends, the organizations we belonged to, the memory of medals and awards that we gained, and everything else that relates to earthly concerns. We now are together collectively with everyone from our earth and whatever other earths in the universe that are inhabited by human beings. Everyone now spontaneously and without apparent awareness of it, speaks a universal thought-language that is spiritual and not natural.

People who have formed a habit of doing things for the sake of others and not just self, find themselves in the afterlife in beautiful heavenly surroundings and societies where people live together in gardens and cities, enjoying all their heavenly desires and feeling peace from all their former troubles that they discarded.

Shortly after resuscitation everyone is instructed in spiritual truths. These are necessary in order to open or operationalize fully the spiritual mind. Spiritual truths in the mental world of eternity are just as important as natural truths in the physical world. Those who come with the habit of loving self for the sake of self only reject that instruction and are unwilling to acquire them or even to think of them and figure them out, let alone to love them and see them as the true reality. And so they walk away from instruction and instead, pick up whatever ideas and principles agree with and support the traits they love more than anything. They hang on to these falsified truths, which allow them to enter the life dedicated exclusively to hellish enjoyments.

Experiencing Regeneration

With the above knowledge you can now see why it is so critical for us as adults to acquire spiritual truths from *Sacred Scripture* and conscience formed from it, so that we may apply relevant criteria in evaluating spiritually the traits by which we live. And this task would be impossible for us to achieve on our own because we love our hellish enjoyments and traits to such an extent that we even hide most of them from our self-monitoring or conscious evaluation. This is why it is necessary for God to manage this process of personality recovery, which is also called "salvation" through rebirth and regeneration.

Regeneration requires our willingness to cooperate with God in this recovery process.

We must be willing to face spiritual combat called "temptations" by using spiritual truths in our understanding to evaluate (or "judge") our own intentions and motivations, our thoughts and reasonings, and our overt activities. When we find something in ourselves that we analyze as being "hellish" or "not heavenly," we must then stop doing it for the reason that it is contrary to God and to our heavenly life in eternity. This is not easy. This is very difficult. So we must consciously talk to God and receive more courage and power. Gradually the difficulty decreases and we have a new outlook, new loves, new desires, new motives, new goals that keep us happy and peaceful, uncluttered, untroubled, and successful.

Consider a hobby you might have, like collecting little rocks or, climbing big rocks. Hobbies are considered to be something we do for ourselves. We are choosing to do this rather than that, to spend time and money on it. It is personal and represents our affection or love for that activity or involvement. But there are two ways of performing any hobby: for the sake of self only vs. for the sake of self and others. For example, some hobbies have risks associated with them, like flying, parachute jumping, driving, mountain climbing, surfing, playing contact sports, and so on. Even golf can be dangerous as some people can testify who dislocate a joint or injure their back while swinging the club. Some people get hit in the head by a golf ball.

So now what matters in the heaven vs. hell decision process is to consider the manner in which you perform your sport and exercise activities. When you perform the activity "for the sake of self only" (hellish motive) you are going to consider your desires and wants only. You might not be as careful as you need to be. You might take risks that you shouldn't. If you perform from the motive of doing it for the sake of self and others, you would not take those risks because you would be balancing what you want to do and how others will be affected if you get injured or if you pass on.

Take another example. You are considering having sex with someone and all you can think about is the attraction you feel, which often is lust rather than love. If you are considering this for the sake of self only you are going to have sex with this person if you have the opportunity. Nothing else matters to you, except perhaps safety and protection, which you are considering also for the sake of self only, being scared of disease. Also, if the partner is under the protection of someone else who might retaliate against you, you might be deterred if you are scared or don't want to deal with the trouble afterward. But if you are considering this for the sake of self and others, you will be thinking of what you want, and also, what is potentially hurtful to the partner or to your future relationship with another partner.

Suppose you depend on others for your daily financial needs. The others are sharing their resources with you. Now you might want to buy something for yourself. If you think about it in a hellish way you would think about what you want and you would get it for yourself whenever you can. This is doing it for the sake of self only. But if you're doing it for the sake of self and others, you will also consider whether you can afford it, or whether others will have to give up something as a result, and whether it would not be better for you to give it up. After considering all this you might still decide to go ahead and buy it for whatever reason you think is justified in this case. In that case your decision-making was consciously involved, and that is a good thing.

Here is another example to consider. You are an unmarried young woman and you like to dress in a style that many young women call 'sexy style', just like your friends. You can consider doing it for the sake of self only, so that you will only think about yourself. You will think that you have the right to wear these outfits because you look good in them, and as a result you will feel better about yourself, especially when others notice and give you compliments, even strangers. But if you think about it for the sake of others as well as self, you will think about the principles or attitudes that dressing this way promote. One issue in your mind would be how this will

270

affect your current or future partner, or how dressing this way may affect your younger sister or cousin or neighbor.

You might decide that it's all right for you to do this and that you are not hurting any conjugial principle in yourself or corrupting the morals of other girls, or encouraging various men to think about you in a sexual way. The point is that *whether you are doing something for a hellish motive or a heavenly one has to be your decision made with reflection in the light of your conscience and values.*

This applies to everything you do in the course of a day. It is important for your spiritual development not to oppose your conscience and your principles. If you do, there will be a risk of possible injury to your spiritual mind. Remember that you want to protect your spiritual mind and foster its growth and development. That's the mind you need for heavenly life in eternity. And that's the mind you need now in order for your natural mind to experience happiness and self-confidence.

The more your spiritual mind is "opened" or matured the more it can give happiness and intelligence to your natural mind now.

What can be more important to you in the long run than to make sure that your spiritual mind is being opened more and more? At stake is the quality of your life in eternity, which means endlessly into the future. Nothing else relating to you can have this much importance.

It is instructive and useful to always remind ourselves on a regular basis that no one is born for oneself but that everyone is born for others.

This is an amazing spiritual truth to know and enlightening to understand as a universal principle. Consider that all of humankind as a whole is to God gathered together in one view and forms an image and anatomical structure of a single individual. No cell can remain disconnected from a body. *Every cell fulfills a physiological function that is not for itself but for other cells.*

Every human being is born to fulfill a particular unique *mental* function in the whole of humanity, and contributes that uniqueness to the entire human race so that everyone is enriched by that individual's unique contribution. Countless numbers of individuals die on the countless number of planets every day and join the numberless communities of the afterlife. Each new addition to one of the spiritual societies brings a specific type of mental enrichment to all in that society. There is then the ripple effect that continues to all the other societies. In this way God is enriching the mental state of the human race on a continuous and never-ending schedule.

So if we know that we are born for the sake and enrichment of others we can better see how inhuman and mentally sick it is to love self only. This is the experiencing of life upside down, thus what is spiritually insane. When we love ourselves only and do everything for the sake of self our spiritual mind gradually closes and no longer active. No spiritual truths can now be perceived, known, or understood. What we love is then called good, and what we think is then called intelligent and true. All ability to understand spiritual truths is thereby arrested. Regeneration is impossible.

Remember that there is no sliding line or curve between the love of self only vs. the love of others as well as self. It does not make sense to think that you can split the difference, or balance one side with the other, when at certain times you love yourself only and at other times you appear to be loving others as well as yourself. From this balance sheet you cannot correctly think that you therefore sometimes love your self and sometimes love others. You must apply the test with each instance of your love.

When you love self only at certain times it is not possible for you to love self and others at other times.

For instance, you may love yourself only today but could it be that yesterday you loved others more than yourself when you volunteered to do the dishes three times in a row that day when you didn't have to do it more than once. Why did you volunteer to do it the extra two times? You might say that you wanted to give the family a treat since they work hard and deserve it.

Now you need to witness yourself volunteering. What is the love that motivates it? Could it be a selfish love? Could it be that if no one knew that you are the one who did the dishes all day you would actually not be motivated to do it. We often do things apparently for the sake of others, or in the name of others, but we actually do this from a selfish motive such as getting the credit for doing it.

Experiencing Regeneration

If you examine many situations in which you do things for others it may tujrn out that you are motivated to do this for the sake of some benefit to yourself. Many of our apparent "good deeds" such as being generous, volunteering, being supportive, are actually done for the sake of some personal benefit that might come from them. And if it is clear to us that no benefit will come to us then we lose the motivation to do it. This is proof that we love ourselves only even when we display our being nice personality.

The fact is that since the Fall of humankind from spiritual consciousness we are all born into natural consciousness and inherit our parental mental traits that consist of numberless loves that extend only to self and for the sake of self only. Altruistic behavior and giving charity can be learned as things to be done for the sake of self only, such as maintaining our reputation, obtaining status, receiving praise, gaining an advantage, increasing our popularity, influencing others, and so on. So we have an enormous task to accomplish by which we reverse this inborn situation and learn to install new anatomical programs of thinking and conduct. This process is called rebirth and regeneration because we are going from our inborn natural consciousness back to the earlier spiritual consciousness of the human race.

This is then our life task. Nothing else matters unless it is connected to this task and promotes it. We don't have many minutes to waste in this process for it takes a lifetime to get rid of numberless selfish loves that are deadly to our happy future.

Is Being Good Difficult?

We have two distinct states of consciousness in daily life: natural and spiritual. Until we reach adulthood we are in natural consciousness, but those who then undergo regeneration begin to alternate between natural and spiritual consciousness. With regeneration we are able to operate mostly in spiritual consciousness.

In natural consciousness the idea of "being good" as here defined seems a very difficult thing to achieve, perhaps too difficult, maybe even unrealistic and idealistic, and certainly no fun! But in spiritual consciousness we recognize the reason for this reticence and cool reception to the idea of "being good" all the time. Thinking that being good is difficult or impossibly unrealistic comes from the expectation that to be good one must cease to have fun in life. But this is an illusion and a false belief.

In natural consciousness we feel free when we do what we want. We do not realize that when we want to think or do something that is not good, we are not free but a slave. As will be discussed in more detail in later chapters, we do everything in conjunction with some spiritual society in the afterlife to which we are anatomically connected. We are kept in freedom of choice by equilibrium in our mind between the forces of doing what is not good and the forces of doing what is good.

In spiritual consciousness we can understand that our mind is created in a certain organic anatomical order that God has revealed through *Sacred Scripture*. Wanting to be good means deciding to adopt heavenly loves for our personality. Wanting to be bad means deciding to adopt hellish loves for our personality. In one case we want what is in the created order, but in the other case we want what is contrary to the created order. To want to be good is defined as freedom, while to want to be not good is defined as hellish slavery.

We can be slaves in our selfish loves and their false materialistic beliefs, or we can be free in our heavenly loves and their spiritual-rational truths. It's a matter of anatomy, not judgment. There is no "discretion" of choice here. We are locked into the anatomy into which we were created and in which we are maintained.

Now to return to the question, "Is it difficult to be good", the answer is that it is easy and pleasant and peaceful to want to be good, while it is difficult and disturbing to want to be bad. Wanting to be good is operating with the mental "software" for which our anatomy was built. Wanting to be bad is trying to operate our mental anatomy by using some other software that enslaves us, takes away our freedom, our happiness, our rationality.

And yet there is the strong illusion that being good means to give up all the fun in life. If we like to eat whatever we enjoy, we are told that we need to give that up for the sake of our health and for the sake of the poor animals that are being slaughtered to satisfy my craving. If we enjoy the

Experiencing Regeneration

relationship adventures that go with being promiscuous we are told that we must give that up and choose just one partner for life. If we enjoy playing violent video games in which we can drive over some pedestrians and spill blood, we are told that that kind of fun is hellish and must be given up. If we like exaggerating our stories and tell a few lies to impress our friends, we are told that this is disrespectful and untruthful, thus harmful. If we have the satisfying habit of swearing, we are told that it is from hell and we must give it up. And on and on it goes in this manner throughout our personality. Does it not look difficult to give all these enjoyments up, and is it even right or healthy to do that, and can anyone really be happy afterwards when deprived of any of these enjoyments?

Someone pointed out to me that most of the commandments God gives are negative, telling us what we may not do. Why is this? The commandments reveal to us what our personality is before it is regenerated. It is equipped for hell. But if we obey the commandments we are equipping our personality for living in heaven. Human beings have been in this upside-down situation since the Fall of Humankind. This occurred when people began to prefer experiencing selfish and ego boosting loves. Until then they had been happy in mutual love and love of God. Ever since the Fall people have been acquiring more and more ways of pursuing their selfishness. As a result of wanting to be bad, people have lost all experiencing of spiritual consciousness since this is possible only when we are in the created anatomical order. As a result, life on this earth turned from a peaceful and pleasant paradise to a war-filled hell of suffering, disease, stupidity, mutual hatred and cruelty. In consequence, all spiritual knowledge of the afterlife and of God was lost by being doubted and rejected.

God has provided a lawful anatomical procedure for getting ourselves out of this spiritual mess. It is the experiencing of regeneration. We experience ourselves in full freedom when we resist temptations for the sake of being good and avoiding being bad. To give in to a temptation is to fall into emotional and intellectual slavery again. This process will be discussed throughout this book.

Heaven and hell are mental states. This means that our consciousness can be raised or lowered, and this alternately and repeatedly. When our consciousness is lowered to its lowest level and we are aware of it, we are in the experiencing of hell. When our consciousness is raised to its highest level and we are aware of it, we are in the experiencing of heaven. The experiencing of hell is the awareness of our mental states when our consciousness is lowered. The experiencing of heaven is the awareness of our mental states when our consciousness is raised.

While we are still attached to the physical body in this world we experience hell and heaven not directly but mediately through others who are in their own mental states that are half way between heaven and hell. But after resuscitation when we are fully conscious in the spiritual body, we are less and less able to be in in-between states and gradually descend to hell or ascend to heaven in our mind. Only then are we fully in one or the other with absolutely no overlap. Those whose consciousness is raised to the higher levels of their mental states are said to "enter heaven" and to live there forever without ever descending again to lower states. Similarly with those who "enter hell" in their mind, living there and never ascending again.

This pattern is the result of the anatomy of the spiritual body or mind. Prior to death of the physical body our mind's physiology is able to contain both types of influx from heaven and from hell. You know this when you reflect on a good day when things are running splendidly and efficiently and you feel like you're in your heaven. Then later or the next day you feel like you fell back into hell with everything going wrong and all sorts of negative thoughts and feelings going on. But after resuscitation the ruling love that lies hidden in our personality until the afterlife now externalizes itself by taking over the hierarchy of loves, arranging them under itself, and exiling all positive loves and truths that are antithetical to the ruling love. If the ruling love is positive all negative thoughts and feelings are shut down as the person's consciousness is raised even to heaven. If the ruling love is negative all positive thoughts and feelings are shut down as the person's consciousness is lowered even to hell.

Equipping our personality with positive loves under the motivation of loving God and being useful to society begins the anatomical strengthening of a positive ruling love that will arrange all positive loves under itself and suppress and extinguish all negative loves. This is accomplished through the experiencing of regeneration in this life. This positive ruling love, which is our very own, is the means of our salvation as it raises our consciousness after resuscitation and betakes us upwards to heaven.

Experiencing Regeneration

Without experiencing regeneration and victory in the spiritual temptations that are involved, the ruling love remains such as we were born, thus negative and selfish.

Chapter 5
The Poetry of Experiencing

The purpose of experiencing the poetry of living is to be able to draw on the endless treasury that thinking makes available to us. People believe that information is something that comes in from outside in the physical environment and is stored in our memory for later recall and use. But in actuality information comes in from both sides of the mental anatomy, natural and spiritual, outside and inside. The availability of spiritual information to our thinking is limitless.

Everyday experiencing is the awareness of the inflow of spiritual information that takes place continuously in our mind.

Poetic discourse is the language of experiencing. The awareness of experiencing is consciousness. All possible human knowledge from past to future is accessible to consciousness. Describing the content of our consciousness generates poetic discourse. People communicate their consciousness to each other by constructing and sharing poetic discourse.

The following entries are insights contained in this book. See if you can provide a rational justification for each entry. Circle the items you can justify. Discuss them with a friend. As you progress in the book, come back here from time to time and see if you can circle more items. Happy experiencing!

Experiencing Regeneration

It's a useful practice of experiencing to write down or record insights during the course of the day. Reviewing these later, as well as much later, provides new insights and delights. It is also something you can share with a friend.

It is a useful exercise for building up our spiritual understanding to go through each numbered proposition in the list, reviewing in the mind what the item means and how it is true. One useful way of describing what the item means is to paraphrase it by saying the same thing in your own words or metaphors. Another useful way is to tell a friend how you interpret the item and discuss what might be its implications for everyone's life.

You might also deepen your knowledge or perceptions by adding to the list new items that represent your own insights regarding experiencing God and regeneration. Keep each item short and self-contained. You might need to enter several items separately, that together make up a larger view or principle. Discuss it with a friend. See how you need to alter the wording or to add additional items.

The word "correspondence" in theistic psychology refers to the relationship between spiritual and natural things in the created universe. After reading some of these correspondential equations between what is physical and what is mental or spiritual, you might like to produce a list from your own experiencing. See if some of your friends want to play the game with you. You can also do a web search of your phrases in quotes to see who else has used that phrase before.

For example, if you search for "the trees of perception" there are only three or four uses having to do with people's opinions. On the other hand, "the heat of love" has thousands of uses but most of them seem to be related to music lyrics and bands. "The pearl of gratitude" has just a handful of prior uses relating to discussions on feeling gratitude. However, "the silver of comprehension" has no occurrences and is thus a "neologism" or new coined expression. "The wood of goodwill" has only one use involving an Abbey. See how many of your productions are actually neos that have not been thought of by anyone before. "The ugliness of selfishness" has thousands of prior uses by others, but "The clothes of illusions" is a neo with no one ever having used this phrase before. Other neos in the list include: "The shove of unpleasantness" and "The mud of involvements".

Experiencing Regeneration

Experiencing God is always a surprise. It is the easiest thing in the world. God stands at the door of our conscious awareness and waits to be acknowledged and admitted in reciprocation. Throughout this book there is a focus on the importance of initiating and maintaining a reciprocal relationship with God. This makes everything possible and easy. Part of this process is to recognize our mental negativity and to strengthen our positive experiencing.

You might benefit by practicing writing down or just reflecting on your relationship to God. This experiencing is the source of all that we know directly about God. As you practice a little you will be able to make your own list of struggles and victories. The doing of this deepens the knowledge and the relationship. The following list recapitulates many of the assertions and descriptions of God and regeneration found in this book. You can read line by line or groups of lines by four and five for additional depth.

1. There is only experiencing.

2. Life is experiencing.

3. The actual and real human life of everyone is in the experiencing of spiritual consciousness.

4. Experiencing is the all of life, the all of reality. Experiencing is God, who is the provider of every experience.

5. If you know experiencing, you know God.

6. Truth and good come to us only through experiencing.

7. All love exists only in experiencing.

8. All knowledge, all possibilities exist in experiencing, and nowhere else.

9. Consciousness is the awareness of experiencing. Therefore such as is the quality of awareness such is the consciousness.

10. Experiencing is what happens. There is no other venue for anything to happen.

Experiencing Regeneration

11. Experiencing exists in the human mind, and nowhere else.

12. Mental states in experiencing are real. All else is appearance.

13. Self-witnessing is the monitoring of our awareness of experiencing.

14. An individual's experiencing is unique as a whole but contains similitudes and dissimilitudes in relation to other individuals.

15. Natural communities are organized externally or physically. Its collective members can be both similitudes and dissimilitudes in experiencing. Spiritual communities are organized internally or mentally. Its members can be only similitudes since dissimilitudes in experiencing repel each other, while similitudes attract each other.

16. Natural marriage and its consciousness provide the couple with the experiencing of unlove and quasi-friendship in marriage. But spiritual marriage and its consciousness provide the couple with the experiencing of eternal love and inmost friendship in marriage.

17. Experiencing is eternal, spiritual, mental, human, and unique. Therefore it is infinitely variable.

18. God may be said to be experiencing itself because an individual's experiencing is within God.

19. Experiencing is the never ceasing framework that maintains the person from birth to eternity.

20. The immortality of the person is nothing else than the flow of experiencing that cannot cease.

21. The experiencing of spiritual conscience is unique to human beings and defines what it means to be inwardly and truly human.

22. Spiritual conscience is a form of consciousness. Through spiritual conscience we can regenerate and be conjoined to God.

Experiencing Regeneration

This conjunction provides us with immortality and eternal happiness.

23. Experiencing restores all relationships into the present.

24. Spiritual consciousness provides the experiencing of rational faith, which is theistic psychology drawn from the correspondential sense of *Sacred Scripture*.

25. Selfish love will not allow the consciousness of spiritual truths. This is an anatomical effect. In regeneration we resist selfish love and acquire mutual love, and this provides the consciousness of spiritual truths, which is enlightenment.

26. If you are experiencing being in hell, you are there.

27. The physical body has no life of its own, containing only chemical and electrical materials. Experiencing is in the mind and gives our physical body the appearance of living, *as if life were its own.* This is only an externalized appearance, thus false in itself, because mental objects such as sensations, feelings, and thoughts occur and exist only in the mind and nowhere in the physical body.

28. Regeneration is the experiencing of spiritual salvation, that is, of inner liberation from the tyranny of inherited and inborn selfishness. Without salvation, experiencing devolves into the eternal hells that exist in the human mind.

29. To love self more than others provides the experiencing of natural consciousness. To love others as much as self and God above all things, is the experiencing of spiritual consciousness. The first is like that of animals; the second is truly human.

Experiencing Regeneration

30. The experiencing of selfishness produces only natural consciousness that is based on the appearances of the senses, and this is filled with false ideas and evil intentions.

31. Communities of people in the experiencing of natural consciousness lead to living conditions that we can witness around us – war, cruelty, hatred, harshness, lack of compassion, deceit, abuse of children and women, denial of freedom and due process, unhealthy lifestyles leading to sickness and a miserable life.

32. Natural consciousness organically leads to the devolution of human mind and consciousness to ever lower and sub-human levels. In its devolved stage, natural consciousness becomes nothing but pure rage, mad fury, and explosive insanity.

33. In regeneration we are experiencing the stream of Divine Providence carrying us through the healing of our character.

34. Salvation is the experiencing of mutual love in community, and consists of wishing others well and treating them with respect.

35. To love others as much as loving oneself, and God above all, is the experiencing of spiritual consciousness.

36. The unlove of natural marriage produces the experiencing of cheating and unchastity, either in deed or in thought.

37. The conjugial love of spiritual marriage produces the experiencing of faithfulness and chastity.

38. Chastity in marriage is the voluntary constriction of sexuality solely to the married partner. This involves the experiencing of avoidance and aversion for sexually relevant interests, fantasies, thoughts, and noticings about any other person than the partner.

Experiencing Regeneration

39. Every boy and man is a husband, either currently, or in the future. It is the same with every girl and woman being a wife.

40. Natural marriage provides the experiencing of natural consciousness in love, in friendship, in trust, in communication, fun, and happiness.

41. The initial love, friendship, and trust that may exist in natural consciousness devolve into their opposites when the partners are experiencing a power struggle or a betrayal.

42. Natural marriage becomes spiritual marriage when the partners perceive their union to be eternal and immortal, desiring to become one mind together.

43. One mindedness between spouses provides spiritual consciousness for the experiencing of conjugial love, inmost friendship, and total trust that organically evolves by deepening every day even while the married partners are experiencing a power struggle, or even a betrayal.

44. The deepening of the conjugial union involves each partner continually willing to become one mind with the other. This involves disallowing any mental distance or disjunction that is produced by disagreeing, getting angry, or showing disrespect. In the afterlife this deepening process or evolution continues to eternity in a heavenly society.

45. The belt of unchastity binds the awareness of our experiencing to un-pleasure, which is known as "lust". This in itself is dead, having no permanence.

46. The central feature of heaven is conjugial love, or the mental unity between husband and wife. This unit of life in heaven,

whereby two minds constantly will to be just one mind, is the ultimate goal of human evolution and perfection.

47. In the conjugial couple rests the unit of human evolution. This is the completion of creation of human beings. Hence it is that the heavenly regions of the human mind are populated by conjugial couples, each evolving to an endless future of increasing happiness and intelligence.

48. There is nothing mentally in a husband that is the same as anything mentally in the wife. Husbands think and react by facing the world through the truth-substance in their cognitive system. Wives think and react by facing the world through the love-substance in their affective system.

49. A husband loves what he understands. A wife understands what she loves.

50. In order to understand himself, a spiritual husband relies on his wife.

51. Anatomically viewed, a husband and a wife together make up one complete human being. The conjoined pair is the complete person. She is his heart and he is her lungs.

52. In a conjugial love relationship, intimacy is based on mutual exclusivity in the mind and body.

53. Chastity in marriage exists when all sexuality is restricted to the spouse, both physically and mentally in the privacy of one's own mind.

54. A husband acquires truth according to the love of his wife. A wife acquires love according to the truth of her husband.

55. The best way for a husband to avoid disagreements with his wife is to agree with her.

Experiencing Regeneration

56. When the husband agrees with his wife she listens to his masculine intelligence, which is what she needs and wants from him.

57. When the wife talks seriously and the husband laughs, it is a sign that he is erasing her words in his mind.

58. A wife feels safe and feminine when her husband is being polite with her, but unsafe and cautious when he is being rude or disrespectful.

59. Such as are the uses that spouses do for one another, such are the bonds of their marriage.

60. The deepening of conjugial love over the decades brings emotional closeness and inmost friendship such as there is between young lovers.

61. Being a conjugial husband makes a man smarter than he is.

62. Spouses love each other when they each strive to become one will with the other.

63. Without his wife a husband is not a complete person.

64. Alone I am a divided or half man; with my wife I am a whole man.

65. Conjugial love unites eternally.

66. A husband's wisdom is to see things as his wife sees them.

67. When a husband loves himself more than his wife, her voice when she speaks to him is like a babbling brook.

68. If a husband constantly pretends to be loving and peaceful to his wife, he eventually becomes that.

69. In conjugial simulation by the husband, cluelessness is foolproof in keeping the conjugial peace and its blessedness.

70. A husband's anger towards his wife separates and disjoins them. A wife's zeal towards her husband that just looks like anger outwardly, protects them and binds them together.

Experiencing Regeneration

71. The inner happiness of togetherness that is experienced by a conjugial couple bans all restlessness in their heart.

72. Mutual regard between spouses gives birth to the conjoint self with conjugial couples.

73. A photograph's beauty is one-dimensional; a wife's beauty is multidimensional.

74. The idea of God is inherited and inborn. It is also innocent and normal, except when it is counteracted, as when discussion about God (not just religion) is banished in public schools and in science literature.

75. God is an all-encompassing idea. It is broader and earlier than religion or science. Confusing God with religion leads to the exclusion of God from public life. This exclusion binds people to natural materialistic consciousness. This mental state opposes regeneration.

76. To love others as much as oneself, and God more than oneself, is the experiencing of heavenly life now and in eternity.

77. The promotion of materialistic thinking in science education and science news reporting restricts human consciousness to the materialistic level of thinking and feeling. This natural consciousness opposes spiritual-rational ideas such as God and the afterlife, and can inhibit the development of a reciprocal relationship with God.

78. The experiencing of spiritual consciousness is not possible without a reciprocal relationship with God. This is because God uses this reciprocal relationship with the individual as a vehicle for enlightening the person with spiritual ideas.

Experiencing Regeneration

79. A reciprocal relationship with God is acquired by dialogue, which involves daily acknowledging God's co-Presence in our mind, and sharing with God thoughts and feelings with the expectation of being enlightened and reassured by God.

80. Deepening our reciprocal relationship with God involves the daily effort of acquiring similitudes with God. This involves resisting and suppressing inconsiderate thoughts and intentions for the sake of God who is the opposite of selfish.

81. God stands by the door of awareness in our experiencing, and knocks, asking to be admitted into full conscious co-Presence with the individual. This availability is the salvation from the Fall. It is the elevation of our experiencing back into the mode of spiritual consciousness and sanity that humans had before the Fall. It is arriving back home.

82. God's love that is in me is also God's love that is in you. God is the same in everyone and in all things He created. The difference is caused by unique reception of each individual.

83. A reciprocal relationship with God makes rational sense given that every detail of our daily lives is produced and managed by God. This is the meaning of "omnipotence". God's purpose in this close contact with each human being is to benefit the individual with eternal happiness, conjugial love, and unending creative intelligence.

84. The idea of God is implanted into every human being from birth. It cannot be removed, but it can be denied.

85. The denial or doubting of God produces resistance to the inception of spiritual consciousness. The experiencing of denying

God involves immersing one's thoughts in materialistic ideas, such as that there is no afterlife, or that mind is just an activity of the physical brain and dissipates at death.

86. The process of ridding ourselves of negative emotions is the experiencing of regeneration. It is a joint and reciprocal interaction between you and God.

87. In spiritual consciousness the denial of God is perceived as spiritual insanity. Natural consciousness cannot conceive of eternal marriage, nor of heaven and hell in an afterlife. It denies the reality of these things, seeing them as fantasies of an immature person.

88. Truth by itself is not capable of seeing whether it is genuine truth or falsified. But when good flows in, it gives life and light to truth. We can then tell from spiritual conscience whether some truth is genuine or false

89. God instructs human societies by giving them the text of *Sacred Scripture* that He dictates to the mind of prepared individuals known as "prophets". The literal meaning of these verses refers to the conditions and events in natural life on this earth, such as the history of particular followers and God's relationship to them.

90. The literal or historical meaning of *Sacred Scripture* provides a natural-rational understanding of God and His Commandments. Hence spiritual ideas like sinning, undergoing regeneration, and life after death are interpreted in physical terms.

91. When *Sacred Scripture* is considered analytically through body-mind correspondences, a hidden spiritual meaning is perceived regarding spiritual truths that until then were

comprehended only naturally through the literal or historical meaning alone.

92.   Heavenly secrets that we derive from the correspondential sense of *Sacred Scripture* gradually produce in our mind the spiritual consciousness that we need for our eternal evolution and fulfillment.

93.   The same theistic psychology content is derived from the *Sacred Scripture* of all cultures when applying body-mind correspondences to the literal verses. This is because God speaks to all humanity with one voice.

94.   Body-mind correspondences represent cause-effect laws that God created and built into the physical world of time and into the mental world of eternity. The two worlds are held in synchronous cause-effect action by means of the built-in laws of natural-spiritual correspondences.

95.   Every human being speaks and thinks with body-mind correspondences because these are built-in anatomically in our mind. When we describe *mental* situations we use *physical* ideas to communicate them.

96.   Examples of body-mind correspondences found in the speech of all speakers include: "deep" thought (=involved reasoning), "strong" loyalty (=consistent, dependable character), "sweet" girl (=pleasant, attractive), "sour" deal (=bad exchange), "broken heart" (=sad, unhappy), "sharp tongue" (=critical and hurtful), "pig" (=rude, bad manners), "dog" (=inconsiderate, gross), "mouse" (=fearful), etc. Everyone knows these *mind-body correspondences* as part of knowing how to talk.

Experiencing Regeneration

97. To talk to our rational mind God uses physical events, history, and people of a certain character to describe mental events such as sinning, punishment, repentance, rebirth, regeneration, selfishness, innocence, mutual love, conjugial love, spiritual reward, mental substance, meritoriousness, unchastity, and so on. *These spiritual topics constitute theistic psychology*, that is, psychology derived from God's *Sacred Scripture* when reconstructed in its correspondential sense.

98. Feeling bad and being bad provide the experiencing of unreality that is centered in natural consciousness. The created reality is positive. Being in order with reality is the experiencing of feeling good and being good. This higher mental state provides us with spiritual consciousness, which is the true state of being human.

99. Experiencing restores all relationships into the present. Everything you've experienced in this life returns to you in the afterlife, even as you continue immortal life with ever new experiences. No experience is ever lost.

100. God's own living and immortal substances inflow and form our anatomical organs of the mind, which give us the ability to think, plan, interpret, love, interact, and enjoy everything that God has placed before us as experiencing.

101. Meaning is a vehicle for consciousness.

102. All the knowledge of theistic psychology is embodied in the Writings of Swedenborg.

103. The geography of the mental world gives a map of our involvements.

Experiencing Regeneration

104. We each have one ruling love that controls all our thoughts and decisions.

105. Altruistic feelings make us wise and useful.

106. The afterlife is the mental world of eternity. The loves we have acquired determine what our afterlife is like in eternity.

107. In regeneration we are experiencing the fact that it is not our own power that produces our character change. We are experiencing the stream of Divine Providence carrying us through the healing of our character.

108. Follow up the mental strands that you find in your experiencing. This is your solid rock. Experiencing cannot lie.

109. To love self more than others is the same as to love self only.

110. In spiritual consciousness we make objective determinations based on human anatomy.

111. Both heaven and hell are located in every individual's mind. It is a matter of mental anatomy.

112. There is no other task that is as important as the task of regeneration. If any other task is set before it in importance, regeneration ceases and is destroyed.

113. In daydreams we can see in clear light what is the content of our affections.

114. Until we separate in our mind the idea of God and the idea of religion we are not able to elevate our consciousness to the spiritual level.

115. Mental traits are anatomical properties of mental operations in our mind. Mental operations fall into two distinct categories. One involves what we feel, and the other involves what we think.

Experiencing Regeneration

116. Nothing is more important in regeneration than to understand how feeling and thinking are distinct yet operate together.

117. Such as is our love to God, such is our happiness and intelligence.

118. Wherever life is present or active, God's life is there.

119. Our finite spiritual consciousness is co-present with God's infinite spiritual consciousness. Thus we can dialog with God and share each other to each other.

120. Such as is the personality of the individual, such is the reciprocation to God, and consequently such is the regeneration and the salvation.

121. There is a three-way anatomical connection between God, *Sacred Scripture*, and every person's mind. The entire human race is interconnected by mental fibers to each other and to God and God's *Word*.

122. The will is primary in the mind and is our very life. We love what we will and we will what we love.

123. Such as are our loves, such is our intelligence, and consequently such are we.

124. We change our loves by changing our thoughts. These new loves then change our thoughts.

125. Unless we teach ourselves in daily life how to love doing and thinking what is heavenly, we cannot be in heaven in eternity.

126. We are at war against our self and within our self.

127. What God calls good is what can take us to heaven.

128. What God does, that I love.

129. Wisdom produces beauty from love.

Experiencing Regeneration

130. Without spiritual temptations we would never be able to perceive that we are inverted.

131. Every evil love has sway over every human being – until regeneration.

132. Our life is in our loves, and to remove our loves is to remove our life.

133. Loving self more than others is the same as loving self-alone.

134. By loving others we are mentally enriched with new intelligence and new loves or motives.

135. When we stop loving our self more than others, we move on to loving others as much as self.

136. To love self some of the time, and to show consideration for others at other times, is not yet to love others as much as self.

137. Loves can be consummated by either an overt act or an interior act. By saying things to yourself you are actually consummating an inner love through a mental speech act.

138. When a love is consummated it is appropriated, that is, integrated permanently into our personality. It will be there in our afterlife.

139. By seeing and perceiving our loves in our daydreams we are presented with our temptations, and hence opportunities for spiritual growth.

140. Human life is mental life from beginning to end. Mental life is our life. We have no other life.

141. Loving someone is the experiencing of connectedness.

142. Disagreeing with my wife is experiencing lack of love.

Experiencing Regeneration

143. When the husband loves his wife he is experiencing mental connectedness with her. When a husband gets angry with his wife he is experiencing disconnectedness or distance and separation.

144. For a husband to overtly express disagreement with his wife is to stop loving her.

145. To create time God had to be apart from time. To create space God had to be apart from space. From this duality is God's omnipresence.

146. To be mentally adjoined is to be co-Present.

147. God integrates the whole human race to function as one human being. No one can exist outside this Divine matrix.

148. To think freely from our own affection is our very life. If the affections are those of selfish delights, our life is a hell. But if we delight in mutual love, our life is a heaven.

149. If we abide in our selfish loves we cannot be elevated into spiritual consciousness. We remain natural in this life, as if animal. And in the afterlife of eternity we abide with those in hell.

150. Feeling good requires being good, which consists of loving God above all things and loving others as oneself.

151. Feeling negative is being in company with those who are in hell. We can escape from that mental state by finding reasons for feeling positive.

152. Human beings live in their thoughts according to their loves.

153. All that is living exists in what is mental.

154. There is nothing living in the physical world.

155. Each person is an anatomical part of other persons.

156. All human minds are organs in a mental world.

Experiencing Regeneration

157. The entire mental world is an anatomical construction and everything therein is connected anatomically to the whole.

158. God is not part of any human being but is within every human being as the infinite is within the finite.

159. The same infinite God is within every finite human being.

160. God is not a stranger to us. God is our intimate companion who is always present and is a co-participant in every detail of our lives.

161. The anatomical relationship between God and each human being is our condition and situation from birth to eternity. It is what makes human beings to be born immortal.

162. Our experiencing of God's Human mind brings order and peace into our daily life.

163. The human mind as a spiritual body is the highest of all created forms in the universe.

164. By denying God as a Human person from whose influx we can have feelings and thoughts, we are denying reality and making ourselves to be spiritually insane.

165. All relationship of love must be reciprocal.

166. Since God is Human and person it makes sense to talk with God, one on one, face to face, mind to mind.

167. A direct reciprocal relationship to our Creator is independent of any cultural or religious background.

170. Human immortality is an anatomical property of the spiritual body, which is our mind containing our mental organs and structures of personality.

Experiencing Regeneration

168. (b) From my higher nature I do things that are useful to society. From my lower nature I do things that are harmful to others and to myself.

169. What we think is the result of what we love. For such as are our loves, such are our thoughts.

170. To change our thinking we must change our love.

171. Love well. For you become that love forever.

172. Respect for others keeps the peace.

173. Anger shuts out love. Love dissipates anger.

174. To be sincerely considerate is to love the neighbor.

175. Respect takes courage. Disrespect is cowardly.

176. Good things end so quickly. But more are on their way.

177. Inner and outer stimuli rekindle passion that it may be consummated again and again.

178. Clothes for the body. Truths for the mind. They correspond.

179. Food and air for the body. Knowledge and understanding for the mind. They correspond.

180. To my cat I am God. I tried to explain who is actually God. I don't think he got the idea.

181. Having a good relationship with a human being raises a cat's consciousness.

182. Uses that people perform are the bonds that hold society together.

183. Everyone in community is born for others. No one is born for self. Therefore self-fulfillment comes from being useful to others.

184. When I avoid inconveniencing others out of respect or compassion, I am practicing mutual love and love to God. My personality is being equipped for heavenly life in eternity.

185. I harm society when I am being self-centered, egotistical, or selfish.

Experiencing Regeneration

186. Selfish behavior is harmful to society and to self. It brings suffering, sickness, and poverty to innocent others.

187. By being in a bad mood we give ourselves permission to be hostile and nasty to family, friends, and strangers.

188. When you feel a bad mood coming on, you are standing at the gates of hell. Quick, turn around by pretending you're in a good mood.

189. To be considerate to others is against my lower nature. Therefore my higher nature must overcome my lower nature. This is experiencing regeneration.

190. My personality is a battleground between my lower and higher nature.

191. Love has power by wisdom. Good has power by truth. The will has power by the understanding.

192. Truth without good within it is not truth but only something fake that appears as truth.

193. Truth by itself without love in it is dead, harsh, and cruel. Putting love or good into truth makes it to be living, gentle, and compassionate.

194. Thinking that the mind is physical is reductionism. Thinking it is spiritual is dualism.

195. Death is part of time. What is spiritual is in eternity and apart from time. The mind is immortal because it is apart from time and in eternity.

196. My mind is not on earth, but in eternity. That's why I am immortal. Born into eternity.

197. Love is life. Life is willing, thinking, and doing. Without love for someone or something, we have no life.

198. Love is a striving for mental conjunction with someone.

199. Love is spiritual gravity. They correspond.

Experiencing Regeneration

200. Discipline brings achievement. Achievement provides the experiencing of success.

201. Sunday. Time to pray and affirm – Monday. Time to practice.

202. My inner self can observe my outer self. The unexamined self can be harmful.

203. Have you listened in on yourself today? -- What you said to yourself about others and about what is happening.

204. The instant we decide that all human beings are born to live forever, our higher rational understanding is activated and provides us with the experiencing of spiritual consciousness.

205. Soaring on the wings of beauty. Opening up deeper passions.

206. Beauty is the face of intelligence.

207. Missing someone brings the two minds closer.

208. Daydreams are predictions of our own future when seen through the meaning of correspondences.

209. The future is not ahead of us, but within us. For such as is our love within us, such is our future ahead of us.

210. Desire is opportunistic. It can silence our conscience.

211. Resentment and discontent in my heart. Time to let go of illusions. And turn back to the East.

212. Heaven and hell are not places somewhere but mental states in our mind.

213. I hear an inspiring song without words. It is the voice of heaven.

214. Angels forgive, but do not forget. To forgive is rational; to forget is not.

215. Innocence and modesty have their own inspiring inner beauty.

Experiencing Regeneration

216. Innocence knows no rancor, plans no evil, is content and happy in the here and now.

217. Runaway passion catapults us into trouble.

218. The courage to be other-centered always pays off.

219. Can I love others as much as I love myself? I must continue to try.

220. Altruism and selfism struggle within me.

221. Every human mind is born with anatomical roots to heaven and hell.

222. We can change our future by changing our loves now. This is regeneration.

223. If you don't stop pretending to be a nice person, eventually you'll become one.

224. The body is the visible mind. The mind is the form of eternity.

225. Do not step on the road to perdition. Face your temptations with the spiritual truths of Sacred Scripture.

226. I listen to the sound of the night. Awake. Alone. Everyone else has departed to his or her dreams. Time to have a chat with God.

227. When I look beyond myself I see nothing.

228. Love consumed is love nourished. Without consummation love starves, forever longing and hungry.

229. Healthy loves need to be consumed. Unhealthy loves need to be starved to death.

230. Life is the will to love someone. To love is to be joined together, to be happy and productive.

231. A good love conjoins with truth to produce something useful to others. A bad love conjoins with untruth to produce something harmful to self and others.

Experiencing Regeneration

232. Looking a great photograph or painting gives us a respite and lets us breathe more deeply.

233. Heed the children in your car. Don't let the back seat become their road rage nursery.

234. Altruism goes against my nature. Therefore I need to change my nature. This is regeneration.

235. Eating something I enjoy calms me down.

236. The day is slipping away. I can't slow it down. So much to do.

237. In the sweetness of celestial scenery.

238. I want to be good even if I don't feel like it. This is regeneration.

239. Some day I'm going to enjoy being good all the time.

240. Outwardly we can believe what we don't understand, but inwardly we only believe what we understand.

241. In this life our outer personality shows and our inner personality is hidden. In the afterlife of eternity it is the reverse.

242. Outwardly we act for show; but inwardly for keeps.

243. Altruism is the delight of doing something that is useful to others as well as to self.

244. To walk the talk – that is my ambition.

245. To love unselfishly, that is my goal.

246. To love what is good as much as I love myself – that is my duty.

247. Driving is a good time to practice altruism. Two million people worldwide die in traffic every year. Think how many die like that in 10 or 20 years!

248. In the silence of the night I can hear the wind rushing through the leaves and rattling the garage door.

Experiencing Regeneration

249. When bright dawn arrives all the shades of night self-destruct. Time to be happy again.

250. We are immortal because our mind is born into eternity.

251. Love is an attachment, either to something good or to something bad.

252. If you know the body you know the mind because the two correspond.

253. Body and mind correspond but exist in different realms.

254. I eat, therefore I am.

255. I am, therefore I think.

256. I love, therefore I think.

257. Love is life, and without love there is no life.

258. Love without action is nothing.

259. Action without love is impossible.

260. I am more than I know.

261. Everyone is their own love.

262. Everyone's love is uniquely them.

263. Love is mental heat and is the source of physical heat.

264. Truth is what we think when it corresponds to what is real.

265. Memory is a footprint in time.

266. Memories are footprints in the mind.

267. Truth uncovers what is kept hidden.

268. No two moments can ever be the same. This represents God's infinity.

269. Aging and dying would be unbearable if I didn't know that I was immortal.

270. Plants unfurl themselves from within. So our loves unfold from within our desires.

Experiencing Regeneration

271. Holding fast to principles helps steer clear of life's many traps.

272. Searching for something undefined and sublime to liberate our soul.

273. Hanging on to what love offers. Reaching upwards, beyond ourselves.

274. Dawn chases away the night demons from the mind.

275. A tree is created in the image of a human.

276. The courage to behold what is larger than ourselves.

277. Beauty is a window into our soul.

278. The sky mirrors what is in the heart.

279. I promise you love.

280. To appreciate beauty and harmony is the essence of being human.

281. We search for truth in appearances. We seldom know what lies deeply in our heart.

282. Salvation comes at twilight.

283. True love forgives but does not condone.

284. Compassion is from love. Cruelty is from selfishness.

285. The mind points out what the heart desire.

286. Hope soars above longing.

287. Evening. Then night. At last, Dawn.

288. Anticipation feels unbearable, at times.

289. Sand. Ocean. Mountains. Clouds. Sky --- so many layers of our mind.

290. Everything in nature is a theater for what lies in human minds.

291. Clouds in my horizon. Peace is in the heart.

292. In my failing body I am continuously comforted by the warmth that awaits us on the other side of time.

293. Community fosters individuality. Individuality that is in harmony with community.

294. Love and truth -- my foundation.

295. And now my heart is troubled, but it shall quickly pass.

296. I think humans think too much.

297. Nightfall. The hour of challenge. Dawn. Light chases away the darkness.

298. Promise of a new day. Morning intensity strengthening. Calm and peace. Protection from above.

299. Calling all dawns. Sunrise begins. Midday. Passion's love. Sunset. Light hangs on as darkness approaches. The mystery of night.

300. The body is an image of the mind.

301. Light is to its heat as truth is to its love.

302. Patriotism makes the heart noble and more truly human.

303. When I am humble I am wise, but a fool when I am arrogant.

304. Beauty remains hidden, then suddenly appears with a breath taking surprise.

305. The highest bravery there is for a man is to listen to his wife.

306. I strive to make my wife's will to be as if my own.

307. Feeling old is to take appearances for real.

308. Love is truth's inner power. Truth is love's outward shield.

309. Becoming adult is learning how to wait.

310. Love is the invisible portion of truth. Truth is the visible portion of love.

311. If you love something, you are connected to it forever, even if you now hate it.

312. Love truth so that you may receive good.

313. To be a safe and happy driver, cultivate an attitude of gratitude.

314. Human beings are born into eternity. But we only get to see that after death.

315. Enchanted evening, promising romance and friendship.

316. I must stop thinking the wrong thing, before I can think the right thing.

317. Heaven is a state of mind, not a place, and so is hell.

318. Love binds us to what we like. Hate binds us to what we do not like.

319. Appearance reflects reality.

320. The talent we are born with is a treasure that enriches others.

321. Love kindles interest that chases away the blahs and the blues.

322. Husbands often wait while the wife shops. But now I learned how to shop with her.

323. The husband's mind flows. The wife's mind pulsates.

324. The husband's mind flows on the outside and pulsates on the inside. A wife's mind pulsates on the outside and flows on the inside.

325. I outsmart myself and win by putting someone else's wants ahead of mine.

326. I can't win by fighting myself, but I can, by outsmarting myself.

327. When sweethearts quarrel it is better to give in than to win.

328. Beware! Don't let the backseat of your car serve as road rage nursery. We are models to our children.

329. Reality is far more amazing than any fiction.

330. The human mind is vaster than any ocean.

331. Spiritual light is truth in the mind. Enlightenment is to recognize truth and to love it.

332. What faces outward protects what faces inward.

333. To worship and love God is the essential part of being human.

334. After the storm comes clean up.

335. When I quiet down my outward self, I can hear my inner self. It's nice and peaceful.

Experiencing Regeneration

336. Our standards regulate our desires. Without standards our desires take us to trouble. Heeding our principles protects us from troubles brought by runaway desires.

337. Death is only a transition to a world without time or decay.

338. The eyes reflect our inner loves and reveal them.

339. Desire is opportunistic. Lust is promiscuous.

340. Love is spiritual gravity. It binds souls together.

341. My outer self follows my nose; my inner self follows my eyes.

342. Heaven is not a place, but a mental state. So is hell.

343. Conjugial love unites eternally.

344. My wisdom is to see things as my wife sees them. My courage is to love that.

345. To a man a woman's voice is a babbling brook -- until he wizens up.

346. Outwardly I am restless. Inwardly I am calm.

347. The ocean speaks secrets to the human mind. Listen.

348. Experiencing the past and future simultaneously.

349. Every individual is tied to community roots. No one is born for self but for others.

350. Love in truth is the daily food that our mind needs in order to survive.

351. Beauty is endless because it is from eternity.

352. The experience of trepidation, anticipating the infilling of our body and mind.

353. As things get smaller their complexity increases.

354. The closer we get the more we see how little we know.

355. The inner and the outer must correspond.

Experiencing Regeneration

356. The spiritual and the natural must correspond.

357. Celestial nuptials. Inner Harmony. Peace, enthusiasm, and above all LOVE.

358. We tuck our illusions deep in our mind so they appear real to us.

359. Human inventiveness is inexhaustible.

360. Light and shadow. Truth and half-truth.

361. Getting a larger view helps to clear our mind.

362. Getting a closer view helps to ease our worries.

363. Nature is an image of what we are inside.

364. Nature is a theater for exhibiting God's wisdom and love.

365. When the mind is visible to us, the heart is still hidden.

366. Placing our lives on solid principles. God. Truth. Love.

367. The heat of the sun originates from the love in human hearts.

368. We branch out and expand to what we were born to become.

369. Every individual is born for heaven. Every man or woman is a potential angel.

370. The endeavor to reach our goals makes us human.

371. Dreams immerse us in a virtual world through our dream body avatar.

372. Rest from the clutter in our mind.

373. Predictability brings hope as well as certainty.

374. Nature unfolds its secrets for the mind to recognize God's wisdom and love.

375. Human beings are created as the center of the universe. God creates each thing for a use to humanity. Nothing can exist that does not have this use.

Experiencing Regeneration

376. Light without heat is cold. Truth without love is cruel.

377. Sand absorbs water, but only so much. There is no limit to how much spiritual light our mind can absorb.

378. Clouds of passion connecting to our heart. There is mystery within.

379. The closer the view the more spectacular it is.

380. Nature speaks beauty and order to each of us. God creates every thing for a use.

381. Endeavor bubbles up from deep inside the spirit.

382. Beauty springs up at you everywhere you look for it.

383. Layers of interaction complicate our lives.

384. Happiness and beauty depend on order.

385. Does the dog see the sunrise, or only the sand?

386. Imagination transforms make-believe into virtual reality.

387. Discipline brings rewards.

388. Some flowers open at sunrise and close at sunset.

389. Probing sacred secrets, uncovering truth.

390. Reflection brings new insights.

391. Light shapes objects as truth shapes our understanding.

392. God's perfect wisdom is seen in uses.

393. Beauty corresponds to intelligence, and fragrance to pleasing moments in our lives.

394. When we get angry we can see the trees but not the forest.

395. Our large ego projects even a larger shadow.

396. Foresight includes hindsight.

397. To be in God's mind is to exist forever.

Experiencing Regeneration

398. Striving upward to our higher destiny. Walking in the quiet dawn. Drama in the sky.

399. The light of truth stays dark without the heat of love attached to it.

400. Intelligence becomes foolishness in a person who loves self only, but wisdom in a person who loves others more than self, and God above everything.

401. Dark sayings of old. Correspondences. The spiritual uncovered.

402. Morning. Morning Meditation. Early morning ocean. Purple dawning. Sunrise, sunset. Dusk falling at the beach. Night approaching. Silent darkness into light. Morning. Purple dawning.

403. What faces outward protects what faces inward.

404. To worship is part of being human.

405. The mystery of night. Calling all dawns.

406. Our standards regulate our desires. Without our standards, our desires take us to trouble.

407. When I quiet down my outward self, I can hear my inner self.

408. Death is only a transition to a world without time.

409. The eyes reflect our inner loves.

410. Can I love others as much as I love myself? I must try.

411. If you pretend to be a nice person, eventually you become one.

412. The body is the visible mind. The mind is the form of eternity.

413. I listen to the sound of the night. Awake. Alone. Everyone else has departed to their world of dreams.

414. The inner happiness of togetherness bans all restlessness.

415. Cosmic Prayer. Do not step on the Road to Perdition.

416. With couples, a man's anger separates and threatens, while a woman's zeal protects and conjoins.

417. Healthy loves we want to nourish. Unhealthy loves we want to starve to death. Agreed?

418. Innocence and modesty have their own special inner beauty.

419. The peace that passes all understanding. God gives it freely.

420. Innocence knows no rancor.

421. The courage to be other-centered always pays off.

422. A photograph's beauty is cold and one-dimensional. A woman's beauty is warm and multidimensional.

423. The day is slipping away. I can't slow it down. So much to do.

424. A good love conjoins with truth to produce something useful, but a bad love with untruth, producing harm.

425. Eating something I enjoy calms me down.

426. Conscience keeps us human.

427. My mind is not on earth, but in eternity. That's why we are immortal.

428. Our inner self can observe our outer self.

429. When we decide that everyone is born to live forever, our inner sight is immediately activated.

430. Being in a bad mood means allowing ourselves to be mean to others.

431. In this life our outer personality shows and our inner personality is hidden. But in the afterlife of eternity, it is the reverse.

432. Outwardly, we can believe what we don't understand, but inwardly we believe only what we understand.

Experiencing Regeneration

433. I want to be good, even when I don't feel like it. Some day I'm going to enjoy being good all the time.

434. Outwardly we act for show, but inwardly, for keeps.

435. Altruism or mutual love is the delight of doing something that is useful to others as well as to self.

436. Love has power only through truth.

437. The useful thing people do are the bonds of society.

438. To love unselfishly – that is my goal. To love what is good as much as myself – that is my duty.

439. Faces exhibit the types of love.

440. The heat and redness of blood comes from love. They correspond to each other.

441. Alone I am a half man. With my wife I'm a whole man.

442. Love is a striving for conjunction. Without love for someone, we have no life.

443. We are immortal because our mind is born into eternity.

444. Mutual regard in relationship gives birth to the conjoint self.

445. When bright dawn arrives, all the shades of the night self-destruct. Time to be happy again.

446. To walk the talk --- that is my ambition.

447. Emotional closeness is inmost friendship between sweethearts.

448. A woman feels safe and feminine with a polite man, but unsafe and cautious with a rude one.

449. The self is a battle ground for our lower and higher nature.

450. What we think is the result of what we love.

451. To be considerate is love

452. Respect for others keeps the peace.

453. Respect takes courage. Disrespect does not.

454. The best way not to disagree with my wife is to agree with her.

455. She is my heart and I am her lungs.

456. The man is truth from love. A woman is love from that truth.

457. A man's mind flows. A woman's mind pulsates.

458. My mind is my entertainment.

459. I eat, therefore I am. I am, therefore I think. I love, therefore I think. I am more than I know.

460. Love without action is nothing. Action without love is impossible.

461. Gentleness takes courage.

462. Love is life and without love there is no life.

463. Love is mental heat, and is the source of bodily heat.

464. Everyone's love is uniquely them.

465. Everyone is their own love.

466. Perspective puts things in order.

467. Truth is what we think when it corresponds to what is real.

468. Love is an attachment – either to something good, or bad.

469. If you know the body, you know the mind because the two correspond.

470. Physical and mental exclusivity is essential for true love.

471. What we love, that we do if not hindered.

472. How much we know about ourselves is tiny compared to what we don't know about ourselves.

473. Sometimes we want to tell. Sometimes we want to listen. And sometimes, neither.

Experiencing Regeneration

474. We don't know ourselves. Therefore we need others as reflectors.

475. You know more than you're conscious of.

476. Cruelty is the source of suffering, for self and others.

477. Everything in the universe has its opposite. All things are connected to a series.

478. Nature mirrors the mind by correspondence.

479. The less I talk the more people understand me. (A lesson I still need to learn.)

480. Everything in existence has been created for the sake of human beings.

481. Better I be silent than to say the wrong thing.

482. To be coherent I must have the love of being taken for normal.

483. When I get offended I need to file it away in my short-term memory.

484. Love is nothing without its delight.

485. When we love something, we become spiritually attached to it.

486. A little of something good is better than a lot of something mediocre.

487. Impatience views things head on, while patience looks all around.

488. Experience is an act of living through an event.

489. When dieting to lose weight, the slower the weight loss, the longer it stays off, and vice versa.

490. Meaning is alive when it is exciting.

491. Best friends can't disagree, even when they see things differently.

Experiencing Regeneration

492. All appearances are real appearances. All fantasies are real fantasies.

493. All action springs from some love.

494. We suffer. Therefore our spirit can grow and evolve.

495. Love drives and directs what we think and do.

496. Love's principle venue is the sense of touch.

497. Sunrise in my heart sings for my beloved.

498. Regrets are like hauntings.

499. Love is mental glue.

500. A love can be defeated only by another love, either a better one, or a worse one.

501. Love does not allow doubt.

502. Fear is insufficient love.

503. Passion is the absence of inner conflict.

504. Things that take longer to finish, need more interruption.

505. Disorder brings suffering.

506. Your mental world is my mental world is every one's mental world.

507. Emotionally intelligent thinking empowers drivers.

508. Spiritual marriage. Entering the unity phase of affective intimacy.

509. Eternity is not something "later" -- it is now.

510. External particulars of natural life. Externalized products of inner behavioral phenomena.

511. Anger released is anger increased. Anger transformed is anger dissolved.

512. Drive smart. Put a smile in your heart.

313

Experiencing Regeneration

513. Feeling that we are alone struggling, but knowing that the Lord is close by.

514. God makes sure that we are not tempted beyond our ability or readiness to resist.

515. A conjugial couple. He was stupefied by this celestial appearance and reality. He witnessed their conjoint self, shining from their faces, their beauty, and their wisdom.

516. Heavenly loves are living mental substances.

517. Heavenly loves possessed by human beings are dead without the Divine Love within them.

518. Hell is a physiological or medical issue.

519. Hellish societies in our vertical community serve the Divine Love by providing a balance in the natural mind between good and evil traits.

520. I remind myself daily about heaven and hell.

521. I now realize that the possibility exists that I may forget that I am already enlightened.

522. In the *Swedenborg Reports* God reveals a new scientific theory, which is theistic psychology.

523. It is a mental substance flowing out of the Spiritual Sun, which is from the Mind of God.

524. Knowing our excellent future, knowing how to get there.

525. Love directs cognitive operations to formulate a plan or method of attaining its fulfillment.

526. Love invents what is pleasing to it.

527. Mental technology of spiritual self-witnessing. Mental vehicles of delivery.

Experiencing Regeneration

528. Varieties of religion under one Divine Human Person.

529. Experiencing. Visible to consciousness for only a split second in sudden memory.

530. All knowledge already exists. The higher we raise our consciousness, the more access we have to that knowledge.

531. All knowledge that can exist is present in consciousness to God. The more we strive to stay in God's established order, the more of that knowledge is shared with human beings.

532. Science exists at two levels of discovery: natural science and theistic science. Our rational mind ties these two together.

533. What we choose from our own love, remains forever as ours.

534. A man is normally scared of the idea of conjunction with the same woman forever. But if he wishes, he can discover the heaven of onemindedness provided by such eternal unity.

535. The completed human being is the oneminded married couple.

536. Onemindedness is the anatomical fusion of the two married partners. They look like two, but they are really one.

537. A spiritual husband loves his wife spiritually as well as naturally.

538. Affections are eternal in the mind. They remain deep seated.

539. Creation and the universe exist for the purpose of fostering this love between a husband and a wife.

540. From birth to eternity, mental development continues in its evolution towards the perfection of what is purely human in us, which is to love God and others more than self.

541. Love is consummated when it conjoins itself to a thought. Then action flows forth wherein love is fulfilled through a use.

Experiencing Regeneration

542. Loves are the origin of all uses; good uses from mutual love, and evil uses from love of self.

543. Evil uses are good uses turned into their opposites by selfish loves that are united to falsified truths.

544. Mental conjunction requires reciprocal organic structures in the mind.

545. With oneminded husband and wife passionate love does not diminish, but continues increasing daily to eternity.

546. She burns with longing for affective intimacy. She can only obtain this if he wants to have that with her.

547. She receives conjugial love from God directly, and then he receives it from her to the extent that he desires onemindedness with her.

548. The conjugial wife just knows things about their union because she perceives them from that conjugial love from God. Therefore he is wise who fulfills his wife's wishes.

549. Experiencing spiritual meaning is by appropriation of spiritual truths from Sacred Scripture in its correspondential sense.

550. Spiritual development is upward cyclical and sideways recursive.

551. A heavenly love is fulfilled when it perceives its own good in another human being. A hellish love is fulfilled when it recognizes its own evil in another human being.

552. The heavenly and hellish societies battle each other inside our thoughts and feelings. The outcome of that battle determines our eternal fate.

Experiencing Regeneration

553. The love of our conjugial partner gradually disengages us from the un-reality of selfhood as an individual.

554. As the self is allowed to die, the as-of self is born and develops to eternity.

555. The meanings we perceive and become conscious of are those that are selected by our loves.

556. The psychology of spiritual self-witnessing is the experiencing of regeneration.

557. The purpose of theistic psychology is to acquire systematic, rational, and practical knowledge about regeneration. It gives us the ability to equip our personality for living in the afterlife. Such as our personality is at death, such is our fate in eternity.

558. The same Spiritual Sun is in every person's mind as there is only one mental world.

559. Be aware that when you talk to yourself in your mind, there are listeners.

560. Those who would profane are not enlightened. Guard yourself against swearing and profaning.

561. To be consumed is the purpose of love's existence.

562. To be good, you must love being good.

563. We have a choice whether we are going to love the hell in us or the heaven in us.

564. What God calls good is what can take us to heaven.

565. With respect to experiencing consciousness, individual development recapitulates collective evolution.

566. Consciousness is the vehicle for human contact.

567. Dreams are covered up. Daydreams are naked.

568. Sunrise Conflagration. Molten Sunrise. Sunrise fantasy.

569. Sunset Quietude. Sunset Intensity. Sunset painting.

570. Sunrise Love. Molten Gold pouring over the ocean.

571. Sunrise in Blue. Hot dreams.

572. Sunrise brightens the heart. Renewal in Sunrise.

573. Sunlight pouring through a crack in the door. Sunrise penetrates to the heart.

574. A tree is like a person's mind.

575. What is new will get old. Only our spirit never ages.

576. Orchid plant without flower promises a beautiful future to those who know the secret.

577. Looking through a tree, seeing a house.

578. Ocean. Sky. Beach. Tree. Light. Air.

579. Tree in the light. Sunset tree symmetry. Palm trees glowing in the night.

580. Moon light Ti Leaf Plant. White ginger in the night. Good Morning!

581. Good night sky. The day is ending. A new day is now possible.

582. Night is the lessening of light in our mind, the diminishing of love, the lowering of our humanity.

583. Good morning. Good evening.

584. Sunrise over the ocean, so warm and comforting. Full Glory unfiltered. Heavenly Passion.

585. Sunrise Tree. Sunrise Explosion.

586. Early Sunrise Beach. Peaceful quiet morning on the canal.

587. Sunset Cloud. Evening is brewing in the sky.

588. Good morning. Morning waves. Morning clouds.

Experiencing Regeneration

589. Inviting ocean at dawn. Burning fire in the morning sky over the dark cold ocean.

590. Secrets that only the eyes of the blind can see in the dark. An emotional firestorm in the self.

591. Dawn arising cold purple just before turning red hot and peach. Waiting for the Glory to burst open. Here it is at last!

592. God and human. God and tree. The eye of God.

593. Darkness above, light below. Heaven descending.

594. Night is slowly descending in many colors. Good night secret garden.

595. Attachment demands reciprocation. It is irresistible.

596. Everyday experiencing is the awareness of the inflow of spiritual information that takes place continuously in our mind.

597. Poetic discourse is the language of experiencing.

598. The awareness of experiencing is consciousness.

599. All possible human knowledge from past to future is accessible to consciousness.

600. Describing the content of our consciousness generates poetic discourse. People communicate their consciousness to each other by constructing and sharing poetic discourse.

601. The trees of perception.

602. The road to happiness.

603. The window of opportunity.

604. The clouds of uncertainty.

605. The face of happiness.

606. The heat of love.

607. The light of truth.

608.   The song of redemption.

609.   The sun of love.

610.   The moon of faith.

611.   The arm of sustenance.

612.   The finger of accusation.

613.   The heart of charity.

614.   The waters of turbulence.

615.   The waters of peace.

616.   The rock of perdition.

617.   The rock of salvation.

618.   The pearl of gratitude.

619.   The bread of goodness.

620.   The wine of spirituality.

621.   The gap of willing.

622.   The appearance of beauty.

623.   The flame of compassion.

624.   The cold of hatred.

625.   The ugliness of selfishness.

626.   The steps of consciousness.

627.   The sound of awakening.

628.   The call of loyalty.

629.   The gold of generosity.

630.   The silver of comprehension.

631.   The wood of goodwill.

632.   The field of doctrine.

633.   The mountain of love.

634.   The ocean of doubt.

Experiencing Regeneration

635.   The waves of uncertainty.

636.   The darkness of understanding.

637.   The sharpness of rationality.

638.   The knife of discernment.

639.   The odor of welcome.

640.   The touch of pleasure.

641.   The embrace of conjoining.

642.   The path of righteousness.

643.   The city of learning.

644.   The ground of instruction.

645.   The serpent of deception.

646.   The house of goods.

647.   The temple of worship.

648.   The blindness of self.

649.   The bush of hiding.

650.   The hill of faith.

651.   The coldness of hatred.

652.   The heat of passion.

653.   The burning of anger.

654.   The power of truth.

655.   The holiness of God.

656.   The greeting of friendship.

657.   The gift of intelligence.

658.   The cup of knowledge.

659.   The clothes of illusions.

660.   The nakedness of innocence.

661.   The hairiness of prejudice.

662. The muscle of assistance.

663. The shoulder of support.

664. The leaf of culture.

665. The flower of delight.

666. The flower of recompense.

667. The flower of romance.

668. The perfume of vanity.

669. The scent of agreeableness.

670. The grey of absence.

671. The blue of presence.

672. The brown of complaint.

673. The black of disappointment.

674. The yellow of service.

675. The hand of friendship.

676. The clasp of peace.

677. The handshake of agreement.

678. The signature of personhood.

679. The check of contribution.

680. The line of attention.

681. The hole of depression.

682. The money of reassurance.

683. The money of avarice.

684. The money of success.

685. The bank of possessions.

686. The appointment of doom.

687. The shoes of poverty.

688. The sandals of uncleanness.

Experiencing Regeneration

689. The socks of promises.

690. The violence of cruelty.

691. The softness of caring.

692. The spring of inventiveness.

693. The iPhone of relationships.

694. The iPad of productivity.

695. The desktop of steadiness.

696. The jewels of foolishness.

697. The touch of passion.

698. The warmth of friendship.

699. The growth of independence.

700. The wheels of stereotypes.

701. The mirror of feelings.

702. The blindness of self-love.

703. The walk of destiny.

704. The cats of hiding.

705. The pets of indulgence.

706. The crash of impatience.

707. The crush of persuasion.

708. The rush of consummation.

709. The push of self-interest.

710. The shove of unpleasantness.

711. The torque of self-deception.

712. The slavery of indulgences.

713. The sleeplessness of discontent.

714. The protection of prudence.

715. The Bible of soteriology.

716. The God of salvation.

717. The God of mercy.

718. The God of reassurance.

719. The endlessness of eternity.

720. The temple of faith.

721. The rituals of worship.

722. The automobile of escape.

723. The cars of doom.

724. The airplane of promises.

725. The filter of organization.

726. The gesture of conciliation.

727. The replenishment of determination.

728. The train of planning.

729. The dictionary of meanings.

730. The thesaurus of synonyms.

731. The list of connectedness.

732. The painting of fantasy.

733. The art of imagination.

734. The language of thought.

735. The writing of communication.

736. The message of relief.

737. The email of exploration.

738. The Web of information.

739. The birds of freedom.

740. The corpse of disbelief.

741. The grating of obnoxiousness.

742. The barking of disobedience.

743. The vomit of hypocrisy.

744. The sweetness of romance.

745. The steadiness of integrity.

746. The imbalance of injustice.

747. The aloneness of rejection.

748. The health of precaution.

749. The sickness of indulgences.

750. The stink of disrespect.

751. The sting of disloyalty.

752. The attack of indiscretion.

753. The rescue of innocence.

754. The falling of morality.

755. The failing of immorality.

756. The bench of conscience.

757. The bracelet of devotion.

758. The earrings of belonging.

759. The ring of conjunction.

760. The necklace of propriety.

761. The gift of friendship.

762. The flow of perseverance.

763. The choppiness of hypocrisy.

764. The paralysis of fascination.

765. The movement of synchrony.

766. The immobility of conflict.

767. The flight of self-confidence.

768. The hammer of dominance.

769. The needle of honesty.

770. The pressure of expectations.

771. The fight of disagreements.

772. The glue of similarity.

773. The weight of evidence.

774. The lightness of being.

775. The shovel of service.

776. The pitchfork of distinctions.

777. The axe of sinfulness.

778. The acts of selfishness.

779. The performing of unchastity.

780. The performing of chastity.

781. The escape of hell.

782. The escape of heaven.

783. The river of prayers.

784. The waters of humility.

785. The fountain of revelation.

786. The keyboard of discursiveness.

787. The click of agreement.

788. The productivity of uses.

789. The chamber of privacy.

790. The roof of know-how.

791. The wall of disagreement.

792. The door of acknowledgment.

793. The door of perception.

794. The entrance of dreams.

795. The mud of involvements.

796. The pollution of the "I".

Experiencing Regeneration

797.   The prickliness of temptations.

798.   The shadow of doubt.

799.   The shadow of illogic.

800.   The darkness of materialism.

801.   The brilliance of spirituality.

802.   The colors of semantics.

803.   The dispersion of lies.

804.   The framework of analysis.

805.   The bedrock of faith.

806.   The morgue of envy.

807.   The saltiness of tears.

808.   The reversal of directionality.

809.   The receiving of luxury.

810.   The resolution of differences.

811.   The excitement of romance.

812.   The pleasures of marriage.

813.   The excesses of abandonment.

814.   The engagement of communion.

815.   The posture of mutuality.

816.   The posture of availability.

817.   The circle of creation.

818.   The inclusiveness of love.

819.   The acknowledgement of reciprocation.

820.   The interdependence of living.

821.   The dependency of good.

822.   The acceptance of order.

823.   The holiness of the infinite.

Experiencing Regeneration

824.   The anatomy of the word.

825.   The conjunction of love.

826.   The sin of rejection.

827.   The insanity of self.

828.   The reality of as-of-self.

829.   The murder of innocence.

830.   The suffering of obedience.

831.   The experiencing of regeneration.

832.   The backbone of reliance.

833.   The shattering of silence.

834.   The ending of aloneness.

835.   The living of kindnesses.

836.   The holy of flame.

837.   The eternity of eternity.

838.   The love of totality.

839.   The absence of punishings.

840.   The absence of anger.

841.   The absence of abandonment.

842.   The infinite of our finite.

843.   The relationship of reciprocity.

844.   The God of service.

845.   The permanence of belonging.

846.   The friend of concerns.

847.   The surprise of surprises.

848.   The Providence of plenitude.

849.   The perfection of everything.

850.   The beauty of omniscience.

Experiencing Regeneration

851. The reassurance of omnipresence.

852. The confidence of omnipotence.

853. The inkling of infinity.

854. The rationality of wisdom.

855. The truth of intelligence.

856. The love of liberation.

857. The love of salvation.

858. The love of unification.

859. The gift of love.

860. The enlightenment of truth.

861. The awe of awesomeness.

862. The vision of reality.

863. The death of ego.

864. The restoration of remains.

865. The fructification of good.

866. The multiplication of truth.

867. The Divine of Human.

868. The Human of Divine.

869. The Son of Father.

870. The Father of Son.

871. The trinity of aspects.

872. The creation of all.

873. The salvation of all.

874. The salvation of regeneration.

875. The rebirth of character.

876. The resuscitation of mind.

877. The separation of physical.

Experiencing Regeneration

878. The immersion of spiritual.

879. The departure of goodwill.

880. The arrival of hatred.

881. The falsification of truth.

882. The adulteration of good.

883. The hatred of love.

884. The lust of hatred.

885. The mending of hearts.

886. The lending of Proprium.

887. The abandoning of proprium.

888. The love of mutuality.

889. The community of saints.

890. The society of spirits.

891. The society of angels.

892. The Grand-Human of heaven.

893. The grand-monster of hell.

894. The voice of accusation.

895. The voice of mercy.

896. The grating of falsities.

897. The insanity of doubt.

898. The experiencing of certainty.

899. The spiritualization of everything.

900. The Song of Songs.

901. The music of forgiveness.

902. The music of praise.

903. The music of worship.

904. The harp of acknowledgment.

Experiencing Regeneration

905.   The trumpets of oneness.

906.   The cymbals of reminder.

907.   The drums of initiation.

908.   The organ of repentance.

909.   The flute of wisdom.

910.   The shouts of enthusiasm.

911.   The secrets of heaven.

912.   The mysteries of revelation.

913.   The heaven of devils.

914.   The sufferings of hell.

915.   The insanities of lusts.

916.   The lusts of excesses.

917.   The atonement of sin.

918.   The immortality of soul.

919.   The immortality of self.

920.   The language of humanity.

921.   The unification of humanity.

922.   The evolution of humanity.

923.   The humanity of eternity.

924.   The eternity of God.

925.   The God of love.

926.   The love of humanity.

927.   The liberation of captivities.

928.   The freedom of compulsions.

929.   The freedom of charity.

930.   The temple of God.

931.   The temple of worship.

932. The temple of sacrifices.

933. The temple of holiness.

934. The temple of ego.

935. The temple of Dagon.

936. The temple of self-love.

937. The rock of stumbling.

938. The rock of faith.

939. The rock of truth.

940. The rock of rationality.

941. The rock of sustenance.

942. The corporeal of natural.

943. The natural of rational.

944. The rational of spiritual.

945. The spiritual of celestial.

946. The celestial of Divine.

947. The Divine of Human.

948. The Divine of Human.

949. The Father of Eternity.

950. The Sun of Heaven.

951. The immorality of discrimination.

952. The harmfulness of injustice.

953. The corpse of self-love.

954. The insanity of adultery.

955. The rejection of God.

956. The darkness of Godlessness.

957. The doctrine of charity.

958. The doctrine of faith.

959. The doctrine of Sacred-Scripture.

960. The doctrine of Lord.

961. The doctrine of salvation.

962. The materialism of science.

963. The bias of appearances.

964. The aversion of arrogance.

965. The cruelty of pride.

966. The dangers of reasoning.

967. The spiritual of the literal.

968. The celestial of the historical.

969. The Divine of the natural.

970. The blunder of atheism.

971. The costliness of atheism.

972. The consequences of atheism.

973. The faith of charity.

974. The hills of eternity.

975. The fields of desire.

976. The fall of man.

977. The reconstruction of reality.

978. The return of charity.

979. The face of faithfulness.

980. The shield of regeneration.

981. The reality of mutual-love.

982. The conjugial of marriage-love.

983. The non-reality of hatred.

984. The insemination of truth.

985. The company of spirits.

Experiencing Regeneration

986.   The test of temptations.

987.   The link of plantation.

988.   The lake of perdition.

989.   The smudge of sin.

990.   The Commandments of precision.

991.   The contact of caring.

992.   The sweetness of companionship.

993.   The renewal of friendship.

994.   The cold of mercilessness.

995.   The conspiracy of Cain.

996.   The frenzy of self-intelligence.

997.   The crying of hopelessness.

998.   The arrow of conscience.

999.   The sword of distinguishing.

1000.   The protection of law.

1001.   The remains of goodness.

1002.   The temptations of regeneration.

1003.   The emptiness of self-hood.

1004.   The insanity of scortations.

1005.   The insanities of lust.

1006.   The punishment of evil.

1007.   The punishment of falsities.

1008.   The law of retribution.

1009.   The breaking of faith.

1010.   The lawlessness of selfishness.

1011.   The inevitability of punishments.

1012.   The mercy of forgiveness.

Experiencing Regeneration

1013. The shamefulness of indolence.

1014. The restitution of wrongdoings.

1015. The promises of truth.

1016. The promises of lies.

1017. The generosity of mutuality.

1018. The value of repentance.

1019. The healing of reformation.

1020. The liberation of goodwill.

1021. The slavery of selfhood.

1022. The sweetness of union.

1023. The tragedy of divorce.

1024. The uselessness of strife.

1025. The epiphany of God.

1026. The opening of possibilities.

1027. The opportunity for reversals.

1028. The welcoming of order.

1029. The wisdom of innocence.

1030. The wisdom of maturity.

1031. The mercilessness of self-interest.

1032. The advantages of partnership.

1033. The mutuality of caring.

1034. The divisiveness of disagreements.

1035. The lust of dominion.

1036. The respect of humanity.

1037. The agreeableness of similitudes.

1038. The disjunction of dissimilitudes.

1039. The violence of adultery.

Experiencing Regeneration

1040. The poison of porn.

1041. The debasement of prostitution.

1042. The cowardice of forced-sex.

1043. The dishumanity of rape.

1044. The rationality of virtues.

1045. The goodness of morality.

1046. The orderliness of civility.

1047. The pearl of generosity.

1048. The diamond of integrity.

1049. The platinum of sharing.

1050. The gold of goodwill.

1051. The silver of honesty.

1052. The brass of appearances.

1053. The steel of perseverance.

1054. The aluminum of light-heartedness.

1055. The chromium of learnedness.

1056. The crystal of innocence.

1057. The glass of open-mindedness.

1058. The field of desires.

1059. The tent of holiness.

1060. The tent of the covenant.

1061. The tabernacle of sacrifices.

1062. The temple of God.

1063. The temple of prayers.

1064. The den of thieves.

1065. The lake of condemnation.

1066. The well of truth.

Experiencing Regeneration

1067. The serpent of lies.

1068. The horn of self-intelligence.

1069. The desert of the few.

1070. The covenant of reciprocation.

1071. The prophet of falsehood.

1072. The dragon of Philistia.

1073. The beast of Babylon.

1074. The whoredom of adulteration.

1075. The vastation of truth.

1076. The mountain of holiness.

1077. The servant of charity.

1078. The brotherhood of unification.

1079. The church of salvation.

1080. The church of perdition.

1081. The marriage of truth.

1082. The wedding of love.

1083. The charity of caring.

1084. The fulfillment of the law.

1085. The hell of selfishness.

1086. The arrogance of self-intelligence.

1087. The dominion of souls.

1088. The darkness of falsifications.

1089. The light of rationality.

1090. The law of belonging.

1091. The sympathy of similitudes.

1092. The antipathy of dissimilitudes.

1093. The simulation of the conjugial.

Experiencing Regeneration

1094. The opposition of destruction.

1095. The regeneration of personality.

1096. The dominion of Babylon.

1097. The self-intelligence of Philistia.

1098. The Satan of self-delusion.

1099. The Lucifer of arrogance.

1100. The devil of temptation.

1101. The angel of justice.

1102. The restitution of remains.

1103. The mirror of representations.

1104. The garden of Eden.

1105. The north of floods.

1106. The south of enlightenment.

1107. The west of degradation.

1108. The east of salvation.

1109. The increase of remains.

1110. The growth of heaven.

1111. The Father of omnipotence.

1112. The Son of liberation.

1113. The Spirit of regeneration.

1114. The sheep of obedience.

1115. The goats of disobedience.

1116. The frogs of devastation.

1117. The devastation of love.

1118. The adulteration of good.

1119. The falsification of truths.

1120. The doctrine of life.

Experiencing Regeneration

1121. The doctrine of Sacred-Scripture.

1122. The doctrine of charity.

1123. The doctrine of conjugial-love.

1124. The bread of faces.

1125. The altar of holiness.

1126. The veil of profanation.

1127. The cherubim of protection.

1128. The wings of protection.

1129. The earth of support.

1130. The Word of God.

1131. The king of servitude.

1132. The man of the field.

1133. The morning of repentance.

1134. The night of forgetting.

1135. The stars of knowledges.

1136. The clouds of literality.

1137. The glory of spirit.

1138. The wisdom of innocence.

1139. The wisdom of old-age.

1140. The reconstruction of meaning.

1141. The ladder of Jacob.

1142. The blessings of Isaac.

1143. The sacrifice of Isaac.

1144. The sport of love.

1145. The covenant of doctrine.

1146. The revelation of immortality.

1147. The kingdom of heaven.

1148.   The fantasy of shamefulness.

1149.   The scortations of daydreams.

1150.   The remnants of Judah.

1151.   The taught of God.

1152.   The circumcision of hearts.

1153.   The bonds of good-will.

1154.   The bread of poverty.

1155.   The bread of riches.

1156.   The seeds of truth.

1157.   The insemination of truths.

1158.   The collectivity of community.

1159.   The crew of infernals.

1160.   The dragon of dominion.

1161.   The conspiracy of Philistia.

1162.   The hatred of innocence.

1163.   The hatred of good.

1164.   The hatred of truth.

1165.   The sirens of eroticism.

1166.   The violation of innocence.

1167.   The anatomy of mind.

1168.   The eternity of mind.

1169.   The proprium of selfhood.

1170.   The resuscitation of death.

1171.   The richness of rational-faith.

1172.   The poverty of blind-faith.

1173.   The punishment of punishment.

1174.   The punishment of evil.

Experiencing Regeneration

1175. Stairs go up. Stairs go down.

1176. Eyes wander. Eyes settle.

1177. Looks appear. Looks reveal.

1178. Self first. First self.

1179. Others first. First others.

1180. God is love.

1181. God is truth.

1182. God is goodness.

1183. God is life.

1184. God is experiencing.

1185. God provides.

1186. God knows.

1187. God is loyal.

1188. God protects.

1189. God supports.

1190. God never punishes.

1191. God is never angry.

1192. God gives.

1193. God forgives.

1194. God enlightens.

1195. God saves.

1196. God rescues.

1197. God serves.

1198. God is mercy.

1199. God is compassion.

1200. God is friend.

1201. God instructs.

1202. To anticipate. To consume.

1203. To endure. To endure.

1204. To worship. To endure.

1205. To observe. To be aware.

1206. To smile. To connect.

1207. To share. To benefit.

1208. To love. To be completed.

1209. To feel. To think.

1210. To laugh. To stimulate.

1211. To provide. To receive.

1212. To prepare. To perform.

1213. To regenerate. To equip.

1214. To splurge. To regret.

1215. To share. To benefit.

1216. To obey. To follow.

1217. To unite. To merge.

1218. To seek. To find.

1219. To pray. To request.

1220. To ask. To receive.

1221. To need. To be satisfied.

1222. To express. To reveal.

1223. To practice. To strengthen.

1224. To receive. To give.

1225. To buy. To have.

1226. To dominate. To enslave.

1227. To be frugal. To conserve.

1228. To use. To replace.

Experiencing Regeneration

1229. Heavenly pleasures.

1230. Wordily pleasures.

1231. Mutual pleasures.

1232. Infernal pleasures.

1233. Consuming pleasures.

1234. Reformed pleasures.

1235. Insane scortations.

1236. Entrapping eroticism.

1237. Unfettered fantasies.

1238. Loose thoughts.

1239. Captivating sirens.

1240. Promiscuous promises.

1241. Unprotected licensure.

1242. Regretful consummations.

1243. Sinful entertainment.

1244. Forbidden lusts.

1245. Destructive attachments.

1246. Spilling emotions.

1247. Engraved habits.

1248. Sins of the night.

1249. Excesses of the night.

1250. Guilty mornings.

1251. Lost afternoons.

1252. Frightening consequences.

1253. Guilty moments.

1254. Enslaving desires.

1255. Erotic daydreams.

1256. Sexy dreams.

1257. Slippery enamors.

1258. Chaining obsessions.

1259. Clean thoughts.

1260. Clean fantasies.

1261. Conjugial sport.

1262. Steadfast loyalty.

1263. Respectful intimacies.

1264. Lawful conjunction.

1265. Eternal relationship.

1266. Exclusive embrace.

1267. Heavenly partnership.

1268. Angelic couplehood.

1269. Listen to God.

1270. Listen to conscience.

1271. Listen to rationality.

1272. Listen to love.

1273. Listen to truth.

1274. Broker truth.

1275. Embrace truth.

1276. Love truth.

1277. Seek truth.

1278. Think truth.

1279. Obey truth.

1280. Do good.

1281. Do uses.

1282. Do loving.

1283. Do truthing.

1284. Be loyal.

1285. Be straight.

1286. Be charitable.

1287. Be lawful.

1288. Acknowledge God.

1289. Reciprocate God.

1290. Admit God.

1291. Invite God.

1292. Love wife.

1293. Honor wife.

1294. Embrace wife.

1295. Kiss wife.

1296. Have children.

1297. Raise children.

1298. Love children.

1299. Protect children.

1300. Read Sacred-Scripture.

1301. Study Sacred-Scripture.

1302. Remember Sacred-Scripture.

1303. Obey Sacred-Scripture.

1304. Listen to God.

1305. Listen to conscience.

1306. Listen to rationality.

1307. Listen to love.

1308. Listen to truth.

1309. Broker the truth.

Experiencing Regeneration

1310. Embrace the truth.

1311. Love the truth.

1312. Seek the truth.

1313. Think the truth.

1314. The natural mind is the spiritual body.

The Q&A of Experiencing Regeneration

Questions (click individual questions to see specific answers)

1) Why do we need to be saved?
2) What's so bad about loving yourself?
3) What if I don't believe in the afterlife?
4) What happens to me then if my personality is selfish?
5) Is that so bad that I need to avoid it through salvation?
6) How does salvation change that?
7) Why is loving God also necessary?
8) What if I don't believe in God?
9) Can I choose and pick which religion and God I should believe in?
10) How do I acquire such a relationship with God?
11) Do I have to love all people even if they are dishonest, cruel, and hostile to me?
12) What about unconditional love, which is to accept people as they are without wanting to change them as a condition of our love and respect?
13) Shouldn't people love their children and their spouse even if they have weaknesses and selfish traits?
14) Are we to love our country even if there is corruption and injustice present?
15) Should public schools teach about God and salvation?
16) How can God be taught in science courses?
17) What is theistic science and how can it be justified?

Experiencing Regeneration

18) Why does God allow evil to occur since it could be stopped by Divine omnipotence?

19) How do you know these things about God and what God does and wants?

20) Aren't these different versions of Sacred Scripture contradictory to each other, and are they not often used to justify dissent and attacks against those with different beliefs.

21) Some people have given up on God because it seems wrong to them that God punishes people to eternal hell simply for not believing something or for having done something wrong. Can theistic psychology resolve this concern?

22) How is evil defined in theistic psychology, given that similar activities that are allowed in one culture are defined as evil in another: does it not seem relative?

23) How is evil related to our afterlife?

24) What is sin and what is the punishment of evil?

25) Since God intervenes and manages every detail what is the point of praying and asking?

26) Is atheism detrimental to the individual?

27) Can good people be atheists, or are all atheists bad people?

28) What is the view of theistic psychology on human immortality?

29) From Sacred Scripture people have concluded that each individual is in company with angels. Can you explain that?

30) What kind of people are heavenly people or angels? Are they sexless?

Experiencing Regeneration

31) Some people have concluded on the basis of Sacred Scripture that angels are sexless and that there are no marriages in heaven. How does theistic psychology resolve this issue?

32) How much good do I need to do before I can earn my way into heaven? And what if I don't have the right religion?

33) How bad do people have to be before God condemns them to a life of suffering in hell forever?

34) People are disturbed by many parts of Sacred Scripture that describe wars between nations and tribes, and the resultant cruel treatment of the victims, including children, women, old people, and their domestic animals. Much of this is commanded and promoted by God. How does theistic psychology justify such intentions attributed to God?

Answers

1. *Why do we need to be saved?*
   **Because we inherit a love of self above all things.

2. *What's so bad about loving yourself?*
   **Loving ourselves above all things creates a selfish personality that remains with us in the afterlife of eternity.

3. *What if I don't believe in the afterlife?*
   **When you wake up in the afterlife following the two-day dying-resuscitation procedure you will think otherwise.

Experiencing Regeneration

4. *What happens to me then if my personality is selfish?*

   **You seek out the company of other selfish people in the afterlife who have similar habits of thinking and interacting with others.

5. *Is that so bad that I need to avoid it through salvation?*

   **A community of all-selfish individuals creates a social and mental environment of pure hell in which people's greatest delight is to dominate each other and to punish with fiendish cruelty all those who resist them.

6. *How does salvation change that?*

   **Salvation is the procedure of equipping your personality with traits of mutual love, which is to love others as much as oneself, and to love God more than anything.

7. *Why is loving God also necessary?*

   **If we compel ourselves to love God more than anything, we receive the power to fight and resist our inborn selfishness, and without this power we are unable and unwilling to stop being selfish.

8. *What if I don't believe in God?*

   **You will continue to think and interact with others as you do now.

9. *Can I choose and pick which religion and God I should believe in?*

   **Salvation is not dependent on any culture and religion but on an individual and reciprocal relationship with God.

10.   How do I acquire such a relationship with God?

**By talking to God every day, by wanting to know God's commandments of how we are to think and interact with others, and by compelling ourselves to consider the welfare of others as much as our own.

11.   Do I have to love all people even if they are dishonest, cruel, and hostile to me?

**It is contrary to our salvation to love people as they are because we are to love only their good traits.

12.   What about unconditional love, which is to accept people as they are without wanting to change them as a condition of our love and respect?

**In selfish love we accept others who favor us or are a part of us, even if they have some bad traits; but mutual love with love of God considers distinctions, loving and respecting good traits in a person, while rejecting the bad traits.

13.   Shouldn't people love their children and their spouse even if they have weaknesses and selfish traits?

**We are to love providing for their needs even if they have some bad traits, but we are not to love these traits in them, but try to modify them through modeling, instruction, and relationship.

14.   Are we to love our country even if there is corruption and injustice present?

**We are to love and protect our country for the good it does in protecting us and providing for our necessities, but we are to make distinctions and not to love or to cooperate with injustice and discrimination.

15.   *Should public schools teach about God and salvation?*
**Children in public schools should be instructed about God through science courses, not religion, as this is rightly prohibited by the constitution to avoid national conflict and loss of freedom of expression and freedom of lifestyle choices.

16.   *How can God be taught in science courses?*
**This can be done when science gives up its biased materialistic philosophy and becomes theistic science, a new trend that is now growing among intellectuals and scientists.

17.   *What is theistic science and how can it be justified?*
**Materialistic science is justified and maintained by requiring physical proof that God exists and intervenes in cause-effect phenomena, while theistic science requires rational proof and systematic methods of rational investigation that show how natural phenomena are caused, not by other natural phenomena, but by the laws of correspondences built into the created universe.

18.   *Why does God allow evil to occur since it could be stopped by Divine omnipotence?*
**God's omnipotence manages all details in the universe, including natural disasters and people's evil thoughts and actions, by rational laws that insure people's ability to equip their personality with good traits that give them a happy and blessed life in eternity. These theistic rational laws

include the laws of individual freedom of choice to love self more than anything or to love others and God as much as self. God prevents all evil from occurring in the world or in the mind when it does not contribute to individual salvation.

19.   *How do you know these things about God and what God does and wants?*
**God provides every culture and nation with its own written *Sacred Scripture* that reveals to people what God wants and how God is active in their salvation.

20.   *Aren't these different versions of Sacred Scripture contradictory to each other, and are they not often used to justify dissent and attacks against those with different beliefs?*
**God dictates Sacred Scripture to prophets who write down what they internally hear using words of their natural language, and this spells out the religion of each culture through the literal and historical sentences and meanings of their Sacred Scripture. In this way God's rational and spiritual ideas are translated into natural ideas that make sense to ordinary people so they can have their religion and rules of life. The translation process from God's spiritual ideas to natural cultural ideas is automatically effected through the laws of correspondence that God built into the created universe. Theistic science allows us to discover these laws of correspondence between spiritual and natural, so that we can reconstruct God's spiritual ideas from the literal natural sentences of Sacred Scripture. When this is done there is complete agreement in the correspondential

meaning of the Sacred Scripture in all religions and cultures.

21.   *Some people have given up on God because it seems wrong to them that God punishes people to eternal hell simply for not believing something or for having done something wrong. Can theistic psychology resolve this concern?*

**The literal sentences of Sacred Scripture declare both that God punishes and gets angry, and that God never punishes and never gets angry. But in the correspondential sense we receive the explanation that it is only an appearance that God punishes and gets angry, and speaking about this appearance in Sacred Scripture is for those who attribute everything to God, both their good fortune and their misery and tragedies. In this way they continue to acknowledge God and God's intervention in their lives. Maintaining this acknowledgement is necessary for their eventual regeneration and salvation. In reality God's mind is pure love-substance, infinite and perfect, and it is impossible for God to experience animosity or resentment, even less the desire to punish and keep punishing. Neither does God want to be worshipped for the sake of glory, as this would apply only to some mere human dictator. In reality God continuously works on behalf of those in hell to give them the opportunity to give up hatred of others, which is what keeps them in their mental hell. Yet they continue to refuse, and might do so to eternity, such is the insanity of their hatred for mutual love and love of God and what is good and true.

22.   *How is evil defined in theistic psychology, given that similar activities that are allowed in one culture are defined as evil in another: does it not seem relative?*

Experiencing Regeneration

**Evil is a spiritual idea that originates in Sacred Scripture. Differences in defining what is evil occur in the literal historical meaning found in Sacred Scripture from different religions and cultures. These differences and contradictions reflect the cultural and historical differences among the peoples of the world. The spiritual idea of evil does not change and is in agreement with all the versions of Sacred Scripture when interpreted through correspondences. This is called the universal definition of evil and is given in terms of the mental anatomy of the human race. Evil is what connects the mind to the hell societies in the afterlife of eternity. This is an actual anatomical connection by affective, cognitive, and sensorimotor fibers in the spiritual body.

23.   *How is evil related to our afterlife?*

**Defined anatomically, doing evil is to strengthen our inherited ties with the hell societies in the afterlife. These ties determine our fate in eternity. We cannot simply wish them away because we actually don't want to get rid of them. We love our evils. God has provided the procedure of regeneration in this life by which we can get rid of those ties, both inherited and acquired. This involves our constant fighting to suppress thinking and doing evils. To fight them means to compel ourselves to stop doing and thinking them. This ability to suppress our evil loves is given to us when we maintain a daily reciprocal relationship with God.

24.   *What is sin and what is the punishment of evil?*

**All the loves and thoughts that we have are either in the good or evil category. Sin is an idea presented in the literal historical meaning of all Sacred Scripture. In the literal historical meaning it is said that God punishes evil and sin. However, in the correspondential sense it is clear that God never punishes and never condemns. In the correspondential sense sin refers to loving our evil traits. Evil loves carry their own built-in anatomical punishment in the spiritual body, just as lack of physical cleanliness or the ingestion of poisonous chemicals carry their own anatomical punishment or negative consequences in the physical body. It is said in Sacred Scripture that the "wages of sin are death" because "death" in the correspondential sense refers to life in hell. To love our evil traits is to condemn ourselves to a life in hell. God continually and ceaselessly out of mercy tries to bend the individual away from sin.

25.   *Since God intervenes and manages every detail what is the point of praying and asking?*

**Praying to God, asking for things, expressing appreciation, worshipping and adoring, are all ways of maintaining a reciprocal relationship with God. God knows what we are praying and what we are thinking and wishing because these are mental states and events that God manages for our benefit. God flows into our will and understanding with love-substance and truth-substance, and this inflow gives us the ability to think, to pray, and to express appreciation. We can ask for things anyway because it is normal for mere human beings to do this. Expressing our felt appreciation is a reciprocating act that conjoins us closer to the Divine Human. As is revealed in Sacred Scripture, God desires this closer conjunction through which we can be blessed with happiness and intelligence to eternity.

26.   *Is atheism detrimental to the individual?*

**God takes care of atheists as much as believers but in different ways.

Experiencing Regeneration

The ability of atheists to construct arguments against God's existence is given to them by God, regardless of whether they are willing or able to admit this. God loves every human being and is present in the mind of every person equally and fully. God's purpose as revealed in Sacred Scripture, is to sub-consciously bend the person's thoughts and intentions as much as the individual is willing to be affected by what is good and true. The closer the reciprocation relationship with God is, the more the individual is capable of being affected by what is good and true. To be so affected is the condition for regeneration, by which we equip our personality for living in heavenly happiness in the afterlife of eternity. Atheism as a belief system, even as a new religion, removes the individual's ability to undergo regeneration, which is an anatomical process of personality change effected by God within a conscious reciprocal relationship with the individual.

27.   *Can good people be atheists, or are all atheists bad people?*
**No one is good and everyone is born with numerous inherited selfish loves and evil enjoyments. People who profess a religion and participate in collective worship with others, are not better than atheists or agnostics. But it's completely different with people who are willing to undergo regeneration. They maintain a daily reciprocal relationship with God, which gives them the ability to fight their inborn and acquired evils. To the extent they are willing to resist their own evils, regenerating individuals are gradually changed within their personality from loving self more than others to loving others as much as self. This takes a lifetime to complete, and even after that, regeneration goes on to eternity since no one can be

perfect except God.

What is the view of theistic psychology on human immortality?
**The correspondential meaning of Sacred Scripture reveals that to God the entire human race past and present is like one human being. This indicates that God wills to unify everything in the universe into the human form, which is that of our body and mind. This result is because God is the only original and infinite Human. Everything God creates relates to this Human form in one way or another. The greatest perfection of the Human form in creation is achieved in individual human beings who love others as much as self and God more than anything. In the afterlife of eternity these human beings form for themselves mental communities or psychic societies and live with each other in eternal conjugial happiness and always growing in intelligence. The two-day dying resuscitation procedure drops the physical body, whereupon we awaken in our spiritual body, continuing our daily lives in the afterlife of eternity where are located the numberless cities and communities that are formed by all those who have preceded us in death-and-resuscitation over the centuries and millenniums from this and numberless other planets.

The human mind and its spiritual body is anatomically adjoined to God. The Divine Human is adjoined to the finite human but the two can never be conjoined as one, but only adjoined, so that God dwells in what is Divine adjoined to the individual and is never a part of an individual as this would mean that God is no longer infinite.

28.   *From Sacred Scripture people have concluded that each individual is in company with angels. Can you explain that?*

Experiencing Regeneration

**While our spiritual body is still attached to a physical body our consciousness is immersed in concepts and thoughts that are based on the physical conditions that we experience through our physical body, namely time, place, origin, quantity, and measurements. Materialistic science does not allow rational proof of God and the revelations in Sacred Scripture concerning the spiritual world of the afterlife in eternity. Hence science today is ignorant of human immortality and any of the anatomical facts of the two-day dying-resuscitation process. In actuality however our mind or spiritual body functions synchronously at both a natural consciousness level and a spiritual consciousness level. In natural consciousness, we seem to ourselves to be alone in our thoughts and dreams, but in spiritual consciousness we perceive that we are mentally always in a collectivity of others, breathing and thinking in synchrony and harmony with them, even though uniquely so for each individual. This result is anatomical and comes from God's desire to mentally enrich every individual with the mental riches or capacities of all the other individuals. Hence it is that during our regeneration here on earth, God keeps our mind in balance between good and evil, or between an other-directed focus and a self-involved or selfish focus. This mental balance insures that we can choose our personality traits in freedom. This balance in our mind is achieved when God connects the individual's mind to heavenly people in the afterlife, called angels, and to hellish people, called evil spirits and devils. When we are fighting in spiritual temptations in our regeneration, the heavenly people that God connects us to, call up the principles of good conscience and morality that we believe in, while the evil spirits call up in our mind the selfish things we enjoy. Now it's up to us to decide in mental freedom whose way we are going to practice. In theistic psychology the phrase "vertical community" is used to refer to the anatomical connections we experience to others in the afterlife.

29.   *What kind of people are heavenly people or angels? Are they sexless?*

**When we awaken from the two-day dying-resuscitation procedure, we discover that our spiritual body is exactly like our physical body except more perfect, more beautiful, and in the state of vitality of early adulthood. Those who have undergone regeneration are now fully equipped with the personality that can live in the highest consciousness region of the mental world where collectivities of people have formed heavens for themselves, and live in unimaginable to us, happiness and intelligence. Their spiritual body is perfect and immortal, never sick, full of vitality and energy. They form marriages in which husband and wife are mentally one minded and unified. They do not produce children, which must be done on earth where children can grow and undergo regeneration in adulthood. Heavenly couples are in "conjugial love" and experience in exquisite intensity everything that married couples on earth experience.

30.   *Some people have concluded on the basis of Sacred Scripture that angels are sexless and that there are no marriages in heaven. How does theistic psychology resolve this issue?*

**Some parts of the literal historical meaning of Sacred Scripture declare that God is angry, vengeful, and desires glory for His sake. Other parts declare that God is pure love and unable to punish or condemn anyone, but always wishes to save everyone and to bless them with happiness and intelligence. Clearly, we need to go deeper into the meaning of Sacred

Experiencing Regeneration

Scripture in order to resolve these apparent contradictions. This is what we do when we focus on the correspondential meaning, which identifies the spiritual ideas that God wants us to think about. It is from this spiritual meaning of Sacred Scripture that we derive all the knowledge of theistic psychology.

31. *How much good do I need to do before I can earn my way into heaven? And what if I don't have the right religion?*

**No one can earn their way into heaven because heaven is not a place somewhere to enter but a state of mind to experience. Every human being is born with the capacity to experience the mental state of heaven. However, the heavenly mental state is not possible in natural consciousness, but only in spiritual consciousness. In contrast, the mental state of hell is possible in natural consciousness, but not in spiritual consciousness. We are born and are raised in natural consciousness, but in early adulthood we can begin the regeneration of our personality by rejecting what we want that is selfish and hurtful to others, and adopting what is of mutual love to others for the sake of God. As we progress in our regeneration we are more and more immersed in spiritual consciousness by which we can see that heaven refers to the happy and vital states of our immortal and constantly developing mind. What is amazing to realize is that countless others are also in that mental state in the afterlife of eternity. These are the heavenly people that form communities of similitudes with each other in which each is enriched by the thoughts and feelings of the other. Heaven is this mutually enriching mental state that develops in our mind more and more daily to eternity. So it does not matter what religion you come from or how much good acts you have done in your life on earth.

Experiencing Regeneration

If you have undergone regeneration of personality, you love to be in the traits in which are the heavenly people. This is what connects you do them and gives you the capacity to be in the heavenly mode of experiencing.

32.   *How bad do people have to be before God condemns them to a life of suffering in hell forever?*

**God never condemns anyone because God is pure love and mercy, loving everyone and striving constantly to guide the person to their eternal happiness in the afterlife. No one is condemned to hell, contrary to what many people believe. Hell is a mental state that people choose voluntarily for their life in eternity, in order to avoid contact with their heavenly mental states. People who were unwilling to undergo regeneration of character in this life, enter the afterlife of eternity with the personality that they provided for themselves through what they had thought and done in this life. Their chief love and inmost enjoyment of life is to dominate all others and to harshly punish those who resist serving them, or do not favor them. This result came about because they thought and did everything for the sake of their own benefit, while having no regard for the inconvenience and suffering of others who did not favor them. Such is the psychological nature of selfishness. In the afterlife, when unregenerate people explore their heavenly mental states and come into contact with mutual love and love of God, which are prominent in that mental state, they feel suffocated and as if losing the vitality of living. They quickly realize that their future in eternity lies in their hellish mental states in company with others who are similar. They then spend an eternity with each other, alternating between inmost enjoyment while able to dominate and cruelly punish others, and utmost suffering when others take their turn to dominate and cruelly punish them.

33.   *People are disturbed by many parts of Sacred Scripture that describe wars between nations and tribes, and the resultant cruel treatment of the victims, including children, women, old people, and their domestic animals. Much of this is commanded and promoted by God. How does theistic psychology justify such intentions attributed to God?*

**The words of the literal historical sense of Sacred Scripture accurately describe the historical events of the times. The barbaric cruelty that is described reflects the mentality of the people involved in those places and times. In order for them to accept a religion by which they could eventually be amended and saved, Sacred Scripture had to reflect their mentality, or else they would have rejected accepting any religion, and this would have condemned them to eternal hell. But Sacred Scripture is universally for all times and places and states, when understood in its correspondential sense. This correspondential sense is the basis of theistic psychology. Through such analysis of Sacred Scripture, we can develop our spiritual consciousness in which we can clearly see that God did not and could not order some people to massacre other people because of their race or culture and religion. In actuality, all wars and events of wars mentioned in Sacred Scripture refer to spiritual wars. These are the wars every person experiences when undergoing regeneration. The nations, tribes, categories of people, types of acts, and specific animals are all correspondences to mental states in regeneration. The variety of evil nations and activities mentioned correspond to evil intentions and falsified beliefs that we maintain during our regeneration. Hence God in Sacred Scripture commands us to kill in our mind all those varieties of evil thoughts and barbaric intentions against others. Not one of these evil loves is to be left surviving in our mind, if we are to succeed in equipping our personality for heaven. When you read Sacred Scripture think of these wars and cruelties not as people and their awful acts, but as irrational thoughts and selfish intentions that each of us has and favors. You will then appreciate God's loving kindness and perseverance in helping us to get rid of the selfish personality that we were born with. If unregenerated, this personality is inevitably taking us to a life of eternal hell.

Experiencing Regeneration

God, Immortality and Theistic Psychology Series
by Dr. Leon James

Jung and Swedenborg on God and Life After Death (2015) (Print and digital versions)

Reality Is Spiritual: Jung and Swedenborg on Dreams, Religion, Immortality, and Love (forthcoming 2016)

Biology of Consciousness and Immortality: Knowledge That Holds the Key to Our Eternal Destiny in the Afterlife (forthcoming 2016)

Eternal Romance: The Role of God in Marriage (forthcoming)

Theistic Psychology Hidden in the Bible (forthcoming)

Experiencing Regeneration: Equipping Our Personality For Living In The Afterlife (2015)
(Print and Kindle Digital versions at Amazon.com)

The Conjoined Pair: Natural and Spiritual Marriage (2012)
(Print at amazon.com)

The Correspondential Sense of Sacred Scriptures: Proving that there is a Unified Theistic Psychology Hidden within the World's Historical Sacred Writings (2009)
On the web: http://www.theisticpsychology.org/books/ssss.htm

Best Friends in Love and Together Forever: The Natural and Spiritual Dimension of Marriage (2008)
On the web: http://theisticpsychology.org/books/best-friends-in-love.htm

Principles of Theistic Psychology: The Scientific Knowledge of God Extracted from the Correspondential Sense of Sacred Scripture (18 Volumes) (2004-2008)
On the web: http://theisticpsychology.org/books/theistic/index.htm

Experiencing Regeneration

A Man of the Field: Forming the New Church Mind in Today's World (3 Volumes) (2002-2014)
(Print and Kindle version at amazon.com)

Moses, Paul, and Swedenborg: Three Steps in Rational Spirituality (1999)
On the web: http://theisticpsychology.org/books/rationality/moses.html

Swedenborg Encyclopedia of Theistic Psychology: The Ideas of Emanuel Swedenborg (1668-1772) Expressed In Modern Scientific Psychology (1995-2010) (multiple Volumes)
On the web: http://theisticpsychology.org/gloss.html